POSSESSION OF LAND

Nothing is more important in English land law than 'possession'. It is the foundation of all title, rights and remedies. But what exactly is it, and why does it still matter?

This book is about the meaning, significance and practical effect of the concept of possession in contemporary land law. It explains the different meanings of possession, the relationship between possession and title, and the ways in which the common law and equity do, and do not, protect possession.

The rights and remedies of freeholders, tenants and mortgage lenders, between themselves and against third parties, are all to some extent dependent on questions of status and possession. This book shows how. It is designed to provide an understanding of the basic principles for the student, and the answers to difficult problems for the practitioner.

MARK WONNACOTT is a property litigator at Maitland Chambers, Lincoln's Inn, London.

POSSESSION OF LAND

MARK WONNACOTT

CAMBRIDGE
UNIVERSITY PRESS

CAMBRIDGE
UNIVERSITY PRESS

University Printing House, Cambridge CB2 8BS, United Kingdom

Cambridge University Press is part of the University of Cambridge.

It furthers the University's mission by disseminating knowledge in the pursuit of education, learning and research at the highest international levels of excellence.

www.cambridge.org
Information on this title: www.cambridge.org/9780521868990

First published 2006

A catalogue record for this publication is available from the British Library

ISBN 978-0-521-86899-0 Hardback

CONTENTS

PREFACE AND ACKNOWLEDGMENTS

At University College London, undergraduate lawyers are traditionally told the story of its first two Professors. John Austin, Professor of Jurisprudence and the Law of Nations, taught dry legal philosophy to an empty room. But, Andrew Amos, Professor of English Law, knew his market. His first lecture was on the rules of accretion to and diluvian from land, and his lectures were packed.

He knew then, as every property litigator knows now, that few things evoke more passion and litigation than possession of land. Every week, in county courts up and down the country, there are people spending £50,000 or more, fighting domestic boundary disputes, typically over six inches of residential back-garden, and counting the money well spent if the judge decides that the boundary is where they say it should be.

But English law has never produced a proper theory of possession.

What exactly is it to be 'in' possession of land? What is it that is possessed? What is its relationship with a freehold or leasehold title? How is it acquired, and how is it lost? How does the common law protect it? What difference does equity make? What happens when a mortgagee takes possession, or if the possessor becomes insolvent or ceases to exist? What exactly is the effect of a possession order? In short, how does it all fit together?

This book is an attempt to answer that question.

Thanks are due to my former pupil-master, Robert Ham QC, and to Martin Hutchings, both of Wilberforce Chambers, who looked over the final version of the manuscript. Philomena Harrison, of Maitland Chambers, did likewise. My former pupil, Mark Sefton, of Falcon Chambers, saw and commented on an early draft, and Gabrielle Higgins, of Maitland Chambers, made useful observations about every page. They have all, at various times, been forced to take part in dull conversations about my hobby-horse, and, if those conversations were sometimes held in one of the many wine bars near Lincoln's Inn, that can only have done a little to alleviate the tedium.

Thanks are also due to the various clients of Central Law Training Ltd. For ten enjoyable years, I provided continuing professional development lectures for them, up and down the country, on property law subjects. On many occasions, what had started as a discussion of a current legal problem, turned into a lecture on the history of the point, or some tangentially related point; and, if anyone thought that odd, at least nobody ever complained.

Many of the problems discussed in this book have a provenance in the real world. In most cases, it would not have occurred to me that there was a problem at all, had a solicitor not instructed me to provide a solution to it for a client. So thanks are due to them too; and, in particular, to Christopher Dalton, of the Mary Ward Legal Centre, a free-thinker, who is always willing to challenge legal dogma.

Finally, thanks are due to the Cambridge University Press, for agreeing to publish this book at all, and for putting up with the eccentricities of my word processing system.

TABLE OF CASES

King's Leasehold Estates, Re (1873) LR 16 Eq 521 51
Kingsalton v Thames Water Developments [2002] 1 P & CR 15 2, 47
Kooltrade v. XTS Ltd [2001] FSR 158 155
Kumah v. Osbornes (a firm) [1997] 1 EGCS 1 80

Ladupt Ltd v. Williams & Glyn's Bank [1985] 2 All ER 577 152
Lambeth LBC v. Blackburn [2001] EWCA Civ 912 134
Lanecrest v. Asiwaju [2005] EWCA Civ 117; [2005] 1 EGLR 40 93
Leeds Industrial co-op v. Slack [1924] AC 851 103
Leeds Permanent BS v. Mansfield, 16 June 1993, unreported 65
Leicester BS v. Shearley [1950] 2 All ER 738 147
Leicester (Earl of) v. Wells-next-the Sea UDC [1973] Ch 110 102
Leigh and Sillivan v. Aliakman Shipping [1986] 1 AC 785 100
Letang v. Cooper [1965] 2 QB 232 92
Liverpool Corporation v. Chorley Union Assessment Committee [1912] 1 KB 270 8
Lodge v. Wakefield [1995] 2 EGLR 124 132
London Diocesan Fund v. Phithwa [2005] 1 WLR 3956 50
Long v. Tower Hamlets LBC [1996] 2 All ER 683 3
Lord Advocate v. Balfour 1907 SC 1360 38
Lowe v. J. W. Ashmore Ltd [1971] Ch 545 38
Lowe's Will Trust, Re [1973] 1 WLR 882 122
Luganda v. Service Hotels Ltd [1969] 2 Ch 209 68
Lyons v. Anderson (1886) 13 R 1020 51

Mabo v. Queensland (No. 2) (1992) 175 CLR 1 37
Malone v. Laskey [1907] 2 KB 141 6
Manchester Airport v. Dutton [2000] QB 133 72
Mander v. Falcke [1891] 2 Ch 554 57, 87, 138
Mann v. Stephens (1846) 15 Sim 377 138
Mannai Investment Co. Ltd v. Eagle Star Life Assurance Co. Ltd [1997] AC 749; [1997] 3 All ER 352 50
Marchant v. Charters [1977] 1 WLR 1181 68
Marshall v Charteris [1920] 1 Ch 520 20, 116, 154
Matadeen v. Caribbean Insurance Co. Ltd [2002] UKPC 69 83
Matthews v. Usher [1900] 2 QB 535 97
MCC Proceeds Inc. v. London Bros International [1998] 4 All ER 675 101
McCabe v. Bank of Ireland (1880) 14 AC 413 148
McClymont v. Primecourt Property Management [2000] EGCS 192 72
McPhail v. Persons Unknown [1973] Ch 447 157
Metall & Rohstoff v. Donaldson Lufkin & Jenrette [1990] 1 QB 391 155
Midland Bank v. McGrath [1996] EGCS 61 79

TABLE OF STATUTES

Land Registration Act 2002
s. 2(a)(iv) 144
s. 11(7) 47
s. 23 77
s. 29 49, 139
s. 51 75, 77
s. 60 142
s. 79 37
s. 87 149
s. 96 42, 141
s. 96(1) 141
s. 131 2
Sch. 4 para. 2(1) 47
Sch. 4 para. 3 48
Sch. 6 para. 4 141
Sch. 6 para. 5 142
Sch. 6 para. 6 141
Sch. 6 para. 9(2) 49, 139
Sch. 8 para. 1 48
Sch. 12 141
Land Transfer Act 1875 76
Land Transfer Act 1897 12, 109
Landlord and Tenant Act 1730 61
Landlord and Tenant Act 1954
s. 67 82, 114
Landlord and Tenant (Covenants) Act 1995
s. 1 99
s. 3 138
s. 5 54
s. 15 88, 90
s. 15(1) 99
s. 15(3) 87
s. 15(4) 87
s. 15(6) 87
s. 17 55, 58
Landlord and Tenant Law Amendment Act (Ireland) 1860
s. 3 50
Law of Distress (Amendment) Act 1908 57
Law of Property Act 1925
s. 1(1)(a) 74
s. 1(1)(b) 74
s. 1(2) 75, 144

TABLE OF STATUTORY INSTRUMENTS

1

Meaning of possession

Introduction

It has been said, rightly, that there is no law of ownership of land in England and Wales, only a law of possession.[1] Yet 'difficult problems arise in English real property law on the concept of possession'.[2] The following chapters explore some of these problems, and suggest some solutions. But this chapter is concerned with the principal cause of those problems; the different meanings, and inconsistent usage, of the term 'possession' in English land law.

Different meanings

In English land law, we use the term 'possession' in three quite distinct and separate senses: first, in its proper, technical sense, as a description of the relationship between a person and an estate in land; secondly, in its vulgar sense of physical occupation of tangible land; and, thirdly, to refer to fictional 'constructive' possession, which is almost, but not entirely, of historical interest only.[3]

First meaning: a relationship with a corporeal estate

This is the proper, technical meaning of the word 'possession' in English land law.

[1] G. Cheshire and E. Burn, *Modern Law of Real Property* (15th edn, London, Butterworths, 1994), p. 26. Oliver Wendell Holmes, in *The Common Law* (ed. M. Howe, Boston, Little Brown & Co., 1963), p. 163 said: 'possession is a conception which is only less important than contract': and this is true, for 'throughout the history of English land law the operative concept has been possession rather than ownership'; K. Gray and S. Gray, 'The Idea of Property', in *Land Law Themes and Perspectives* (ed., S. Bright and J. Dewar, Oxford, Oxford University Press, 1998), p. 21.

[2] Per Harman J in *Stokes* v. *Costain Property Investments* [1983] 1 WLR 907, 910.

[3] For a different suggested nomenclature, see J. Hill, 'The Proprietary Character of Possession', *Modern Studies in Property Law* (ed. E. Cooke, Oxford, Hart, 2001), vol. 1, p. 25.

The fundamental point about 'possession' in this sense is that it does not describe the relationship between a person and any tangible property, such as a field, or a building, or a road. The combined effect of the doctrines of tenures and of estates is that there is no absolute ownership of land; only ownership of greater or lesser rights in it.[4] Consequently, 'possession' in this sense describes a relationship between a person and a corporeal estate in land (a fee simple, a lease or, stretching the point, a profit à prendre) rather than the relationship between a person and any physical feature of the land.

There are two types of relationship described by the term 'possession' in this sense; a relationship of *right* and a relationship of *fact*.[5]

A relationship of right

A person has a *right to possess* an estate if he or she has acquired a title to it which is 'vested in possession'. If someone has a present fixed right only to begin enjoying[6] it at some point in the future, then it is vested only 'in interest'. It is 'vested in possession' when someone has a present fixed right to enjoy it now.[7]

The distinction between an estate that is vested in possession and one that is merely vested in interest is illustrated by the distinction between a concurrent (or 'overriding') lease and a reversionary lease.

A concurrent lease is a lease that takes effect immediately, but is granted in reversion upon and subject to a prior occupational lease. A concurrent lease is vested in possession because it grants an immediate fixed right to enjoy an estate in land. The estate is the concurrent lease itself, and it is

[4] There is one exception to this. Land held by the Crown as part of the residual royal demesne could be described as owned by the Crown absolutely. But no private individual or person can ever own land absolutely. Even an unencumbered freehold must technically be held as a tenant of the Crown, whether mediately or intermediately. See ch. 3.

[5] It is important to keep the two concepts distinct. The Court of Appeal failed to do so in *Kingsalton* v. *Thames Water Developments* ([2002] 1 P & CR 15) when deciding that the right of a new registered proprietor to take possession of the registered estate was sufficient to make that person 'the proprietor who is in possession' for the purpose of s.82(3) Land Registration Act 1925. If that had been correct, then any registered disposition during an incomplete period of adverse possession would have reset the clock to zero. See now s.131 Land Registration Act 2002.

[6] 'The word "enjoy" used in this connection is a translation of the latin word "fruor" and refers to the exercise and use of the right and having the full benefit of it, rather than deriving pleasure from it': per Pearson LJ in *Kenny* v. *Preen* [1963] 1 QB 499, 511.

[7] *Fearne's Contingent Remainders* (4th edn, London, Strahan & Woodfall, 1844), vol. 1, p. 2, cited with approval in *Pearson* v. *IRC* [1981] AC 753, 772.

immediately enjoyed by receiving the rent reserved by, and enforcing the covenants contained in, the extant prior lease.

A reversionary lease is a lease which is granted to begin at some time in the future, usually after an existing lease has expired.[8] A reversionary lease is 'vested' as soon as it is granted,[9] but until the term begins it is vested only 'in interest', and not 'in possession', for, although it already exists, it gives no present right to enjoy any estate in land.[10] The right to enjoy the estate is postponed to some future date, when its term will start.

Consequently, whilst someone can have a 'right to possess' a concurrent lease, no one can have a 'right to possess' a lease that is still reversionary. The most he or she can have is a right to possess it at some point in the future.

A relationship of fact

In contrast to the relationship of right, the relationship of fact – being 'in' possession (or 'having' or 'entering into' possession) – exists when a person is, as a matter of observable fact, actually enjoying the rights and incidents of an estate in land.[11]

Whether a person is 'in' possession is a pure question of fact, for factual possession is not necessarily rightful possession. It is quite possible, common even, for the right to possess an estate to be vested in one person, but for someone else actually to be 'in' possession of it. That is what happens every time a squatter ousts the true owner from land. As we shall see in chapter 8, there is a mental element in this, in that the possessor must intend to possess, but that is itself ultimately a question of fact too.

[8] A lease of a reversion granted to take effect immediately is a 'concurrent' lease (nowadays, often called an 'overriding' lease) and not a 'reversionary' lease. A reversionary lease is a lease, whether of a reversion or not, granted to begin at some date in the future. The two concepts are often confused, and lawyers frequently talk about a 'reversionary lease' when what they mean is a 'concurrent lease': see e.g. *Bell* v. *General Accident* [1998] 1 EGLR 69.

[9] A reversionary lease cannot be granted so as to begin more than twenty-one years in the future: s.149(3) Law of Property Act 1925.

[10] *Long* v. *Tower Hamlets LBC* [1996] 2 All ER 683.

[11] Oliver Wendell Holmes said in *The Common Law* (ed. M. Howe, Boston, Little Brown & Co., 1963), p. 170: 'To gain possession, then, a man must stand in a certain physical relationship to the object and to the rest of the world, and must have a certain intent.' The intent, Holmes thought, was an intent to exclude all others from that relationship (p. 174). It is perhaps more accurate to say that the intent is to enjoy the incidents of a particular estate, which might or might not involve excluding all others from physical enjoyment of the thing, depending on the nature of the estate.

But a person cannot 'have' or be 'in' or 'enter into' possession of an estate that is merely vested in interest, such as a reversionary lease, any more than he or she can have a right to possess it. By its very nature, an estate that is vested only in interest carries no right of present enjoyment of anything. There is nothing to enjoy, and therefore nothing to possess, until the right to the estate becomes vested in possession.

Possession of an estate: summary

The concept of 'possession', in this sense, can thus be summarised by four rules. First, what is possessed is a corporeal estate: a lease, a fee simple, or, stretching the point, a profit à prendre; rather than the physical land itself. Secondly, only estates capable of present enjoyment are capable of being possessed; an estate which carries only a right of future enjoyment is not capable of being possessed. Thirdly, a person has a right to possess such an estate when he or she has acquired a title to it. Fourthly, the person who is, as a matter of observable fact, enjoying the benefits of the estate, 'has' or is 'in' possession of it, irrespective of whether he or she has any externally verifiable title to it or not.

Orthodoxy

Although it is not often stated in these terms, this is entirely orthodox land law, as it has been understood by property lawyers since at least the seventeenth century. Before the Civil War, William Noy wrote *A Treatise on the Law of Tenures, Estates and Hereditaments.*[12] He is an unimportant figure now, because, as Charles I's attorney-general, he devised the writ for raising ship-monies, and was personally responsible for many other abuses of prerogative power, which made him unpopular, even with other lawyers.[13] His treatise, however, included a well-thought-out discussion of the concept of possession.

Noy made two points about it.

[12] The treatise is bound in with *Noy's Grounds and Maxims of the Law of England* (9th edn, reprinted Oxford, Professional Books Ltd, 1985).

[13] His contemporary, Sir Edward Coke, did not suffer the same fate. Coke was an equally difficult man, but had the good fortune (or political foresight) to switch from supporting the Crown to supporting Parliament – eventually becoming leader of the parliamentary opposition between 1620 and 1629 – instead of making the switch the other way, as Noy did. As a result, it is Coke's personality that is imprinted on every page of the common law; see S. Thorne, 'Sir Edward Coke', *Seldon Society Lectures* (New York, William S. Hein, 2003), pp. 1–18.

His first point was 'all estates which have their being are in possession, reversion, remainder or in right; but to all these, possession is the principal, because it is the full fruition of the estate'. In essence, this is the same distinction as that drawn above between estates which are vested in possession, and which can therefore be enjoyed now, and estates which are merely vested in interest, which can only be enjoyed at some time in the future. The one point of divergence is that, unlike Noy, we would now treat an immediate reversion upon a lease as an estate capable of present enjoyment and therefore capable of being possessed.[14]

Noy's second point was that there is a distinction between 'possession in *fait*' and 'possession in law': the first meant actual enjoyment of an estate capable of being possessed; the second meant the right of actual enjoyment of an immediate estate. Although the terminology is different, Noy was again making the same basic point as one that has already been made above, namely, that there is a distinction between 'having' or being 'in' possession of an immediately enjoyable estate, and merely having a right to do so.[15]

The way property lawyers have understood the concept of 'possession' in its technical sense has, therefore, changed little in the last 300 years.

Second meaning: occupation

The second meaning of possession is its common or vulgar meaning, which is physical occupation of tangible land.[16]

[14] Noy was willing to accept that a reversioner might have seisin, but ruled out the possibility that the reversioner might be described as being possessed of the reversion: *Noy's Grounds and Maxims of the Law of England* (9th edn, reprinted Oxford, Professional Books Ltd, 1985), p. 64.

[15] Pollock and Maitland said of Bracton that he 'never tired of emphasising the contrast' between possession and the right to possession: *History of English Law* (2nd edn, Cambridge, Cambridge University Press, 1911), vol. 2, p. 33. *Cowel's Interpreter of Words and Terms* (3rd edn, London, Place, Churchill & Safe, 1701) makes much the same point: 'Possession is twofold, actual and in law: actual possession is when a man actually enters into lands and tenements to him descended. Possession in law is when lands or tenements are descended to a man, and he hath not yet actually entered into them.'

[16] This concept is sometimes referred to in the cases as 'actual' possession, so as to distinguish it from 'legal' possession; e.g. *Prasad* v. *Wolverhampton BC* [1983] 2 All ER 140, 153. But this is itself capable of causing confusion, because 'actual' possession is sometimes used to denote the state of being 'in' possession of an estate, rather than merely having a right to possess it or having constructive possession of it. The term 'natural' possession is also sometimes used instead of occupation.

Occupation itself is not a legal term of art. It does not have a single and precise meaning.[17] The meaning varies according to the subject matter and context.[18] But the core concept is not in doubt. A person who is physically present on land is in occupation of it. The presence might be personal, or through goods and chattels or agents or employees. In exceptional cases, a person who does not have a present physical presence on land might, nonetheless, be treated as occupying it;[19] but cases on the edge do not change the core concept, and the core concept is physical presence.

Although occupation is the vulgar sense of the word 'possession', it is quite common even for property lawyers to use the word 'possession' in its 'broader popular' sense of 'use and occupation'[20] rather than its technical sense describing the relationship between a person and an estate. For instance, in *Anchor Brewhouse* v. *Berkeley House* ,[21] Scott J said:

> A landowner is entitled, as an attribute of his ownership of the land, to place structures on his land and thereby to reduce into actual possession the air space above his land.

Plainly, what he meant by 'actual possession' was occupation.

In some ways it is quite natural even for property lawyers to use the word 'possession', when what they really mean is 'occupation', because a person in possession of an estate in land is also often in occupation of it. Indeed, if an estate carries with it a right of occupation, then a person's possession of the estate is frequently made manifest by occupation.

But, although a person in occupation of land is often also in possession of an estate in it too, there is no necessary connection between the two. A person in occupation of land is not necessarily in possession of any estate in it, and a person in possession of an estate is not necessarily occupying any tangible land in which that estate subsists.

[17] 'The difference between possession and occupation is rather technical and, even to those experienced in property law, often rather elusive and hard to grasp': per Neuberger LJ in *Akici* v. *LR Butlin Ltd* [2006] 1 WLR 201, 207.

[18] Per Lord Nicolls in *Graysim Holdings* v. *P & O Property Holdings* [1996] 1 WLR 109, 110. The same point was made by Lord Cooke in *Hunter* v. *Canary Wharf* [1997] AC 655, 712: '[O]ccupier is an expression of varying meanings.' See also *Paterson* v. *Gas Light and Coke Co.* [1896] 2 Ch 476, 482 and *R* v. *Tao* [1977] QB 141, cited by Lord Cooke in *Hunter* v. *Canary Wharf* [1997] AC 665, 712; cf. per Gorell Barnes P in *Malone* v. *Laskey* [1907] 2 KB 141, 151: 'right of occupation in the proper sense of the term'.

[19] *Bacchiochii* v. *Academic Agency Ltd* [1998] 1 WLR 1313; cf. *Esselte* v. *Pearl Assurance* [1997] 1 WLR 981, and *Barnett* v. *O'Sulivan* [1994] 1 WLR 1667.

[20] Per Sir Douglas Frank QC in *Tulapam Properies* v. *De Almeida* [1981] 2 EGLR 55, 56.

[21] [1987] 2 EGLR 173.

That there is no necessary connection between possession of an estate in the land and occupation of the physical land itself can be demonstrated by considering four different types of estate.

First, the estate might be of a type where there is no right to occupy any land, because the right to occupy it has been granted away to someone else. A good example is the reversion upon an occupational lease. The reversioner has no right to occupy the land until the lease falls in. The reversion is nonetheless an estate and the person who receives the rent is in possession of it.[22] A similar, if more exotic, example is a freehold seigniorial manor.[23] The owner of the manor has a freehold interest in the land, but so too does everyone who holds underneath, and the owner of the manor has no right to occupy the latter's lands unless and until their interests escheat.[24]

Secondly, the estate might be of a type which is incapable of being occupied now or at any time in the future. A profit à prendre (such as a right to fish) cannot be occupied. But it is sufficiently corporeal to be treated as if it were an estate in its own right for this purpose,[25] and may be possessed, in precisely the same way as a fee simple may be possessed. So, if the profit is a fishery and someone else fishes, the person in possession of the profit may bring an action for trespass to the fishery.[26]

Thirdly, even if the estate carries a right of occupation with it, the right may not relate to any certain land. Moveable fees, such as a tidal foreshore, may be held 'in fee simple' but, if the sea permanently recedes, the foreshore moves with it. Whilst there is no definite area which the person in possession may occupy, nonetheless he or she can possess the

[22] Section 205(1)(xix) Law of Property Act 1925.

[23] In theory, it has not been possible to create a new manor in England and Wales since the statute of Quia Emptores Terrarum, 1290. In practice, the title to most manors cannot be traced back before the eighteenth century; these are 'reputed manors'. In Scotland, it was possible to create a new manor by subinfeudation until 2004, when feudal tenure was entirely abolished by s.2 Abolition of Feudal Tenure (Scotland) Act 2000.

[24] Formerly, land escheated if the owner died without an heir or was convicted of a felony. Neither event causes an escheat now: s.45(1) Administration of Estates Act 1925, s.1 Forfeiture Act 1870. An escheat can still occur, however, where a liquidator or trustee in bankruptcy exercises the statutory right to disclaim freehold land: *Scmlla Properties Ltd* v. *Gesso Properties (BVI) Ltd* [1995] EGCS 52; [1995] BCC 793. See ch. 7.

[25] See ch. 8.

[26] *Bristow* v. *Cormican* (1878) 3 App Cas 641. If someone instead pollutes the water killing the fish, the action is in nuisance for interference with the fishery: *Fitzgerald* v. *Firbank* [1897] 2 Ch 96; *Paine & Co.* v. *S Neots Gas & Coke Co.* [1939] 3 All ER 812.

fee simple by exercising the rights of the fee simple owner wherever the foreshore happens to be.[27]

Finally, even if the estate does carry with it a right to occupy particular land, the estate may be possessed without the person in possession being in occupation of any land. He or she might choose to enjoy the estate by leaving the property locked up and unoccupied,[28] or by putting a caretaker into occupation.[29]

Third meaning: constructive possession

There is yet a third sense in which the term 'possession' is used in English land law, namely, constructive possession.

The expression 'constructive possession' is sometimes used in contrast to 'actual possession', so as to mean possession of a thing otherwise than by actual occupation.[30] This is particularly common in cases about land taxes, because the taxation consequences sometimes depend upon whether a person in possession of an estate is also in occupation of the land. But otherwise the distinction is irrelevant, because occupation is neither necessary nor sufficient to be in possession of an estate.

There is, however, another more significant meaning to constructive possession, and that is possession which is entirely fictional. It describes the process by which the law deems a person presently to be 'in' possession of an estate, when, in fact, he or she is not; or which deems that person to have been 'in' possession of it in the past, when, in fact, he or she was not.

Historically, this deeming process was very important. In the past, rights and remedies often depended upon being able to establish who was currently, and who had recently been, 'in' possession of a particular estate.

Title to an estate often depended upon this because long after the Norman conquest it remained common for lifetime transfers of land to be made by a process called 'livery of seisin'. As the name suggests, the transfer was completed by delivering occupation of the land up to the transferee,

[27] *Baxendale* v. *Instow Parish Council* [1981] 2 All ER 620; *Jackson* v. *Simons* [1923] 1 Ch 373; s.61 Land Registration Act 2002.

[28] Per Lush J in *R* v. *St Pancras Assessment Committee* (1877) 2 QBD 581, 588; approved *Liverpool Corporation* v. *Chorley Union Assessment Committee* [1912] 1 KB 270.

[29] *Bertie* v. *Beaumont* (1812) 16 East 33.

[30] An attempt to introduce the concept of 'constructive-actual' possession was rejected in *New York–Kentucky Oil & Gas* v. *Miller* 187 Ky 742, 220 SW 535 (1920).

so that he became physically seized of it.[31] So the transferor could take the transferee onto the land and leave him in occupation, sometimes symbolically handing him a rod or a sod of earth before departing,[32] or the transferor could point to the land and authorise the transferee to enter upon the land and take it. The result was that you could never know who had good title to the land unless you also knew who had recently been in possession of it, and also the circumstances in which possession had been given up.

In the medieval period evidence of recent possession was as important to procedural rights as it was to substantive rights. Henry II's great innovation, the assize of novel disseisin, depended on evidence of it. Novel disseisin was a summary remedy designed to discourage resort to self-help. The principle was that, if someone ousted another from possession of a freehold estate, without first obtaining a court order, then the court would make a summary ruling, requiring possession to be restored to the original possessor, without any investigation of the merits. The defendant could still bring a separate 'real' action to prove that the ouster had been lawful, but in the meantime the position on the ground would be restored to that which it had been before hostilities commenced.[33]

But, as society became more complicated, so relying on evidence of who had formerly been 'in' possession of an estate inevitably became more unsatisfactory for determining rights and remedies. Livery of seisin could not be used to convey a freehold if the land had already been let to a tenant, because a physical entry would not be possible without interfering with the rights of the tenant. Similarly, there was a problem with novel disseisin where someone had been wrongly dispossessed of land but had taken the matter into his own hands and retaken the land by self-help, instead of

31 F. Sullivan, *Lectures on the Constitution and Laws of England* (2nd edn, London, Dilly & Johnson, 1776), pp. 59–60.

32 When William landed at Pevensey in Sussex, he is supposed to have stumbled to the ground, and then turned a bad omen into a good one, by rising, holding a sod of earth in each hand, and explaining that he had seized England. His knights would all have understood the reference: he had tripped because God was anxious to deliver seisin to him immediately, using the traditional Norman form of lifetime conveyance.

33 F. Sullivan, *Lectures on the Constitution and Laws of England* (2nd edn, London, Dilly & Johnson, 1776), p. 292. F. Maitland, *Forms of Action at Common Law* (Cambridge, Cambridge University Press, 1962), p. 22. Pollock and Maitland, in their *History of English law* (2nd edn, Cambridge, Cambridge University Press, 1911), p. 146, described the assize of novel disseisin as 'one of the most important laws ever issued in England', it having been created by a now lost ordinance of Henry II in 1166, perhaps modelled on an already extant practice in London; see H. Chew, *London Possessory Assizes* (London Record Society, 1965), p. xiv.

bringing novel disseisin and recovering the land through the courts. Novel disseisin would then work the wrong way round: the squatter, having been physically dispossessed, would be able to recover the land from the original possessor.

In order to resolve these and other problems the courts developed disparate doctrines of constructive possession, but in each the basic concept was the same: someone would be treated as having taken possession, without ever having done so,[34] or someone would be treated as still retaining possession after having been dispossessed.[35] So a freehold, which was subject to a tenancy, could be transferred by constructive livery of seisin without evicting the tenant, provided that the tenant attorned to the new owner. The attornment stood in place of the physical entry. Similarly, with novel disseisin, the original possessor could retain constructive possession, even against the disseisor's heir, in the following manner:

> if he dare approach the land, then he ought to go to the land, or to a parcel of it, and make his claim; and if dare not approach the land for doubt or fear of beating, or maiming, or death, then ought he to go and approach as near as he dare toward the land, or a parcel of it, to make his claim.[36]

There ought to be little room for any of this sort of nonsense in land law today. In conveyancing, there is one faint echo of livery of seisin, which

[34] Statute could work the same trick. By the Statute of Merchants, 1285, a judgment creditor was deemed to have been in possession of the debtor's land, in order to bring novel disseisin for the purpose of evicting the debtor, selling the land with vacant possession, and satisfying the debt. The statute was not entirely popular. Andrew Horne, a fourteenth-century London fishmonger, who is traditionally credited with having written *The Mirror of Justice*, one of the first textbooks of English law, complained that the statute was contrary to law: A. Horne, *The Mirror of Justice* (trans. W. Hughes, Washington, John Byrne, 1903), p. 287. Coke and Blackstone both thought highly of *The Mirror*, but Sir Frederick Pollock thought that it might have been written as a joke, and the always reliable Maitland said: 'No doubt a well-read and circumspect historian may find valuable hints in this book; but the statements of law that are in it he will construe by "the rule to the contrary", and he will insert a "not" wherever the author is more than usually positive' ((1893) 7 Seldon Soc. p. li). Holdsworth thought it was 'incomprehensible', and, more kindly, 'a legal romance': W. Holdsworth, *Sources and Literature of English Law* (Oxford, Oxford University Press, 1925), p. 32.

[35] Until the doctrine was abolished by the Real Property Limitation Act 1833, a physical ouster was required to dispossess a paper title owner for limitation purposes, even though someone else might have been in possession for all other purposes: *Paradise Beach* v. *Price–Robinson* [1968] AC 1072, 1082; *Pye* v. *Graham* [2003] 1 AC 419, 433.

[36] Littleton's Tenures, sec. 419. See also B. Simpson, *Introduction to the History of Land Law* (2nd edn, Oxford, Oxford University Press, 1961), pp. 38–9.

performs the useful function of allowing a deed to be delivered in escrow.[37] Otherwise all estates and interests now lie in grant, and may therefore be conveyed or transferred without an entry.[38] As a result, the possessory remedies of trespass, nuisance and ejectment (an action for recovery of land) are all available to a person who has a mere right to possess. So a person who has been granted a paper right to possess an estate may rely on that grant in order to recover it, or to prevent intrusions upon or interference with it. It is not necessary to allege also that the claimant is, in fact, in possession of it.[39]

Turning to the substantive law, exceptionally, when it comes to enforcement of the covenants contained in a lease, being 'in' possession does still matter, in two circumstances. First, a personal representative is personally liable upon, and can enforce the covenants contained in a lease, with retrospective effect, but only after entering into possession.[40] Secondly, sometimes a secured lender is not liable to perform, and cannot enforce, covenants attached to the secured estate before taking possession of the security.[41] It also still matters when a landlord forfeits a lease. As we shall see in chapter 4, service of a forfeiture claim form is a notional re-entry; it stands in the place of a physical re-entry. Otherwise, rights and remedies no longer depend upon having, in fact, taken possession.

Of course, a right to possess an estate is not necessarily derived from a paper grant. A person who is 'in' possession of an estate in land, even

[37] A conditional delivery of a deed is ineffective, until the condition is fulfilled, because a conditional entry upon the land would not have been effective as livery of seisin: *Alan Estates Ltd* v. *W. G. Stores Ltd* [1981] 3 All ER 481, 486 per Lord Denning MR. It is a misnomer to describe a deed as being 'sealed in escrow'. 'A deed is not sealed in escrow, it is sealed upon conditions to be satisfied which makes it not a deed but in truth an escrow'; per Harman J in *Venetian Glass* v. *Next Properties* [1989] 2 EGLR 42, 45.

[38] Section 51(1) Law of Property Act 1925, reproducing, with amendments, s.2 Real Property Act 1845. The doctrine of *interesse termini*, which required the tenant of a lease to enter before bringing any of the possessory actions survived until 1926; it was abolished by s.149 Law of Property Act 1925. See, W. Holdsworth, *Historical Introduction to Land Law* (Oxford, Oxford University Press, 1927), p. 120.

[39] Exceptionally, a defendant can plead a prior constructive entry, by someone with a better right to possession, as a defence to an action in trespass or nuisance; see ch. 2.

[40] An assignee of a commissioner in bankruptcy was formerly in a similar position: *Hanson* v. *Stevenson* (1818) 1 Barn & Ald 308; *Copeland* v. *Stephens* (1818) 1 Barn & Ald 593, 606. A trustee in bankruptcy now has a statutory power of disclaimer instead; see ch. 7.

[41] A secured lender normally has a right to take possession of the security immediately, but does not do so prior to having taken possession of the lease (the mortgage term) created by the mortgage, or by exercising the right to be put into the same position as if the security had created a mortgage term, thereby excluding the borrower from dominion and control of the secured estate. See generally ch. 5.

without any colour of title to it, has a bare right not to be disturbed, except by someone who has a better right to possess it than he or she does, and the possessory remedies are available to protect that right.[42] A litigant who wishes to rely on this bare right in order to bring an action to recover the land must, of course, assert that he or she was formerly in possession of it, for that is the basis of the right. Similarly, a litigant who wishes to sue in trespass or nuisance, relying on that bare right rather than any other title, must establish that he or she is now, or was formerly, in possession of the estate, for that too is the basis of the claim.

But whether the right claimed is derived from a paper title or from the fact of possession, there is no longer any scope for a doctrine of constructive possession. In the case of paper rights, neither the grant of the right nor the means of protecting it now depends upon proof of prior factual possession. The right to possess it is enough, so there is no need to pretend that the person with the right has ever in fact been in possession. In the case of rights derived merely from the bare fact of possession alone, there is no reason to extend the right, and the law does not extend the right, beyond those who really are, or who formerly really were, in possession.

Nonetheless, the ghost of constructive possession still continues to haunt some of the attic rooms of English land law.

Perhaps the most surprising example of this in modern times relates to oral wills. Before the industrial revolution, when England was still a largely illiterate society, it was possible to dispose of chattels by an oral will but it was not possible to dispose of freehold land in this way.[43] As writing became more common, the ability to leave even chattels by an oral testament was gradually restricted so that, by 1837, only men in

[42] See ch. 2. A similar rule applies to chattels: *Parker* v. *British Airways Board* [1982] 1 QB 1004.

[43] Freehold land (except for burgage tenements devisable) passed by descent outside the will to the heir-at-law, if there was one, or otherwise escheated to the lord. During the sixteenth century, it became possible to declare an oral trust of land, to take effect on the death of the settlor, but that was stopped by the Statute of Uses in 1536. By the Wills Act 1540 it became possible, for the first time, to dispose of freehold land by a written will. Attestation was first required by the Statute of Frauds in 1677. Land devised by will passed straight to the legatee, subject only to the possibility of disfeasence to pay the deceased's creditors, until the law was amended by Land Transfer Act 1897, so as to vest the land in the deceased's personal representatives instead: Blackstone, *Commentaries on the Laws of England* (11th edn, London, Strahan & Woodfall, 1791), vol. 2, p. 378; F. Sullivan, *Lectures on the Constitution and Laws of England* (2nd edn, London, Dilly & Johnson, 1776), p. 151; W. Holdsworth and C. Vickers, *The Law of Succession* (Oxford, Blackwell & Stevens, 1899), pp. 28-9; *Noy's Grounds and Maxims* (9th edn, reprinted Oxford, Professional Books Ltd, 1985), p. 219.

actual military service (who were unlikely to be literate) were secure in the privilege.[44] Not until after it had been made necessary by the First World War, were men in military service permitted, for the first time, to make oral wills of land too.[45] Nonetheless, in *Sen* v. *Headley*,[46] the Court of Appeal held that anyone who is convinced that he or she is about to die may make an oral gift of land, to take effect on death, by delivering constructive possession of the land to the donee, for instance by handing over the keys to a house. It is hard to see how this can be right because, even when lifetime oral transfers of land were permitted by livery of seisin, it was an absolute rule that the delivery had to be completed by physical entry upon the land before the donor died.

Summary of meanings

To summarise, 'possession' may have one of three meanings: it may be describing a relationship between a person and a fee simple, a lease or a profit à prendre (the person presently using and enjoying it is 'in' possession of it; the person who has a present right to use and enjoy it has a 'right' to possess it); or it may simply mean occupation of the physical land itself; or it may be referring to an old legal fiction, whereby someone was deemed to have been using and enjoying an estate in land, when (in fact) that person was not.

Problem of different meanings

Because the word 'possession' has three different and inconsistent meanings, the truth of any statement made about the law of possession depends upon the context in which it is made. The rights and obligations of a person in possession of an estate are rarely the same as those of a person in occupation, and the position of a person in constructive possession may be different to both.

So, in order to answer the question, 'what is the law of possession?' on any particular point it is first necessary to determine in which of these three senses the word 'possession' is being used. Any answer which does not distinguish between the different meanings of 'possession' is inevitably going to be misleading at best, and simply wrong at worst. For example, the statement 'possession is sufficient in order to bring an action

[44] Sections 9, 11 Wills Act 1837. [45] Section 3 Wills (Soldiers and Sailors) Act 1918.
[46] [1991] Ch 425; [1991] 2 WLR 1308.

for nuisance' is true if the word 'possession' is used in the technical sense of possession of an estate, but is false if the word 'possession' is being used in the sense of occupation.[47]

Wherever the law relating to possession appears to be difficult or inconsistent, it is usually the result of failing to distinguish between the three different meanings, and instead choosing to treat those meanings as if they were simply aspects of a larger, more amorphous concept. It is no exaggeration to say that this single failure is the root cause of most of the difficulties with and confusion about the law of possession.

Errors as a result

The error most often finds expression in an assumption that a person who is in occupation of land is necessarily in possession of an estate.

One of the best examples in recent times can be found in the speech of Lord Templeman in *Street* v. *Mountford*.[48] Mrs Mountford had been let into occupation of a furnished room in Bournemouth under a written agreement. The issue was whether that agreement, properly construed, created a licence or a tenancy. This was a matter of some practical importance, because Mrs Mountford's security of tenure, and her right to have a 'fair rent' fixed, were dependent upon the agreement creating a tenancy.

The argument for the owner, Mr Street, was quite simple, and properly distinguished between the various meanings of the word 'possession'. On behalf of Mr Street, it was said:[49]

> The expression 'exclusive possession' or 'exclusive occupation' can be used in two senses, namely (a) meaning no more than the right of a contractual occupier to prevent, through the grant of an injunction, the owner of the land entering on the land for purposes inconsistent with the contract and (b) in the full sense of the right enjoyed by the owner of an estate in land in possession to exclude all the world.

Properly construed, the argument went, the agreement fell into the first category rather than the second.

As a matter of the actual construction of the agreement, that argument might not have had much merit. But the argument itself was certainly grounded in well-established and orthodox land law. The distinction between a mere contractual right occupy and a right creating an estate in

[47] *Hunter* v. *Canary Wharf* [1997] AC 655; [1997] 2 All ER 436.
[48] [1985] 1 AC 809. [49] *Ibid.*, p. 812.

land had been recognised as early as 1470.[50] So all the House of Lords had to do was to decide whether the agreement, on its proper construction and shorn of any sham terms, granted Mrs Mountford a leasehold estate in the land or only a contractual right of occupation.

Lord Templeman, who gave the only speech, certainly accepted that, as a matter of law, this was the issue. He said:[51]—

> The position was well summarised by Windeyer J sitting in the High Court of Australia in *Radaich* v. *Smith* (1959) 101 CLR 209, 222, where he said:
>
> What then is the fundamental right which a tenant has that distinguishes his position from that of a licensee? It is an interest in land as distinct from a personal permission to enter the land and use it for some stipulated purpose or purposes. And how is it to be ascertained whether such an interest in land has been given? By seeing whether the grantee was given a legal right of exclusive possession of the land for a term or from year to year or for a life or lives. If he was, he is a tenant. And he cannot be other than a tenant, because a legal right of exclusive possession is a tenancy and the creation of such a right is a demise. To say that a man who has, by agreement with a landlord, a right of exclusive possession of land for a term is not a tenant is simply to contradict the first proposition by the second. A right of exclusive possession is secured by the right of a lessee to maintain ejectment and, after his entry, trespass. A reservation to the landlord, either by contract or statute, of a limited right of entry, as for example to view or repair, is, of course, not inconsistent with the grant of exclusive possession. Subject to such reservations, a tenant for a term or from year to year or for a life or lives can exclude his landlord as well as strangers from the demised premises. All this is long established law: see *Cole on Ejectment* (1857) pp. 72, 73, 287, 458.

But, having acknowledged the long-established distinction between a 'personal permission to enter land for some stipulated purpose or purposes' and a 'legal right of exclusive possession', Lord Templeman then decided the appeal on the basis that Mr Street had conceded that Mrs Mountford had 'exclusive possession',[52] and so it necessarily followed that she was a tenant.

But the concession was of 'exclusive possession or exclusive occupation ... meaning no more than the right of a contractual occupier to prevent, through the grant of an injunction, the owner of the land entering on the land for purposes inconsistent with the contract'. If Lord Templeman

[50] *Prior of Bruton* v. *Ede*, YB Edward IV (1930) 47 Seldon Society 31.
[51] [1985] 1 AC 809, 827. [52] *Ibid.*, p. 816.

had kept the concept of occupation separate from the concept of possession of estate, then it is impossible that he could have concluded, as he did, that this concession determined the question of whether Mrs Mountford had been in possession of an estate, and therefore had a tenancy. As a result, although *Street* v. *Mountford* is often cited as the leading case on the distinction between a licence and a tenancy, in fact it decided very little. The principles were already well established and the actual judgment on the facts was premised on the mistaken assumption that Mr Street had conceded that Mrs Mountford was in possession of an estate.

A similar example of the confusion that results from failing to distinguish between possession and occupation is demonstrated by a later decision of the House of Lords on a similar point, the case of *Bruton* v. *London and Quadrant Housing Trust.*[53] In that case, the housing trust had been granted a licence to use some accommodation for housing people who would otherwise have been homeless, and had accordingly granted a sub-licence of part of it to Mr Bruton. Mr Bruton claimed that his sub-licence was really a tenancy because it gave him exclusive possession.

The answer to that could, and perhaps should, have been that, although, Mr Bruton had been granted an exclusive contractual right to occupy, he had not been granted possession of any leasehold estate, because the housing trust had made it clear that it was only a licensee itself, and so had no estate out of which it could have carved a tenancy.[54] Nor could this be changed by the rules of estoppel as to title. Estoppel as to title stops a grantor saying: 'I cannot have granted you what I purported to grant you because I did not have any power to do it.' It does not stop the grantor saying: 'I must have granted you exactly what I purported to grant you because I did not have power to grant you anything else.'[55]

The House of Lords, however, decided that Mr Bruton had exclusive possession, without distinguishing between possession in the sense of occupation and possession of a leasehold estate. It went on to say, as had been said before in *Street* v. *Mountford*, that, because Mr Bruton had 'exclusive possession', it therefore followed that he was a tenant. Having decided that the housing trust had granted Mr Bruton a tenancy, the peculiar (but logical) result was that the housing trust could not deny

[53] [2000] AC 406; [1997] 4 All ER 970. [54] *Torbett* v. *Faulkener* [1952] TLR 659.
[55] *Terunnanse* v. *Terunnanse* [1968] AC 1086.

that it had granted him a tenancy, even though both parties had known from the start that the housing trust had no power to do so. The decision has, therefore, been criticised, rightly, for turning the law of estoppel on its head, and for producing an estate out of nothing.[56]

That is not to say that either *Street* v. *Mountford* or *Bruton* v. *London and Quadrant* were wrongly decided on their facts. On the facts, it is hard to see how the agreement in *Street* v. *Mountford*, shorn of its sham terms, could have created anything other than a tenancy,[57] and the real question in *Bruton* v. *London and Quadrant* ought to have been whether the agreement between the owner and the housing trust, whereby the owner granted the housing trust authority to grant Mr Bruton his 'licence', really authorised the creation of a tenancy. The answer could and should have been that it did, because it expressly contemplated that the interest which would be granted to Mr Bruton would be one whereby he would have the right to control access by strangers, in return for periodic payment of a sum of money, and that, in substance, is a tenancy, even if the parties choose to call it something else; and, if the owner of any property stands by, and allows another to create a proprietary interest in it, then the owner ought to be bound by the disposition, even if the owner is not contractually a party to it.[58]

The reasoning in both cases is, nonetheless, demonstrably suspect, and for the same reason. In both cases, the judges failed to distinguish between the different meanings of the word 'possession'. Both cases proceeded on the assumption that, because someone was in possession in one sense (in both cases, in the sense of occupation), it therefore followed that he or she was in possession in all senses of the word. If the different meanings of the word 'possession' had been kept in mind, it would have been impossible to make that mistake.

Treating occupation as a synonym for possession of an estate is not, however, the only mistake that can be made. It is, for instance, quite possible to turn it round the other way, and conclude that, because someone is not in possession of an estate, that person is not in occupation either. This is rarer because, although the logic is the same, it is more intuitively wrong.

[56] M. Dixon, 'The Non-Proprietary Lease: The Rise of the Feudal Phoenix', [2000] CLJ 25–8; P. Routley, 'Tenancies and Estoppel – After Bruton' (2000) 63 MLR 424–8.

[57] See ch. 4.

[58] *Rimmer* v. *Webster* [1902] 2 Ch 163, 173; *Keech* v. *Hall* (1778) 1 Doug 21.

Examples do, however, exist in the caselaw.

For instance, in *Allan* v. *Liverpool Overseers*,[59] a leading case on rateable occupation, Blackburn J said:

> A lodger in a house, although he has the exclusive use of rooms in the house, in the sense that nobody else is to be there, and though his goods are stowed there, yet he is not in exclusive occupation in that sense, because the landlord is there for the purpose of being able, as landlords commonly do in the case of lodgings, to have his own servants to look after the house and the furniture, and has retained to himself the occupation, though he has agreed to give the exclusive enjoyment of the occupation to the lodger.

The logic of that passage, as a matter of the ordinary use of language, is impossible to follow. How can the landlord be 'occupying' the rooms, and the lodger not, when it is the lodger who is physically present in the rooms, who has goods stowed there, and who has a contractual right of exclusive use of the rooms good against the landlord? It appears to be simply nonsense to say that, in those circumstances, it is the landlord rather than the lodger who is occupying the rooms. No doubt, what Blackburn J meant was that rateable occupation required possession of an estate, rather than mere occupation, and that a lodger is not in possession of any estate, because a lodger only has a contractual right of occupation. But, instead, he appeared to say that, because a lodger is not in possession of an estate, then, in defiance of the known facts, nor is the lodger in occupation either.

These cases all demonstrate the fundamental importance of distinguishing between the different meanings of the word 'possession' when used in English land law. Failing to do so can cause even the most distinguished of judges to decide cases on the basis of a misunderstood concession, or to throw well-established principles into turmoil, or to say things which, as a matter of language, are nonsense. Distinguish between the different meanings, however, and most of the problems with the law of possession either can be resolved, or simply disappear.

[59] (1874) LR 9 QB 180, 191–2.

2

Protection of possession

Introduction

The previous chapter distinguished between the various meanings of the word 'possession', and defined the key concept of possession of an estate. This chapter explores the importance of that concept to legal disputes about the use or enjoyment of land.

The possessory actions

The common law protects the use and enjoyment of land, and the right to use and enjoy land, by three possessory actions.

The first is the action for recovery of land. This is the action by which a person who has a right to possess a freehold, or a lease, or a profit à prendre, may vindicate that right, by using the process of the court to oust the person who is in fact in possession of it, and to require that person to pay compensation (called mesne profits) for the wrongful use of it in the meantime.

The second is the action of trespass to land. By this action, a person who is in fact in possession of a freehold, a lease or a profit à prendre, or who has a right to possess it, may obtain compensation for wrongful physical intrusions which fall short of a dispossession.

The third is the action of nuisance. This is the action by which a person who is in possession of a freehold, a lease or a profit à prendre, or who has a right to possess it (or, indeed, who has a right to any legal interest in the land, except an advowson or franchise) may obtain compensation for wrongful interference with its use or enjoyment which does not involve a physical intrusion.[1]

[1] In a 'seminal article' (per Lord Goff in *Cambridge Water* v. *Eastern Counties Leather* [1994] 2 AC 264, 299), Professor Newark said: 'Disseisina, transgressio and nocumentum covered the three ways in which a man might be interfered with in his rights over land. Wholly to deprive a man of the opportunity of exercising his rights over land was to disseise him, for which he might have recourse to the assize of novel disseisin. But to trouble a man in

These are all common law actions, meaning that they are causes of action developed by common law courts before the enactment of the Judicature Acts, and not by chancery courts administering the rules of equity.

Equity protects the use and enjoyment of land, and the right to use and enjoy land, in two additional ways. First, it provides additional defences and additional remedies, where those common law wrongs have been committed. Secondly, it provides its own remedies (principally, injunctions) where there is no wrong at common law because the interference is with a proprietary right which is recognised only in equity.

What equity does not do, and never has done, is allow someone who has what is only an equitable right to bring an action to recover land, or to sue in trespass or nuisance, on the strength of the equitable right alone.[2]

Actions for recovery of land

An action in which a person who is not in possession of an estate in land claims that he or she should be put into possession of it is called an 'action for recovery of land'. It is the cause of action formerly known as 'ejectment'.[3]

It is a curious historical accident that ejectment is used to recover land. Ejectment began as a type of trespass. It was a tenant's remedy for dispossession, and it was needed because a tenant could not bring novel disseisin.[4] A tenant was not technically 'seised' of the land, and so novel disseisin was only available to a freeholder. Ironically, ejectment became cheaper and quicker than novel disseisin, and so, over time, lawyers adapted it so that it could be used by freeholders too.

At first, this was done by arranging for the freeholder to grant a genuine lease to a friend, who would then attempt to enter upon the land as tenant. If evicted, that friend could then bring an action in ejectment to be put into possession of the lease, relying on the freeholder's title to grant it. Eventually, however, the lease, entry and eviction all became fictional.

the exercise of his rights over land without going so far as to dispossess him was a trespass or a nuisance according to whether the act was done on or off the plaintiff's land' ('The Boundaries of Nuisance' (1949) 65 LQR 480, 481).

[2] See ch. 6.

[3] *Gledhill* v. *Hunter* (1880) 14 ChD 492, 498–500. In England, as late as 1920, it was still 'commonly spoken of as an action in ejectment' (*Marshall* v. *Charteris* [1920] 1 Ch 520, 523) and, in Australia, it still is.

[4] See B. Simpson, *Introduction to the History of Land Law* (2nd edn, Oxford, Oxford University Press, 1961), p. 71.

The freeholder brought the action in the name of the non-existent tenant (usually a Mr John Doe) claiming that Mr Doe had entered pursuant to a non-existent lease and been ousted by a non-existent person in possession. The person who was then, in fact, keeping the freeholder out of possession had to come into the action and defend it, for otherwise the freeholder could obtain judgment in default.[5] But, in order to come in and defend the action, the non-existent lease, entry and eviction all had to be admitted. By this elaborate means, it was possible for the action to proceed solely as a test of the title of the real claimant, the freeholder, against the title of the person in fact keeping the freeholder out of possession.[6] The tenant's action of *ejectione firmæ* thus became the freeholder's action of ejectment.

These fictions were, eventually, swept away by the Common Law Procedure Act 1852, but that did not change the substance of the action, or even its name. The name was changed in 1875, with some lack of imagination, to 'an action for recovery of land' but no change was made to the substance of the action.[7] Another procedural reform, made at the same time, was to allow equitable defences to be pleaded in the same action as a common law claim, provided that they were properly pleaded.[8] Before

5 For the effect of the judgment, see ch. 9. The freeholder had to give the possessor a notice, purportedly written by the non-existent person in possession as 'his loving friend', which read as follows: 'I am informed that you are in possession of, or claim title to, the premises mentioned in this declaration of ejectment, or to some part thereof; and I, being sued in this action as casual ejector, and having no claim or title to the same, do advise you to appear on [date] at [address of court], by some attorney of that court, and then and there, by a rule to be made of the same court, to cause yourself to be made defendant in my stead; otherwise I shall suffer judgment to be entered against me, and you will be turned out of possession.' The person serving the notice had to explain what this actually meant: J. Day, *The Common Law Procedure Acts* (London, Sweet, 1868), p. 141.

6 *Bristow* v. *Cormican* (1878) 3 App Cas 641, 661; *Ocean Estates Ltd* v. *Pinder* [1969] 2 AC 19, 25–6; Blackstone, *Commentaries on the Laws of England* (11th edn, London, Strahan & Woodfall, 1791), vol. 3, p. 203; B. Simpson, *Introduction to the History of Land Law* (2nd edn, Oxford, Oxford University Press, 1961), p. 138.

7 Maitland, *Forms of Action at Common Law* (Cambridge, Cambridge University Press, 1969), p. 49.

8 But not so as to allow an equitable title to be used as the basis of the claim. All that was done was to reverse the rule that the defendant had to go to a court of equity in order to prevent the claimant with the better legal right enforcing it. The old law was explained by Lord Blackburn in *Danford* v. *McAnulty* ((1883) 8 App Cas 456, 462) as follows: 'For a long time an action for the recovery of land at law was brought by ejectment, and it was so established as to be trite law – a commonplace expression of law – that in ejectment, where a person was in possession those who sought to turn him out were to recover upon the strength of their own title; and consequently possession was at law a good defence against any one, and those who sought to turn the man in possession out must shew a superior legal title to his. If, however, they did shew that, still if the person who was in possession

then, the defendant had to bring a separate action in a court of equity, and obtain an injunction to prevent the common law claim proceeding further. But this too was simply procedural. It did not change the nature of the defence. It simply meant that equitable rights and defences relevant to the claim to recover the land could be determined by the court hearing the action instead of by a different court.[9] Thereafter, it was no longer necessary to bring a separate action in a court administering equity to determine that part of the claim.

The result is that, for all practical purposes, an action for recovery of land today is substantively the same as the action of ejectment at the time of the restoration of Charles II. The sole question is whether the person claiming possession of an estate has a better right to possess it than the person defending the claim.

It is important to emphasise at this point – not least because it is something of a recurring theme of this book – that an action for recovery of land (ejectment) is an action to be put into possession of an estate in land. The complaint is that the claimant is not currently 'in' possession of it, and the claimant wants to use the process of the court in order to be put 'in' possession of it. Sometimes, the claimant is asking to be put into possession of a fee simple free of any lease; on other occasions, it is a claim to be put into possession of the fee simple reversion upon a lease. Or, it can be a claim to be put into possession of a lease, free of or subject to a sub-lease;[10] or, if the action is brought by a legal chargee, to be put in the same position as a tenant under a lease granted by the debtor.[11] Or, exceptionally, it is action where the claimant is asking to be put into possession of a mere profit à prendre.[12] But it is never an action in which the claimant is simply asking to be put into physical occupation of tangible land, albeit that the judgment may often be enforced in that way.

Actions for trespass

It is quite possible to intrude upon an estate without acquiring possession of it. There is a qualitative difference between taking possession of the

could shew that although they had shewn a superior legal title to the possession, yet he had an equitable ground for saying that they should not turn him out, he as the law stood was obliged to go to a Court of Equity, and as the plaintiff there, as the "actor" (to use a civil law expression), to make out that there was a sufficient reason for a Court of Equity to interfere, and to prevent his being turned out of possession, on this equitable ground.' See also ch. 6.

[9] *Gledhill* v. *Hunter* (1880) 14 ChD 492; *Danford* v. *McAnulty* (1883) 8 App Cas 456.

[10] See ch. 4. [11] See ch. 5. [12] See ch. 8.

estate itself, and trespassing upon someone else's possession of it, no matter how persistently. For such wrongs, an action to recover the estate would be pointless. At its most basic level, the court cannot compel the intruder to give up possession of something which he or she has not got. Indeed, if the complaint is about an intrusion, the claimant is usually already in possession of it.

For intrusions upon land which fall short of a dispossession, the appropriate action is trespass. The full name of the action is '*trespass quare clausum fregit*' (literally, the complaint is that the defendant has broken into the claimant's close) and, as the name suggests, the essence of the action is a wrongful physical intrusion.[13] The name is misleading insofar as it suggests that in order to commit the wrong it is necessary for the land to be physically closed off. This is not so, for, as Blackstone explained,[14] even open land is notionally separated from all other land in different ownership, and anyone who without lawful authority crosses a boundary, whether vertical or horizontal, commits a trespass.

Trespass is, therefore, a wrong to the enjoyment of an estate in land, and not to ownership,[15] nor to occupation.[16] Consequently, if an estate is capable of being possessed, it is capable of being intruded upon by trespass, even if it is not capable of being enjoyed by occupation.

So, to poach fish from a non-tidal river might, depending upon the circumstances, be a trespass upon the possession of the riparian freehold, or it might equally well be a trespass upon the possession of a profit of piscary.[17] Indeed, it might be both. By standing upon the bank, the poacher intrudes upon the freehold; by casting the line, the intrusion is upon the profit.

Trespass being an interference with possession of an estate, a claimant in possession of it does not also need to prove a right to possess the estate,[18] except against defendants who seek to justify their intrusions by reference to their own titles,[19] or the titles of others through whom they claim.

If the law had remained that only a person who was in fact in possession of an estate could bring the action of trespass, the relationship between

[13] W. Holdsworth, *History of English Law* (2nd edn, London, Sweet & Maxwell, 1937), vol. 7, p. 58.

[14] *Commentaries on the Laws of England* (11th edn, London, Strahan & Woodfall, 1791), vol. 3, p. 209.

[15] Per Scarman LJ in *Hesperides Hotels* v. *Aegean Turkish Holidays* [1978] 1 All ER 277, 294.

[16] Per Blackburn J in *Allan* v. *Liverpool Overseers* (1874), LR 9 QB 180, 191–2.

[17] B. Simpson, *Introduction to the History of Land Law* (2nd edn, Oxford, Oxford University Press, 1961), p. 99.

[18] *Adams* v. *Naylor* [1944] 2 All ER 21, 24.

[19] The plea of *liber tenement*.

trespass, possession and title would have been relatively simple. Title would have been irrelevant, except in cases where intruders sought to justify their intrusions by reference to their own titles, or the title of others by whose right or authority they entered.

The law, however, balked at allowing a squatter to bring the action against an intruder whilst denying it to the person wrongly being kept out of possession by the squatter. It therefore permits the action to be brought by a person who has a mere right to possess too. This naturally complicates the relationship between trespass, possession and title because, in order to protect the intruder from the risk of being sued twice by two different people for the same wrong (first by the person in possession, and then, perhaps, by someone with a better right to possession), the intruder must sometimes be permitted to plead as a defence that someone else has a better right to bring the claim than the claimant; this is the plea of *ius tertii.*

The circumstances in which the defendant is allowed to do so are examined later in this chapter.

Actions in nuisance

The action of nuisance developed out of the assize of novel disseisin, so it is perhaps not surprising that the rules for bringing the action of nuisance should essentially be the same as those for the action of trespass. But there is one difference, which is caught up in the nature of the action. In trespass, the essence of the action is a physical intrusion. But it is not normally possible either to possess or to intrude physically upon incorporeal rights because the rights do not have any physical existence (exceptionally, and stretching the point, it is possible to intrude on a profit à prendre, the thing taken from the land being sufficiently corporeal for trespass to lie). Consequently, the complaint where the interference is with other incorporeal rights has to be of a non-physical disturbance of the right, rather than a physical intrusion upon it, and so the only remedy for an interference with the right is in nuisance.[20]

[20] This has some peculiar results. If the owner of an estate interferes with a right of way, the owner of the right can only complain if the interference is substantial; for the right is an incorporeal hereditament, and so the action must be brought in nuisance. But the owner of the estate can complain about anything done by the owner of the right on the way that is not wholly within the terms of the right, even if the difference is trivial; for if it is not authorised by the right, it must be a trespass on the way, and trespass is actionable without damage.

Otherwise, the rules are the same. In short, for nuisance it is necessary that the claimant should be in possession of, or have a right to possess, an estate in land, or should have a right to a legal interest in land. In *Hunter* v. *Canary Wharf Ltd*,[21] Lord Goff summarised the position as follows:

> It follows that, on the authorities as they stand, an action in private nuisance will only lie at the suit of a person who has a right to the land affected. Ordinarily, such a person can only sue if he or she has the right to exclusive possession of the land, such as a freeholder or tenant in possession, or even a licensee with exclusive possession.[22] Exceptionally however, as *Foster* v. *Warblington UDC* shows, this category may include a person in actual possession who has no right to be there; and in any event a reversioner can sue in so far his reversionary interest is affected. But a mere licensee on the land has no right to sue.

Possessory actions and occupation

For the reasons set out in the previous chapter, a person in occupation of land is not necessarily in possession of any estate in it. This is not merely an academic point. The distinction between possession and mere occupation is a matter of some importance to the common law, because the common law provides no remedy against third party interference with a mere right of occupation.[23]

The clear rule is that even a contractual right of occupation is not protected.

It is not protected by an action for recovery of land (ejectment) because that is the action by which a person is put into possession of a fee simple, a lease or a profit à prendre; and, absent any such a right, no order can be made. As Menzies J observed in *Commonwealth* v. *Anderson*:[24]

> Although it is trite to say so, it is important to remember that ejectment is not so called because it is a process whereby a plaintiff seeks to have the defendant ejected from his land. It got its name because it was an action in which the claimant complained that he had been wrongly ejected by the defendant from land of which he was rightfully possessed.

21 [1997] AC 655, 692; [1997] 2 All ER 426, 436.

22 For what is meant by 'a licensee with exclusive possession', see ch. 4.

23 See *Allan* v. *Liverpool Overseers* (1874) LR 9 QB 180, 191–2 per Blackburn J; *Monks* v. *Dykes* (1839) 4 M & W 567 per Parke B, 569; *Helman* v. *Horsham and Worthing Assessment Committee* [1949] 1 All ER 776; *Appah* v. *Parncliffe Investments Ltd* [1964] 1 All ER 838.

24 (1960) 105 CLR 303, 320.

Of course, if the estate possessed carries with it a right of occupation, then the order will naturally be enforced by physical eviction of whomsoever is in occupation.[25] But it would be a mistake to conclude that, when a sheriff or bailiff enforces the order for possession, the court is protecting the right of occupation in itself. It is not. It is protecting the right to possess an estate, of which the right of occupation happens to be an incident.

The same rules apply to an action in trespass. You cannot trespass upon a licence; the trespass is to the possession of, or the right to possess, the estate out of which the licence has been created. Nor can you commit a nuisance to a licence. The nuisance must to be some corporeal or incorporeal hereditament, not to a mere contractual right.[26]

Notwithstanding that the above is both well-established and orthodox law, judges sometimes express the view that a mere contractual right of occupation can be protected against third parties by one of these actions. Sometimes it is simply assumed. In *Bruton* v. *London and Quadrant Housing Trust*,[27] for instance, the Court of Appeal does not seem to have worried about whether a licensee could obtain an order for possession against its sub-licensee at the end of the sub-licence.[28] Sometimes, the challenge is made more overtly. For example, Lord Hope, in *Hunter* v. *Canary Wharf*,[29] suggested that there are exceptional cases where mere occupation will suffice, and cited *Foster* v. *Warblington UDC*.[30]

But this is a misinterpretation of *Foster* v. *Warblington UDC* . In that case, the claimant sued the council for discharging sewage so as to pollute his oyster ponds on the foreshore. He could not prove that he had any title to the foreshore, but Vaughan Williams LJ said:[31]

> But, even if title could not be proved, in my judgment there has been such an occupation of these beds for such a length of time – not that the length of time is really material for this purpose – as would entitle the plaintiff as against the defendants, who have no interest in the foreshore, to sustain this action for the injury which it is alleged has been done by the sewage to his oysters so kept in those beds.

That does not mean, however, that his occupation was treated as being sufficient to bring the action on its own. The point was that occupation of the oyster beds was enough to establish that he was in possession of

[25] See ch. 9. [26] *Hunter* v. *Canary Wharf* [1997] AC 655. [27] [1997] 4 All ER 970.
[28] The issue did not arise in the House of Lords.
[29] [1997] AC 655, 724; [1997] 2 All ER 426, 468.
[30] [1906] 1 KB 648; [1904-7] All ER Rep 366.
[31] [1906] 1 KB 648, 659–60; [1904–7] All ER Rep 366, 370.

the fee simple in the foreshore. As Lord Hatherley explained in *Bristow* v. *Cormican*:[32]

> There can be no doubt whatever that mere possession is sufficient, against a person invading that possession without himself having any title whatever – as a mere stranger; that is to say, it is sufficient as against a wrongdoer. The slightest amount of possession would be sufficient to entitle the person who is so in possession, or claims under those who have been or are in such possession, to recover as against a mere trespasser.

Another overt challenge was made in *Dutton* v. *Manchester Airport*,[33] where the majority of the Court of Appeal allowed the licensee, in the circumstances of that case, to bring an action to recover land. But, for the reasons explained in chapter 4, the decision of the majority in that case is *per incuriam*. There ought to be no doubt that a person with a mere right of occupation – in other words, a person who has no claim to a freehold or leasehold estate or a profit à prendre – simply cannot bring any of the possessory actions, because they are all actions which protect only those claims.

Perhaps part of the reason for the confusion is that, although a mere occupier cannot bring any of the possessory actions, the actions of trespass and nuisance can certainly be brought against an occupier. An occupier, or anyone else, can be a defendant to an action for trespass or nuisance, because it is not necessary to be in possession of any estate in land oneself in order to intrude upon or interfere with someone else's possession. By contrast, in theory, it ought not to be possible to bring an action for recovery of land against a mere occupier alone (although the occupier might properly be joined, as an additional defendant, for the purpose of ensuring that he or she is bound by the judgment against the actual possessor). The action is an action to recover an estate in land, and if the only defendant is a mere occupier, then there must be someone else in possession of the relevant estate who is a proper and necessary defendant. In practice, of course, few occupiers will take the point, the judge, working through a busy possession list, will not consider it, and the occupier will be evicted by the bailiffs when the possession order is enforced.

Possession and wrongdoer's title

It is a complete defence to an action for recovery of land that the defendant has a better right to possess the estate in dispute than the claimant. But the defendant's possession only gives the defendant a procedural

[32] (1878) 3 App Cas 641, 657. [33] [2000] QB 183.

advantage in this respect, not a substantive one. The claimant does not have to prove an absolute or indefeasible title, simply because the defendant is in possession. It merely throws upon the claimant the burden of showing a better title. So, when making a claim for possession of an estate, the burden is initially upon the claimant to prove the title which he or she claims. Having done so, the burden then shifts to the defendant to show a better right to possess it, either by title paramount, or by virtue of a title which has been carved out of the claimant's title. This was explained clearly by Scarman LJ in *Portland Managements Ltd* v. *Harte*: [34]

> [W]hen an owner of land is making a case . . . against a person alleged to be in possession, all that the true owner has to prove is his title and an intention to regain possession. If the defendant to the action either admits his ownership or is faced with evidence, which the court accepts, that the plaintiff is in fact the owner, then the burden is on the defendant to confess and avoid; that is to say, to set up a title or right to possession consistent with the fact of ownership vested in the plaintiff.

The position is essentially the same in the actions of trespass and nuisance. As between a party in possession, and a party who is not, the burden of showing title is initially upon the person who is not in possession.[35] If that title is shown, then the person in possession must rebut that and show a better title.

So, if the claimant in an action for trespass or nuisance is in possession of the relevant estate, then initially he or she may rely upon the fact of that possession alone. But, if the defendant proves a title to the land which appears to justify what would otherwise be a trespass or nuisance, then, in order to make out the claim, the claimant will be driven to prove either a paramount title or one which is derived from the defendant's title.[36]

In *Delaney* v. *T. P. Smith*,[37] Tucker LJ explained this in its historical context as follows:

> It is no doubt true that a plaintiff in an action of trespass to land need only in the first instance allege possession. This is sufficient to support his action against a wrongdoer, but is not sufficient as against the lawful owner, and in an action against the freeholder the plaintiff must at some stage of

[34] [1976] 1 All ER 225, 231.

[35] There is an exception if the party in possession is in a fiduciary relationship with the person who is not in possession: per Dixon CJ in *Allan* v. *Roughley* (1955) 94 CLR 98, 107; *Lyell* v. *Kennedy* (1889) 14 App Cas 437.

[36] *Stroud* v. *Birt* (1697) Comyns Rep 7.

[37] [1946] 2 All ER 23, 25.

> the pleadings set up a title derived from the defendant. The true position is illustrated in the old forms of pleadings: see *Bullen & Leakes Precedents of Pleading*, 3rd edn, pp. 802, 803, and the cases there referred to dealing with the plea of liberum tenementum. It is sufficient, I think, to refer to the judgment of Patteson J in *Ryan* v. *Clark*, where he explained the nature of this plea as follows (14 QB 65, at p. 71): it admits such a possession as would maintain the action against a wrongdoer, but asserts a freehold in the defendant with a right to the immediate possession. Sutton, in *Personal Actions at Common Law*, I think, correctly states the position at p. 185, where he explains that the plea of liberum tenementum might be thought to infringe the rule that a plea in confession and avoidance must either expressly or by necessary implication confess the plaintiff's claim and says: but it was construed as admitting that the plaintiff had possession of the close in question, which was sufficient to support his action of trespass against a wrongdoer, but was not sufficient to support it against the lawful owner of the property. This being the nature of the plea where the plaintiff relied on a demise from the defendant he had to plead it in his replication and any defence thereto had to be set up by way of rejoinder: see *Wilkins* v. *Boutcher*.

However, as we have already seen, a person may complain of a trespass or nuisance even though he or she is not in possession, has never been in possession, and merely claims a right to possess.[38] Were it otherwise, the law would be most unfair. If a squatter took possession of a house and, before the true owner had succeeded in evicting the squatter, a neighbour pulled down a supporting wall, then the true owner would be left without any remedy against the neighbour, and that would be one misfortune too many. On the other hand, it is plainly necessary to protect the neighbour against having to pay twice for the wrong. The law could not allow the squatter first to recover the value of the house on the basis that he or she was in possession when the nuisance was committed, and then later allow the true owner to recover too, on the basis of a better right to possession than the squatter.

Similarly, it would be wrong if, in an action for trespass, the trespasser could be made to pay twice for the trespass, once to the person

[38] *Ocean Accident and Guarantee* v. *Ilford Gas Company* [1905] 2 KB 493; *Lord Fitzhardinge* v. *Purcell* [1908] 2 Ch 139, 145. It might be thought that Lord Guest held to the contrary in *Wuta-Ofei* v. *Danquah* [1961] 3 All ER 596, 599, where he said: 'In order to maintain an action for trespass, the respondent must have been in possession at the date of the appellant's entry on the land in 1948.' But the point Lord Guest was making was that a common law cause of action must be complete on the date that the proceedings are issued, and the appellant did not have a title at that time, although she later acquired one.

in possession, and then again to a person who had a better right to possession.

In order to reduce that risk, a person who is not in possession of an estate, but who merely claims a right to possess it, ought not to be able to bring the actions of trespass or nuisance in respect of any act done before attempting to take possession, either by physical entry or by action.[39] As a corollary, the wrongdoer may thereafter plead that person's right to possession as a defence to any claim in trespass or nuisance brought by the person who is in fact in possession.

Where a claim in trespass or nuisance is made by a person who alleges a right to possess an estate, but who is not in fact in possession of it, this necessarily has an effect upon the pleading burdens. Neither the claimant nor the defendant has the procedural advantage of being in possession, and so neither of them can rely upon their possession as, *prima facie*, justifying their conduct. The burden is therefore initially upon the claimant both to prove title and to show the attempt to take possession before the trespass or nuisance was committed. The burden then passes to the other party to justify what would otherwise be a trespass or nuisance.

Possessory actions and ius tertii

There is another problem, which is connected with the above, for which the common law has never provided an entirely satisfactory answer, and, indeed, to which every commentator seems to have suggested a different solution. That is the extent to which the defendant in an action for recovery of land, or trespass or nuisance, may rely upon the defence of *ius tertii*, that is, that there is someone else who has a better title to the land than the claimant.

There is no problem with the defence of *ius tertii* if the title which is relied upon is the title of someone else under or by right of whom the defendant claims to be entitled to keep the claimant out of possession. A tenant, for instance, is quite entitled to set up the landlord's title in

[39] A mortgagee's title, it is true, 'relates back'. A mortgagee may recover damages for a trespass or nuisance committed after the mortgage was granted but before the mortgagee took possession of the security: *Ocean Accident and Guarantee* v. *Ilford Gas Co.* [1905] 2 KB 493. But there is little hardship here, for, if the borrower has already recovered damages before the mortgagee gives notice of its intention to take possession, then the mortgagee cannot recover again (s.98 Law of Property Act 1925).

order to justify possession of the lease.[40] Indeed, this was how the action of ejectment was first applied to freehold land.

Nor is there any problem where the defendant admits the root of the title claimed, whether that is a paper root or simply an act of prior possession, but wishes to allege that, by reason of matters which have happened since, the right to recover possession pursuant to that title is vested in someone else rather than the claimant. The defendant might, for instance, point out that the title claimed by the claimant has been conveyed away to someone else, so that the claimant has no title at all, or that the claimant has created a lease out of it, so that the claimant may only recover the reversion upon the lease.[41]

The difficulty only arises where the third party title is a title paramount and is not one under or by right of which the defendant takes. It arises where the defendant wants to plead not only that a stranger has a better right to recover possession, but also that the right is better because the stranger has a title that has an older root than the claimant's, or because the claimant's title has been barred by the stranger's adverse possession.

Holdsworth was firmly of the view that *ius tertii* was a good defence to an action for recovery of land, but that was because he believed that English law had come to recognise absolute titles.[42] The almost universal consensus now, however, is that Holdsworth was wrong, because the ability to plead *ius tertii* would necessarily undermine the rule in *Asher*

[40] In *Roberts* v. *Tayler* (1845) 1 CB 117, 126, Cresswell J said: 'In trespass *quare clausum fregit* the possession of the plaintiff is the foundation of the action; and the defendant is considered sufficiently to deny the plaintiff's right of possession by pleading *liberum tenementum* in himself or a third person; in the latter case justifying as the servant and acting by the command of such third person: and by this anomalous plea the plaintiff is put to show how he has a possession in himself consistent with the freehold being in another, unless he chooses to traverse the title set up by the plea.'

[41] This is also the key that unlocks the solution to a particular problem with adverse possession. Suppose that the freeholder grants a twenty-year lease, and immediately afterwards a squatter begins to occupy the land. There is no difficulty here, for time does not start to run against the freeholder until the lease falls in. But what if the freeholder grants the lease when the squatter is already in possession? Does that mean that the squatter can prevent the freeholder recovering possession for twenty years, on the ground that the tenant of the lease is the proper claimant, and then, afterwards, plead that the right of the freeholder to recover possession has been barred because the lease was created after the squatter took possession? The answer is no, for the existence of the lease only prevents the freeholder recovering possession of the lease during its term. If the squatter will not attorn, the freeholder can stop time running by bringing an action to recover possession of the reversion (the right to receive the rent, and enforce the covenants and conditions contained in the lease).

[42] *History of English Law* (London, Sweet & Maxwell, 1925), vol. VII, pp. 64–8.

v. *Whitlock*,[43] that a claimant must recover on the strength of his or her own title, rather than on any weakness in the defendant's title.

So there is no reason why *ius tertii* should ever be a defence to an action for recovery of land. The position was correctly summarised by Jordan CJ in *NRMA Insurance Ltd* v. *B & B Shipping & Marine Salvage Co. Pty Ltd*,[44] who said:

> The plaintiff could make out a prima facie, although rebuttable, case by proving possession at a date earlier than the defendant's possession, because de facto possession is prima facie evidence of seisin in fee and right to possession: *Doe d. Hall* v. *Penfold* (1838) 8 C & P 536, 537; (173) ER 607, 608. It was once thought that a plaintiff who relied on possession must prove possession for at least twenty years; but it is now well established that proof of anterior possession for any period is sufficient to make a prima facie case: *Asher* v. *Whitlock* (1865) LR 1 QB 1; *Whale* v. *Hitchcock* (1876) 34 LT 136; *Dawson* v. *Pyne* (1895) 6 NSW LR 116; 11 WN 179; *Hawdon* v. *Khan* (1920) 20 SR (NSW) 703; 37 WN 279. The statement in *Richards* v. *Richards* ((1731) 15 East 293 (note a) (104 ER 855) that 'The plaintiff must remove every possibility of title in another person before he can recover' was made in a case in which the plaintiff appears to have relied solely on proof of actual title. As a general proposition, it is clearly not the law: *Dawson* v. *Gent* (1857) 1 H & N 745.

In the actions of trespass and nuisance, the general rule too is that the defendant cannot rely on the defence of *ius tertii*.[45] But there is one exceptional case where something like the defence of *ius tertii* may be pleaded in these actions, even though it cannot be pleaded in an action for recovery of land. The rule was explained by Parker J in *Lord Fitzhardinge* v. *Purcell*:[46]

> An action of trespass is founded on possession, and in order to succeed the plaintiff must show possession of the lands on which the acts complained of were committed at the date of such acts. If possession be shown, the defendant is not at liberty to set up the title of a third party unless he justifies what he has done under a licence from such third party. When,

43 (1865) LR 1 QB 1; S. Wiren, 'The Plea of *Ius Tertii* in Ejectment' (1925) 62 LQR 139; A. Hargreaves, 'Terminology and Title in Ejectment' (1940) 56 LQR 376.

44 (1947) 47 SR (NSW) 273, 279. See also *Allen* v. *Roughley* (1955) 94 CLR 98, and *Wibberley* v. *Insley* [1999] 1 WLR 894, 898.

45 Oliver Wendell Holmes, *The Common Law* (ed. M. Howe, Boston, Little Brown & Co., 1963), p. 166; *Nicholls* v. *Ely Beet Sugar Factory* [1931] 2 Ch 84; *Corporation of Hastings* v. *Ivall* (1874) LR 19 Eq Cas 558, 585.

46 [1908] 2 Ch 139, 145.

> however, as in the present case, a plaintiff in trespass, not being able to prove actual possession, proposes to show possession at law by proving his title to the property, the defendant may, I think, show, if he can, that the title is not in the plaintiff, but in some third party.

But this probably goes too far. Certainly, it must be right that, if the third party has already entered upon the land, or commenced an action for possession, the defendant should be allowed to rely upon the third party's title as a defence to the claim, for otherwise the defendant would be at risk of being sued twice for the same wrong. But there is no such risk unless the third party has entered or brought possession proceedings before the wrong complained of, so otherwise the defendant ought not to be able to plead *ius tertii*; for, if that were possible, the defendant would be able to deny a remedy both to the possessor and to the person with a better right to possess.

Support for this qualification can be found by analogy in the rule which governs the circumstances in which tenants are permitted to plead title paramount (in effect, *ius tertii*) against their landlords. Normally, there is a mutual estoppel as to title between a landlord and a tenant, which prevents both parties denying that the landlord had power to make the lease.[47] This prevents a tenant from pleading title paramount against the landlord. The tenant, having taken a lease, cannot refuse to pay the rent on the ground that the landlord had no power to grant it. There is an exception, however, if someone with title paramount has evicted the tenant or threatened to dispossess the tenant of the lease. In those circumstances, the tenant is entitled not merely to resist any further claim for rent, but also to be repaid all the rent paid from the date upon which the true owner[48] became entitled to possession.[49] The reason is that the true owner is entitled to recover mesne profits, as against the tenant,

[47] This is a principle of general application. The grantor of an estate or interest in land, having made it, cannot later deny that he or she had title to make it; and nor can the grantee, having accepted it, deny that either. The same applies to their successors in title, for they are 'privies' to the estoppel, in precisely the same way as they would be 'privies' to a judgment. See also ch. 9.

[48] The expression 'the true owner' is conventionally used in textbooks and the case law, as a convenient shorthand to describe a person with a better paper title, and that is how it is used here. But, it can be a slightly misleading expression, in so far as it suggests that there can only ever be one 'true owner'; for, as is explained in this chapter and the next, all title is ultimately relative, and so there might be more than one person who could be described, as against a squatter, as a 'true owner'. For the origin of the term, see A. Hargreaves, 'Terminology and Title in Ejectment' (1940) 56 LQR 376, 377.

[49] *Industrial Properties* v. *AEI* [1977] QB 580, 596.

equivalent to the rental value of the property, from the moment when the true owner became entitled to possession.

The same reasoning ought to apply in a trespass or nuisance claim. The defendant should only be able to plead the better right of the third party, if the third party has entered into possession, or attempted to enter into possession, so that the defendant is at real risk of having to pay twice.

3

Possession, title and freehold land

Introduction

The two fundamental building blocks of English land law, notwithstanding compulsory registration, remain the doctrines of tenures and of estates.

The doctrine of tenures is about the ways in which land can be held. It means that no private person can own land absolutely. It is always held as a matter of feudal obligation of some other person, and ultimately of the Crown.[1]

The doctrine of estates is about the ways in which a private person may alienate land so held, in both time and space. It involves 'a recognition that the sum of possible interests in land[2] – the fee simple – may be cut up into slices like a cake and distributed amongst a number of people, all of whom will obtain present existing interests in the land, though their right to actual enjoyment, to seisin in demesne, may be postponed.'[3]

This chapter is about the relationship between possession, title, tenure and estates.

It is, in particular, about the reason why prior possession is necessarily the basis of a title to a freehold estate, and why it really should not be thought at all 'remarkable that the law is prepared to legitimise such "possession of wrong", which, at least in some cases, is tantamount to theft of the land.'[4]

[1] For freehold land the practical consequences of the doctrines were abrogated, first by the Abolition of Tenures Act 1660, and then by s.136 Law of Property Act 1925, though not quite to 'vanishing point' (W. Holdsworth, *Historical Introduction to Land Law* (Oxford, Oxford University Press, 1927), p. 36). For leasehold land, however, it does still matter very much. The landlord's power to distrain for rent, and to treat the lease as determined if the tenant denies the landlord's title, are both consequences of tenure.

[2] Co Litt 18a.

[3] B. Simpson, *Introduction to the History of Land Law* (2nd edn, Oxford, Oxford University Press, 1961), p. 82.

[4] (1998) Law Com No. 254, para. 10.5.

Crown demesne

Modern English land law began with the memorable date of the Norman conquest in 1066. It remains firmly grounded in the premise that William acquired absolute ownership of all the land in England and Wales by conquest.[5] That is how, in the popular imagination, he came to acquire the soubriquet of 'Conqueror'.[6]

It is also pure fiction,[7] not historical fact. William certainly did not think he had acquired anything by conquest – he claimed to be the lawful, if not the legitimate, heir of Edward the Confessor: his claim was certainly no worse than some of those who came after him – and though the estates of Harold and those who fought with him were doubtless forfeited for treason,[8] there is no reason to suppose that there was any wholesale upsetting of pre-conquest titles. Indeed, had William carved the whole kingdom up afresh, the compilation of the Domesday Book twenty years later would have been a somewhat pointless exercise. He would already have known precisely who owned what.

Nevertheless, the fiction that William acquired the whole kingdom by conquest is too firmly grounded in English law to be dislodged by mere historical fact, and the whole point of legal fictions is that, once they have become accepted, the law then not only forbids them to be contradicted, but also follows them through to their logical conclusions, no matter how absurd those conclusions might be.[9]

[5] Blackstone, *Commentaries on the Laws of England* (11th edn, London, Strahan & Woodfall, 1791), vol. 2, p. 53; Co Litt 65a; *A-G (NSW)* v. *Brown* (1847) 1 Legge 312. See also S. Dorsett, 'Land Law and Dispossession' and P. Birks, 'Five Keys to Land Law', in *Land Law Themes and Perspectives* (ed. S. Bright and J. Dewar, Oxford, Oxford University Press, 1998), pp. 282–3 and pp. 479–80.

[6] In fact, it meant something entirely different: see Blackstone, *Commentaries on the Laws of England* (11th edn, London, Strahan & Woodfall, 1791), vol. 2, p. 243.

[7] In *Attorney-General* v. *Brown* (1847) 2 SCR (NSW) App 30 (FC), Sir Alfred Stephen CJ said: 'It was maintained, that this supposed property in the Crown was a fiction. Doubtless, in one sense it is so. The right of the people of England to their property, does not in fact depend on any royal grant; and the principle, that all lands are holden mediately or immediately of the Crown, flows from the adoption of the feudal system merely. That principle, however, is universal in the law of England; and we can see no reason why it shall be said not to be equally in operation here. The Sovereign, by that law, is (as it is termed) universal occupant. All property is supposed to have been, originally, in him. Though this be generally a fiction, it is one adopted by the constitution, to answer the ends of government, for the good of the people.' See also K. McNeil, *Common Law Aboriginal Title* (Oxford, Oxford University Press, 1989), pp. 83–4.

[8] F. Pollock and F. Maitland, *History of English Law* (2nd edn, Cambridge, Cambridge University Press, 1911), vol. 1, p. 92.

[9] The rule that a prescriptive easement can be acquired by a lost modern grant is a good example. It begins, sensibly enough, with an evidential presumption that the explanation

This particular fiction has three logical conclusions, each of which is recognised and accepted as part of English law, and which may be stated as follows: first, that there can be no allodial (unowned) land; secondly, that the Crown is the ultimate feudal overlord of all the land in the kingdom, so that the only tenure recognised is tenure under the Crown; and, thirdly, that title to all freehold estates may be proved by prior possession, even without any evidence of a lawful grant.

The reason why each of these consequences follows, nearly a thousand years on, from the basic premise that William acquired all the land in the kingdom by conquest in 1066, is the subject of this chapter.

No allodial land

There is no unowned land in England and Wales. This is the simplest consequence of the conquest to explain. If the premise is that William acquired all the land in the kingdom absolutely, then it follows that he must have extinguished all private estates and interests which had hitherto existed.[10] If a private person is legitimately to hold an estate in land today, he or she must therefore do so under or by virtue of some grant made by William or one of his successors. The first link in any chain of title has to be a grant made by the Crown subsequent to William's arrival taking the land out of the royal demesne,[11] and into the possession of a private person.[12]

If, for the time being, there is no subsisting estate in any particular parcel of land, it follows that this can only be for one of two reasons: either it is because the Crown has never made a grant taking that land out of the royal demesne, or it is because a grant was once made having that effect, but the estate granted has now determined, and the land has reverted

for long use, which cannot be explained otherwise, might be an old grant which has become lost behind the root of title. In time, that becomes fixed as a legal fiction (W. Holdsworth, *History of English Law* (London, Sweet & Maxwell, 1925) vol. VII, pp. 346–9); and now, it can only be rebutted by showing that such a grant was legally impossible, even if there is good evidence that no such grant was ever made: *Tehidy Minerals* v. *Norman* [1971] 2 QB 528; *Bakewell Management* v. *Brandwood* [2004] 2 AC 519.

10 See *Milirrpum* v. *Nabalco* (1970–1) 17 FLR 141, 245.

11 It became possible to register Crown demesne land for the first time by virtue of s.79 Land Registration Act 2002.

12 The same fiction does not extend to colonies acquired by conquest or treaty, but it is applied to colonies acquired by settlement of otherwise unoccupied and uncivilised land. At the time of its discovery and settlement, Australia was undoubtedly treated as an unoccupied and uncivilised territory, and Crown grants were made on that basis. But native title rights are now recognised as if the Crown had actually treated Australia as a territory acquired by conquest or treaty; see *Mabo* v. *Queensland (No. 2)* (1992) 175 CLR 1.

back.[13] In either event, the land cannot be allodial; if, for the time being, there is no subsisting estate in the land, then it must be Crown demesne land.[14]

Crown overlord

The second result of the fiction that William acquired the whole kingdom by conquest is that the Crown remains as ultimate feudal overlord of the whole kingdom, and the only freehold tenure recognised, even today, is tenure under the Crown.[15] You might think that you are a citizen, but if you own freehold land, in truth, you are a subject.

This follows from the nature of the grants William and his successors are treated as having made following the conquest. For the reason explained above, the only basis upon which a private person can legitimately use or enjoy land today is under or by right of a post-conquest Crown grant, for, without a grant, that person must be intruding upon the royal demesne.[16] But, in feudal theory, if the Crown were to grant away ownership of land absolutely to a private individual, that would necessarily divest the Crown of sovereignty over that territory. In order to retain sovereignty, the Crown must retain its position as ultimate feudal overlord. To put the matter in terms of modern constitutional law, the position of the Crown as ultimate overlord is more a matter of public law than private rights.

[13] Blackstone, *Commentaries on the Laws of England* (11th edn, London, Strahan & Woodfall, 1791), vol. 1, p. 276.

[14] Scotland is not treated as having been acquired by conquest, and certainly not by William; see *Lord Advocate* v. *Balfour* 1907 SC 1360; cf. Co Litt 65(a) n. 1. So the Orkney and Shetland Islands are truly allodial, having been acquired by forfeiture, rather than conquest, in 1472, as is some Scottish church property; see W. Gordon, *Scottish Land Law* (Edinburgh, W. Green & Son, 1999), pp. 41–5. The last vestiges of the feudal system in Scotland were removed in 2004 by the Abolition of Feudal Tenure (Scotland) Act 2000. In Ireland, on the other hand, the rule does apply, notwithstanding that the conquest of Ireland did not even begin until 1171, and was not completed until the seventeenth century. In the Republic of Ireland, it seems likely that the state has, since independence in 1922, occupied the position of ultimate feudal overlord formerly occupied by the Crown; see J. Wylie, *Irish Land Law* (3rd edn, Dublin, Butterworths, 1997), para. 2.03.

[15] '[I]t is fundamental to English land law that nobody save the Crown owns any land: for all others, the subject-matter of ownership is not the land itself but the estates or interests artificially created in that land': per Megarry J in *Lowe* v. *J. W. Ashmore Ltd* [1971] Ch 545, 554.

[16] Co Litt 65a: '[A]ll lands within this realm were originally derived from the Crown, and therefore the king is sovereign lord, or lord paramount, either mediate or immediate, of all and every parcel of land within the realm.'

The result is that the nearest a private person can ever get to absolute ownership of land is tenure of an estate in fee simple. That can never be turned into absolute ownership.

In practical terms, however, the fee simple absolute in possession is almost indistinguishable in the modern state from absolute ownership. The state has gradually come to control land use through statute, not through tenure, and, as the political power of the Crown has declined, so the practical consequences of tenure for land owners have been abrogated.[17] Although the legal structure of feudalism is still largely in place, it does not often have any practical effect on substantive rights. The structure, however, is not entirely irrelevant, for, just as the royal prerogative can still bite at the edges of political power, so at the edges of land law the rights and obligations of land owners can still be dictated by the structure imposed by the feudal system.

For example, the question of whether ownership of a fee simple carries with it the right to exploit minerals often depends on whether the tenure was formerly socage or copyhold.[18] Similarly, until recently,[19] many people experienced difficulty obtaining vehicular access to their houses, because the verge between the road and the house happened once to have been part of the common wasteland of a manor. Likewise, because all land is ultimately held under the Crown, it is impossible for the Crown effectively to exercise its statutory power to disclaim freehold land, except where the land was subinfeudated before 1290; for, on a disclaimer, the land will escheat back to the grantor of that fee simple estate. So, if the land is held as tenant in chief *ut de corona*, the escheat will be back to the Crown.[20]

For present purposes, however, the crucial point to note is this. English law does not recognise any form of land ownership, except tenure mediately or immediately of the Crown. The fiction that William acquired all the land in the kingdom by conquest means that a person's use and occupation of land can only be justified by a post-conquest Crown grant, and the doctrine of feudalism means that the Crown can never grant away its position as the ultimate feudal overlord; it can only grant away lesser estates and interests in it. There are no estates in land, except estates held

[17] The turning point was the Abolition of Tenures Act 1660.

[18] The Law of Property Act 1922 converted copyhold tenure into freehold socage tenure on 31 December 1925 (s.202 Law of Property Act 1925) but the mineral rights were normally retained by the lord of the manor.

[19] *Bakewell Management* v. *Brandwood* [2004] 2 AC 519.

[20] *Scmlla Properties Ltd* v. *Gesso Properties (BVI) Ltd* [1995] BCC 793.

under the Crown as ultimate feudal overlord. That is why the land registry is 'Her Majesty's' Land Registry.

Possession proves title

The third consequence of the fiction that William acquired the whole kingdom by conquest is the one that appears, at first, to be the most surprising, namely, that title to all estates in land may be acquired and proved by prior possession. But this is just as much a necessary consequence of the fiction as the other two, and perhaps, given that the Crown's original absolute acquisition is itself a fiction, it ought not to be thought too remarkable that the law allows lesser estates to be acquired in the same way too.

The reason for the rule is that this is the only way in which a particular problem can be resolved. The problem is this. If, as we have seen, the private use and enjoyment of land is only lawful if permitted by the terms of some post-conquest Crown grant, how can a person prove that grant, and vindicate the right in one of Her Majesty's courts of law, or when registering the estate for the first time at Her Majesty's Land Registry?

The simplest way to do so would be to produce the post-conquest Crown grant, and then trace each link in the chain of title, from the original Crown grantee down to the successor claimant. But it would be impossible to do this in all but a tiny proportion of cases. There are two separate reasons why.

First, there may never have been a post-conquest Crown grant. William's acquisition of all the land in the kingdom by conquest is a legal fiction, not a historical fact. The root of title may be pre-conquest, and there is simply no way of knowing how many titles still have pre-conquest roots.

Secondly, even if there was once an actual post-conquest Crown grant, there is little likelihood of anyone being able to find it or establish its terms, far less being able to prove all the necessary links in the chain of title down to the present day, unless the grant was made very recently. Even then, a provable modern Crown grant would not give an absolute title. To be entirely secure, the claimant would also have to prove a separate negative, namely, that there had been no previous inconsistent Crown grant to someone else.

It being impossible or impracticable, in all but a tiny proportion of cases, to prove the necessary Crown grant, if the law is to protect private rights in property at all, it must allow a person to prove title in some other way. The court is driven to infer the necessary grant and links in the chain of title from the next best evidence, namely, evidence of prior possession of that estate, for 'in order to give adequate protection to ownership, it has been found necessary to protect possession. To prove ownership is difficult, to prove possession comparatively easy.'[21] If it can be shown that particular persons were in possession of an estate on certain dates, then the courts will presume that they had title to what they possessed on those dates, unless and until it is shown that they did not.[22]

This is why, when purchasing an estate in unregistered land, the starting point in any investigation of the title is the search for a 'good root' of that title. The purchaser's solicitor has to check that the vendor has title to sell the property, and the way that is done is to trace the vendor's title back through the deeds until arriving at a sufficiently old[23] good root of it. A good root is a conveyance 'dealing with or proving on the face of it (without the aid of extrinsic evidence) the ownership of the whole legal and equitable estate in the property sold, containing a description by which the property can be identified, and showing nothing to cast any doubt on the title of the disposing parties'.[24] The whole point of searching for such a document is that it provides what is likely to be the best available evidence by which to identify who was in possession of that estate in the land on that particular day. The older the root, the better the title which the vendor has to offer, because prior possession is the best evidence of rightful possession.

This principle of title by prior possession should not be confused with the rules of adverse possession, which are an aspect of the law of limitation, and which are discussed in chapter 8. Briefly, the distinction between the

[21] F. Pollock and F. Maitland, *History of English Law* (2nd edn, Cambridge, Cambridge University Press, 1911), vol. 2, p. 42. In *R* v. *Oxfordshire CC, ex p. Sunningwell PC* [2000] 1 AC 335, 349; [1999] 3 WLR 160, 165, Lord Hoffmann said: 'Any legal system must have rules of prescription which prevent the disturbance of long established de facto enjoyment.'

[22] The rule is similar for chattels. In *Armory* v. *Delamire* (1722) 1 Sta 505, Pratt CJ said: 'That the finder of a jewel, though he does not by such finding acquire an absolute property or ownership, yet he has such a property as will enable him to keep it against all but the rightful owner, and consequently may maintain trover.' See also *Parker* v. *British Airways Board* [1982] 1 QB 1004. Likewise, for incorporeal hereditaments, the rule is that if a person can be shown to have exercised a right for a sufficiently long time, then the doctrine of lost modern grant provides a 'convenient and workable fiction' that there was once a grant which has subsequently been lost: per Fox LJ in *Simmons* v. *Dobson* [1991] 1 WLR 720, 723.

[23] At common law the period was sixty years. It is now fifteen years (s.23 Law of Property Act 1969).

[24] T. Williams, *Vendor and Purchaser* (4th edn, London, Sweet & Maxwell, 1936), p. 98.

two concepts is this. Prior possession is a method by which a person may prove a presumptively good lawful title to an estate, notwithstanding that an actual Crown grant and all the necessary links in the chain of title cannot be proved. Adverse possession is a method by which that person's title to that estate may be extinguished, and acquired unlawfully by someone else.

An example will help to illustrate the point. Suppose that more than twelve years ago 'B' dispossessed 'A' of an unregistered freehold estate. On these facts alone, the courts will presume that 'A' had a freehold title to the land before being dispossessed. The courts will do so, even in the absence of any evidence of a paper title, because 'A' was in possession at the time, and 'A's' possession at that time is otherwise unexplained.[25] But, on the same facts, 'B' will succeed in showing that he or she has extinguished 'A's' title by adverse possession, and that 'B' therefore now has a better right to possess the estate than 'A'.[26]

Relativity of titles

Title, then, can ordinarily be established only by evidence of prior possession. Prior possession is itself evidence of title to that which was possessed.

The practical effect of this is to make all unregistered titles relative. There are no absolute titles to unregistered estates in land, only titles that are more or less good than others.[27] This follows because all titles are at risk of being upset by evidence of prior possession by someone else. A title that begins with possession forty years ago, and where forty years of continuous possession can be shown, is a good title, but it is not absolute. There might be someone else who can show that he or she takes by right of another who was wrongly dispossessed sixty years ago. Adverse possession apart, the title with the sixty-year-old root is the better one. The same principle applies even if we change the time periods to 400 years and 600 years, because 'de facto possession is prima facie evidence of seisin in fee and a right to possession',[28] and the person who can prove the oldest right has the better paper title.

[25] 'It is, in fact, clearly a settled rule of law, that possession, however slender the title to it may be, is sufficient against a wrongdoer'; per Malins VC in *Hastings Corporation* v. *Ivall* (1874) LR 19 Eq Cas 558, 586.

[26] If the land is registered, the position is more complicated, because since 13 October 2003 it has generally not been possible to acquire title to registered land by adverse possession (s.96 Land Registration Act 2002). See ch. 8.

[27] See B. Rudden, 'The Terminology of Title' (1964) 80 LQR 63.

[28] *Doe d. Hall* v. *Penfold* (1838) 8 C & P 536, 537, per Patteson J.

This explains why, as we saw in chapter 2, the issue in an action for recovery of land is always, 'who has the better title?', and not, 'who has title and who does not?' Even if the defendant is a mere squatter, who entered without any colour of title at all, the squatter always has a presumptive title by virtue of being in possession.[29] Similarly, even if the claimant has a title which the most careful lender would accept as security, there is always a risk that there might be someone else who has a better title.[30] So the issue necessarily has to be, who has the better title?

This also explains why *ius tertii* cannot be a defence to an action for recovery of land. If it were, then the law would permit a squatter to grab land, and then prevent the dispossessed owner recovering it by pointing out some wholly irrelevant defect in the true owner's title. That is why the task of a claimant in an action for recovery of land is limited to showing the better right.

A claimant in that action might be able to show a better right than the possessor in one of two ways: first, by showing a better right by title paramount; and, secondly, by showing that the defendant only has a limited interest in the land, which was previously carved out of the claimant's title, and which has now expired or which the claimant can now otherwise determine.

An example again will help make the distinction clear. Suppose that a person claims to be in possession of an occupational lease granted by a freeholder. He or she is at risk of being evicted by title paramount if there is someone other than the original landlord who had a better right to the freehold when the lease was granted. It might be that the landlord had only acquired possession of the freehold recently as a squatter, or that the landlord had previously conveyed it away to someone else. In either event, the person making the claim would be alleging a better right to possess

[29] In *Asher* v. *Whitlock* (1865) LR 1 QB 1, 5, Cockburn CJ said: 'But I take it as clearly established, that possession is good against all the world except the person who can show a good title; and it would be mischievous to change this established doctrine. In *Doe* v. *Dyeball* (Mood & M 346) one year's possession by the plaintiff was held good against a person who came in and turned him out; and there are other authorities to the same effect.' See also per Lord Hoffmann in *Wibberley* v. *Insley* [1999] 1 WLR 894, 898.

[30] This is not a wholly academic point. The Crown, for instance, still claims title to the soil in the streets in the City of London by virtue of a reservation contained in a charter granted by King Charles I: although whether the Crown had any title in the streets to reserve seems unlikely; see G. Norton, *History and Franchises of the City of London* (London, Butterworths, 1829), p. 519.

the freehold than the person who had granted the lease, and consequently the eviction of the tenant would be by title paramount.[31]

In contrast, if a tenant breaches the terms of the lease or holds over after the lease has expired, then the tenant is in danger of being evicted by the person who granted the lease, or the grantor's successor. That claim would not be a claim by title paramount. Rather it would be a claim that the lease had originally been created validly out of the landlord's estate, but that the landlord now has power to end it, or that it had already ended automatically. Neither would involve a challenge to the title under which the lease was granted. On the contrary, both cases necessarily recognise the validity of the title out of which the lease was granted, and the person claiming possession is doing so by reason of ownership of that title.

A title paramount can, of course, be proved presumptively by prior possession, in precisely the same way as any other title. The practical effect of this is that, no matter how old a title is, there is always a possibility that someone else might have a better title, because all titles that rest on possession are presumptive titles only.

The title proved by possession

Possession proves a relative title. In other words, a person acquires a presumptive title to an estate in land simply by using and enjoying it as if he or she owned that estate. There is a problem, however, where the acts done are equivocal, in the sense that there are a number of different estates or interests in the land which could be used or enjoyed in that way.

To take a simple example, suppose that a person is in occupation of the land. That person might be in occupation as the fee simple owner, or as the tenant under an occupational lease, or as an occupational licensee. To which of these, in the absence of an actual grant, is a presumptive title acquired by virtue of the occupation? To put the question more generally, if someone's use and enjoyment of land is otherwise unexplained, to what sort of estate or interest in it does that person acquire a presumptive right?

The answer to this is partly still tied up with the concept of seisin. Seisin originally meant simply undisturbed occupation as of right. But

[31] In *Abbey National* v. *Cann* [1991] 1 AC 56, the House of Lords (overruling *Church Commissioners* v. *Piskor* [1954] Ch 553) held that there was no *scintilla temporis* between the acquisition of an estate using mortgage finance and the grant of the mortgage. If that is right, then the mortgagee takes by title paramount, and, if the debtor subsequently lets the land, the tenant has no remedy on the usual qualified covenant for quiet enjoyment if the tenant is evicted by the mortgagee.

it quickly developed a separate technical meaning, namely, possession of freehold land in demesne. This included a freehold reversion, for a lease was treated as only a chattel interest. An occupier was presumed to have seisin, and therefore (in modern terms) a fee simple absolute in possession; that is, the greatest possible estate.[32] Likewise, a person found to be receiving rent from land was presumed to have seisin, and hence to have a fee simple, subject to the lease in favour of the tenant who was paying the rent. So, in short, the rule is that a person using or enjoying land as though in possession of an estate, is presumed to be in possession of the greatest possible estate in the land which is consistent with that use or enjoyment.[33]

This, however, is only a presumption, and may be displaced in two ways.

First, evidence is always admissible to show that the possessor did acts which were inconsistent with possession of so large an estate, or, indeed, any estate at all. A person in occupation of land apparently has a fee simple, but, if it can be shown that the occupier paid a rent to someone else, that demonstrates possession of no more than a lease. Similarly, if a person in occupation of land acknowledges that a third party has a right of way, then he or she cannot be in possession of more than the fee simple subject to the right of way. This does not breach the rule against pleading *ius tertii* explained in the previous chapter, because this is a rule about the nature of the estate which a prior possessor acquires in the first place, and not about who has the better title to that estate.

Secondly, someone else might show a better title to a particular estate or interest in the land than the possessor. In that circumstance, the possessor

[32] *Peaceable d. Uncle* v. *Watson* (1811) 4 Taunt. 16.

[33] This presumption applies to acquisition of title by *prior* possession. It ought to apply also, as a presumption, to acquisition by *adverse* possession. The Law Commission view is: 'A squatter who commences adverse possession has, from the very beginning, a fee simple absolute in possession, albeit one that is defeasible by a person with a better right to possess. This is so even though the squatter is adversely possessing against a leaseholder' ('Land Registration for the Twenty-First Century: A Consultation Paper' Law Com No. 254, 1998, para. 10.22). But suppose the fee simple owner grants a lease and then unlawfully re-enters upon it. The re-entry does not determine the lease, unless and until the tenant elects to treat it as having that effect. In the meantime, the landlord is in adverse possession of the lease. Can it really be the case that the landlord is in adverse possession of a fee simple in the freehold too? By statute, a tenant is sometimes deemed to be in adverse possession of the freehold (paras. 5-6 Sch. 1 Limitation Act 1980). But, in other cases, there does not seem to be any good reason why someone in possession should not say that he or she only ever intended to bar the right of the tenant, and so has never been in adverse possession of a fee simple, only ever of a lease.

is treated as having been in possession of the greatest estate that might be consistent with that other person's title. So, for instance, if a third party can show that the fee simple was encumbered by an unacknowledged right of support, before the commencement of the acts of possession relied upon, then the possessor acquires the fee simple subject to the right of support.

Registered land

It might be thought or said that there is no need to worry about any of this any more where a title is registered. A perfect system of land registration would completely, conclusively and indefeasibly record the ownership of all estates and interests in land. The title of a prior possessor would be barred upon first registration of the land, and thereafter the title of the registered owner would become absolute. The register would record everything completely, would always be up to date, and only the registered owner would be able to bring an action to recover the land, or complain about a trespass or nuisance. Prior possession would thereby become irrelevant.

But the potential for injustice in such a rigid system would be enormous, and so legal certainty must yield to the practical.

Our system of registration does this in two ways.

First, to some extent it still allows a person who has acquired title by prior possession to prove the title, and be registered in place of an existing proprietor.

The previous registration regime, which applied between 1897 and 2003,[34] did this relatively simply, by providing that, if the court decided that any person was 'entitled to any estate . . . in registered land', then the register might be rectified accordingly.[35] This could be done notwithstanding that the general effect of registration was to deem the legal estate to be vested in the named proprietor.[36] So, where a person proved a better right by prior possession, it made no difference that the estate in the land had been registered in the meantime: the prior possessor was entitled to require the register to be rectified, and to become the proprietor of it; for, although rectification was technically discretionary, it would have been 'difficult to construct any scenario' in which rectification could have been

[34] The Land Registration Act 1925 consolidated the Land Transfer Acts 1875 and 1897. Adverse possession, however, was not possible in the registered system until 1897.

[35] Section 82(1)(a) Land Registration Act 1925.

[36] Section 82(2) Land Registration Act 1925.

withheld,[37] because ownership of the estate was a matter of substantive right.

It is not clear to what extent the right of a prior possessor to require the register to be rectified in this way has been changed by the new registration regime, contained in the Land Registration Act 2002. The court may now alter the register only in three circumstances: either for the purpose of 'correcting a mistake', or for the purpose of 'bringing the register up to date', or for the purpose of 'giving effect to any estate, right or interest excepted from the effect of registration'.[38] The third of these could not apply in favour of a prior possessor, except where what has been registered is a possessory title;[39] otherwise, the general effect of registration applies, and that is to extinguish the unregistered rights of the prior possessor. The second could never apply in favour of a prior possessor. It is intended to deal with changes in substantive rights as a result of things happening after the estate has been registered. The first is more problematic. The 'mistake' consisted of allowing the claim for first registration, when someone else at the time, in fact, had a better claim to be registered by prior possession. Is this a 'mistake' of the type that should lead to an alteration of the register? Probably, it is. The example of a mistake given in the notes published with the Law Commission's draft bill[40] was: '[I]f X has forged Y's signature on a certificate of transfer and has been registered as the proprietor of Whiteacre, the court could make an order for Y to be reinstated as proprietor.' There does not seem to be any difference, in principle, between a registration by 'mistake' as a result of a forged transfer, and a registration by 'mistake' with absolute rather than possessory title. This is reinforced by the Law Commission's original consultation document, which gave this example:[41]

> In the absence of any error or omission in the register, when a court make any determination of substantive rights in or over registered land, it should do so in accordance with the principles of registered land. The principles governing unregistered land should come into play *only* if there is some issue which arises from the time prior to first registration. Following any such determination the register should be amended to reflect its outcome.

[37] Per Scott LJ in *Peterborough BS* v. *Steed* [1993] Ch 116, 139; cf. *Kingsalton* v. *Thames Water Developments* [2002] 1 P & CR 15.

[38] Para. 2(1) Sch. 4 Land Registration Act 2002.

[39] Section 11(7) Land Registration Act 2002.

[40] '*Land Registration Bill and Commentary*' (Law Com No. 277), p. 568.

[41] 'Land Registration for the Twenty-First Century: A Consultation Paper' (Law Com No. 254, 1998), para. 8.40.

That is not quite an end of the matter, because, in order to correct that type of mistake, the court must be satisfied that the proprietor substantially contributed to the mistake, either by fraud or by lack of proper care, or that it would, for any other reason, be unjust not to make the alteration.[42] But, in a case of better title by prior possession, it is hard to see how it could ever be just to refuse to make the alteration. If the land had remained unregistered, and the prior possessor had proved a better right to be in possession, then the subsequent possessor would have been left with nothing. The practical difference that registration makes is that, if that happens in the registered system, then the state pays the subsequent possessor an indemnity for the full value of the estate lost.[43] How, then, can registration make it unjust to vindicate the better right of the prior possessor?

Subject only to the possibility of rectification, a registered title absolute is, as the name suggests, an absolute (rather than relative) title. There cannot be anyone who has a better title to that estate than the person who is registered as the proprietor of it.

But it does not follow that the law only protects the title of the registered proprietor, nor that relative, unregistered titles cannot exist off the register, behind the registered title.

This is the second way in which the rigidity of registration is made to yield to the practical, for the possessory actions protect prior and current possession of both registered and unregistered estates in precisely the same way. There is no special rule for registered land. So a person who has previously been in possession of a registered estate may bring an action to recover possession of it, simply relying on the fact of prior possession. The claimant does not need to plead that he or she is the registered proprietor, any more than it would be necessary to plead a paper title if the land were unregistered. Of course, if the claim is to recover the estate from the registered proprietor, the claim will fail, just as it would if the land were unregistered and the claim were made against someone with a better paper title. But if the claim is made against someone with a worse possessory title (for instance, if the claim is made by one squatter against a later squatter) then the claim will succeed, even though there is a third person who has a better title than either of them, for *ius tertii* is never a defence to an action for recovery of land.

[42] Para. 3 Sch. 4 Land Registration Act 2002.
[43] Para. 1 Sch. 8 Land Registration Act 2002.

Similar principles apply to the actions of trespass and nuisance. The registered proprietor, of course, can complain about an intrusion upon or an interference with the registered estate. But it is not necessary to be the registered proprietor in order to bring those actions. Being 'in' possession of it, or having a right to possess it, is sufficient. Nor need the right to possess the estate be an unqualified right; a right based on prior possession of the estate is quite sufficient.[44]

In practice, what might be described as 'shadow' possessory estates of this kind, subsisting behind a registered estate, have always been rather rare and short lived, because under the registration regime which applied until 2003, a squatter had a right to be registered as proprietor of the estate, once the actual proprietor's title had been barred by adverse possession,[45] and that usually only took twelve years.[46] The shadow estate was destroyed if the registered proprietor recovered possession in the meantime: otherwise, it was upgraded to the registered estate; in either event, it did not last very long. But, upgrading is not, generally, going to be possible under the new regime. The only sensible advice which can be given to someone in adverse possession of a registered estate under the new regime is to keep very quiet about it, for any attempt to upgrade the 'shadow' estate will now almost certainly result in its destruction.[47] So, in the future, it is likely that conveyancers will find themselves dealing with long, unregistered possessory titles of this type, subsisting behind the bare husk of a moribund registered title, and defended by pragmatic if unprincipled estoppels.[48] We have, after all, been here before. The 'dry' legal estate was a familiar problem to the Victorian conveyancer.

[44] See ch. 2.

[45] Section 75(3) Land Registration Act 1925; para. 9(2) Sch. 6 and s.29 Land Registration Act 2002.

[46] Section 15 Limitation Act 1980.

[47] See ch. 8.

[48] See also A. Clarke, 'Use, Time, and Entitlement' (2004) 57 CLP 239, 258–60. For a different view, 'that it will be seen as something more like what used to be called "a mere spes", a hope of ownership rather than the real thing', see E. Cooke, 'The Land Registration Act 2002 and the Nature of Ownership', in *New Perspectives on Property Law, Obligations and Restitution* (ed. A. Hudson, London, Cavendish, 2004), p. 122.

4

Leases and licences

Introduction

The common law of landlord and tenant is neither logical nor entirely intelligible. The reason is that there is a conceptual fissure, which runs right the way through it. We just cannot decide whether it ought to be part of the medieval law of real property or part of the nineteenth-century law of contract.[1] The courts sometimes treat it as part of one and sometimes as part of the other. [2]

Whether a particular problem properly lies within the domain of contract or real property should not always be too difficult to determine. Contract ought to govern issues of interpretation[3] and the extent of obligations.[4] Real property ought to govern issues of transmission and status.[5]

[1] For a good historical explanation, see the judgment of Deane J in *Progressive Mailing House Pty Ltd* v. *Tabali Pty Ltd* (1985) 157 CLR 17, 51–2. In Ireland, the matter appears to have been decided by s.3 Landlord and Tenant Law Amendment Act (Ireland) 1860 which provides: '[T]he relation of landlord and tenant shall be deemed to be founded on the express or implied contract of the parties, and not upon tenure or service, and a reversion shall not be necessary to such relation.'

[2] W. Holdsworth, *Historical Introduction to Land Law* (Oxford, Oxford University Press, 1927), p. 99.

[3] *Mannai Investment Co. Ltd* v. *Eagle Star Life Assurance Co. Ltd* [1997] AC 749; [1997] 3 All ER 352.

[4] *London Diocesan Fund* v. *Phithwa* [2005] 1 WLR 3956.

[5] For this reason, it ought not to be possible to grant or take a lease as agent for an undisclosed principal. In *Fred Drughorn* v. *Rederiaktiebolaget Transatlantic* [1919] AC 203, 206, Lord Haldane put it this way: 'It was held in *Humble* v. *Hunter* (12 QB 310) that where a charterer dealt with someone described as the owner, evidence was not admissible to show that some other person was the owner. That is perfectly intelligible. The question is not before us now, but I see no reason to question that where you have the description of a person as the owner of property, and it is a term of the contract that he should contract as owner of that property, you cannot show that another person is the real owner. That is not a question of agency – that is a question of property.' Thereafter, however, the authorities diverge. In *Epps* v. *Rothnie* [1945] 1 KB 562, the Court of Appeal held that a landlord could contract as undisclosed principal because normal contractual principles applied. But, in *Hanstown*

Sometimes, however, it is not obvious whether the answer ought to lie in contract or real property, and they often suggest radically different solutions to the same problem.

Take, for example, the question of whether it is possible contractually to fetter the power to serve a notice to quit determining a periodic tenancy. As a matter of liberal *laissez–faire* contract law, there is no reason why this should not be possible. But, if a periodic tenancy is viewed as a piece of property, then it might be thought that the ability to determine the tenancy by service of a notice to quit is inherent in the nature of the property.

The property analysis has, in fact, triumphed on this particular question.[6] But the tide is high for the contractual theory, which has already won on the issue of whether a lease may be determined by frustration,[7] and whether a service charge may be reserved as rent,[8] and is winning the debate on whether a lease may be determined by acceptance of a repudiatory breach.[9]

Problems about possession in the law of landlord and tenant tend to occur at precisely those points where the principles of contract and property intersect and suggest different answers. So proper understanding of the contractual and property aspects of the relationship is the key to resolving most landlord and tenant possession problems.

Properties v. *Green* (1978) 246 EG 917, the Court of Appeal subsequently held that a tenant cannot contract on behalf of an undisclosed principal.

6 *Prudential* v. *London Residuary Body* [1992] 2 AC 386. The decision was described by one member of the panel deciding it as 'bizarre': per Lord Browne-Wilkinson, *ibid.*, p. 396. But the court felt driven to it by a series of nineteenth-century and earlier decisions, which appeared to say precisely that. In fact, the reports relied upon only told half the story, because they were exclusively decisions of common law courts. They said nothing about whether the tenant could enforce the contract in equity because none of those courts had any power to grant any equitable relief. In the main case relied on as authority for the proposition that the contract could not be enforced (*Doe d. Warner* v. *Browne* (1807) 8 East 165) we know that the tenant subsequently filed a bill in chancery, and was duly granted an injunction enforcing the contract; for the full history, see the account given by Malins VC in *Re King's Leasehold Estates* (1873) LR 16 Eq 521, 526.

7 *National Carriers* v. *Panalpina (Northern)* [1981] AC 675.

8 *Escalus* v. *Robinson* [1996] QB 231; [1995] 2 EGLR 23.

9 *Highway Properties Ltd* v. *Kelly Douglas & Co.* (1971) 17 DLR (3d) 710; *Shevill* v. *Builder's Licensing Board* (1982) 56 ALJR 793; *Ripka Property* v. *Maggiore Bakeries* [1984] VR 629; *Lyons* v. *Anderson* (1886) 13 R 1020; *Progressive Mailing House Property* v. *Tabali Pty* (1985) 157 CLR 17; *Hussein* v. *Mehlman* [1992] 2 EGLR 87; *Nynehead* v. *Fibreboard* [1999] 1 EGLR 8; *Chartered Trust plc* v. *Davies* [1997] 2 EGLR 83.

Contract and estate

At common law, a lease is a contract between the original landlord and the original tenant by which each usually agrees with the other to perform their respective obligations throughout the term. So, when the original tenant assigns the lease, the incoming tenant may enforce the benefit of the landlord's covenants, for the benefit of those covenants has been assigned with the lease, but the original tenant remains liable as a matter of contract to perform the burden of the tenant's covenants. Likewise, if the original landlord assigns the reversion, the new landlord can enforce the benefit of the tenant's covenants, but the original landlord remains bound to perform the burden of the landlord's covenants. This is perfectly orthodox contract law for, generally speaking, the benefit of a contract may be assigned to a third party, but the burden of its performance always remains with the original contracting party.

The contractual liability of an original tenant at common law is therefore primary. The original tenant is not a surety for the assignee,[10] and defences which are available to a surety are not available to an original tenant. Nor does a landlord owe the original tenant any duty to pursue anyone else liable on the tenant's covenant instead. The landlord's remedies are cumulative.[11]

Landlord and tenant law departs from ordinary contract law, however, in that the burden of the covenants contained in the lease can usually be enforced between the current landlord and the current tenant too. The contract, blessed with the estate, takes on an 'existence as a species of property independently of the contract',[12] with the result that those obligations can be enforced not only against the original contracting party but also against the landlord or the tenant current at the time the obligation accrued due for performance.[13] This is what is meant by 'privity of estate'. It is simply an exception to the normal contractual rule that only an original contracting party can be made to perform the burden of the contract. It means that the person in whom the benefit of the contract

[10] *Allied London Investments Ltd* v. *Hambro Life Assurance plc* (1985) 50 P & CR 207; [1985] 1 EGLR 45.

[11] *Norwich Union Life Insurance Society* v. *Low Profile Fashions Ltd* (1992) 64 P & CR 187; [1992] 1 EGLR 86.

[12] Per Nourse LJ in *City of London* v. *Fell* [1993] QB 589, 604.

[13] The origin of this rule, for the burden of landlords' covenants, is statutory: Grantees of Reversions Act 1540. For tenants' covenants, the origin is the decision in *Spencer's Case* (1583) 5 Co Rep 16a.

(the estate) is vested is also liable to perform the burden of the contract for the period during which it is so vested.[14]

The rules about privity of estate give no remedy to a landlord against an intermediate assignee who has already assigned the term on or before the breach occurs, for the intermediate assignee is not an original contracting party, and the estate is already vested in someone else.

Landlords, as might be imagined, generally found this gap unsatisfactory,[15] and, during the twentieth century, the scarcity of commercial property meant landlords had the whip-hand. So, to fill the gap, it became the invariable practice to include a covenant in the lease forbidding assignment, except to someone who had first entered into a direct contractual covenant with the landlord to pay the rents and perform the covenants contained in the lease throughout the rest of the term. The result was that the landlord would then be able to recover the rent from, or bring an action for damages against, anyone in whom the term had ever been vested: the original tenant would be liable by virtue of privity of contract; any intermediate assignee would be liable by virtue of the direct covenant which had been taken on the assignment to him or her; and the ultimate tenant would be contractually liable for the same reason, and would additionally be liable by virtue of the doctrine of privity of estate, as the person in whom the term of the lease was currently vested.[16]

For so long as everyone remained solvent, it did not matter very much who the landlord looked to for payment; eventually, the ultimate tenant would have to pay. If the landlord brought the action against the original tenant, or an intermediate assignee, then that defendant would have a right of indemnity over against the next assignee,[17] and, on paying the landlord's claim, would be subrogated to all the landlord's rights in respect of that

[14] A modern attempt to do something similar for freehold covenants (*Halsall* v. *Brizell* [1957] Ch 169) was strangled in infancy by *Rhone* v. *Stephens* [1994] AC 310.

[15] If the lease was onerous, the ultimate tenant could always pay a pauper to take an assignment, thereby escaping continuing direct liability to the landlord for the rent and on the covenants contained in it. There was still a risk, however, that the landlord would bring an action against the original tenant, and the liability would then be chased down through the chain of indemnities contained in each assignment.

[16] Most landlords, however, got both their penny and their bun, because it also became common practice for landlords contractually to exclude their liability after a disposal of all interest in the reversion.

[17] Section 77 and Part IX Sch. 2 Law of Property Act 1925; s.24 Land Registration Act 1925.

sum against everyone else further down the chain towards the ultimate assignee, including sureties for them.[18] On payment, anyone further down would then be sub-subrogated[19] to the landlord's rights against those who were even further down the chain, until, eventually, the liability came to rest with the ultimate assignee.

Similarly, if the landlord claimed against a surety, the surety would have an implied right of indemnity over against his or her principal, and would have a right to be subrogated to the same rights against those further down as if the claim had been made against the principal instead.[20]

Those principles have been partly abrogated by the Landlord and Tenant (Covenants) Act 1995. For the purpose of this Act, leases are either 'old' leases or 'new' leases. A lease is an 'old' lease if it was granted before 1 January 1996; otherwise, with a few exceptions, it is a 'new' lease.

For 'new' leases, the purely contractual liability of an original tenant, and of any intermediate assignee who has given a contractual covenant, ends after a lawful assignment over by that tenant; in other words, after a lawful assignment, the estate continues to exist, but the contractual liability of the assigning party is discharged.[21] Thereafter, the assigning tenant can generally be made to guarantee the liability of the assignee under an 'authorised guarantee agreement', but on the next lawful assignment over, that guarantee is discharged too.

So far as 'old' leases are concerned, the contractual liability is preserved but in order to recover a debt from an original tenant who is liable as an original contracting party, or an intermediate assignee who is liable by virtue of a covenant contained in a licence to assign or otherwise, or a surety for either of those persons, a landlord must notify the debtor of the ultimate assignee's default within six months of the debt becoming due using the prescribed form of notice. Upon payment,

[18] *Moule* v. *Garrett* (1871–2) LR 7 Ex 101; [1861–73] All ER Rep 135; *Electricity Supply Nominees Ltd* v. *Thorn EMI Retail Ltd* (1992) 63 P & CR 143; [1991] 2 EGLR 46; *Selous Street Properties* v. *Oronel Fabrics* (1984) 270 EG 743; (1984) 134 NLJ 886; *Becton Dickinson* v. *Zwebner* [1980] QB 208. This was even applied against an assignee where the usual right of indemnity had been expressly excluded from the assignment: *Re Healing Research Trustee* [1992] 2 All ER 481. But it does not extend to a mortgagee in possession (*Bonner* v. *Tottenham and Edmonton BS* [1899] 1 QB 161) except where the mortgagee is directly liable to the landlord on the covenants contained in the lease. For the circumstances in which the mortgagee is so liable, see ch. 5.

[19] There is no conceptual difficulty with 'sub-subrogation': see *Castle Phillips* v. *Piddington* [1995] 1 FLR 783; *UCB* v. *Hedworth (No. 2)* [2003] EWCA Civ 1717.

[20] *Selous Street Properties* v *Oronel Fabrics* (1984) 270 EG 743; (1984) 134 NLJ 886.

[21] Section 5 Landlord and Tenant (Covenants) Act 1995.

the landlord may then be required to grant the debtor an overriding lease.[22]

The Act does not affect a landlord's contractual right to recover against the ultimate assignee, nor any guarantor for the ultimate assignee (except where the lease is a 'new' lease and the guarantor was formerly a tenant of it). Nor does it alter the common law where a landlord is seeking to recover an unliquidated sum under an old lease; in other words, damages for breach of covenant rather than a sum of money payable as a debt.

The common law contractual liability of former tenants and guarantors is also subject to one overriding qualification which is inherent in the nature of the lease. The contract cannot exist without the estate. So, if the landlord destroys the estate by forfeiture, contractual liabilities which have accrued due up to the moment when the estate is destroyed remain enforceable, but all obligations which would otherwise fall to be performed in the future are discharged. So too, if a landlord accepts a surrender from the ultimate assignee, the contractual liability of the original tenant and intermediate any assignees is destroyed, as from that date, because the contractual liability is parasitic upon the continuing existence of the estate.[23]

The rule only applies to a voluntary destruction[24] of the estate, it does not apply the other way around. A release of the estate necessarily releases the contract, but a release of the contract has no effect on the estate. So, if a landlord releases an intermediate assignee from liability under the lease, that does not affect the liability of the ultimate tenant, nor even the original tenant (notwithstanding that the original tenant might have a right of indemnity over against the released intermediate assignee).[25] But the contractual liability only lasts for the period of the contracted-for

[22] Section 17. An overriding lease is a concurrent lease. A concurrent lease is a lease of the landlord's reversion, subject to the rights of an existing tenant. It differs from a headlease, in that it has been carved out of the reversion upon an existing lease, whereas a headlease is a lease out of which a sub-lease has, itself, been carved. The practical difference is that, if a headlease is forfeited, the sub-lease falls with it, because the sub-tenant's rights have been created out of the headlease, whereas, if a concurrent lease is forfeited, the occupational lease is preserved, and takes effect once again as a direct lease of the head-interest. Nonetheless, for so long as the concurrent lease is in existence, the concurrent tenant is the landlord of the occupational lease, and is able to exercise all the rights of the landlord of that lease, including the right to receive the rent or to forfeit the term.

[23] *Clements* v. *Richardson* (1888) 11 LR Ir 535; *Deanplan* v. *Mahmoud* [1993] Ch 151; *Re EWA* [1901] 2 KB 643.

[24] See ch. 7.

[25] *Sun Life Assurance Society plc* v. *Tantofex (Engineers) Ltd* [1999] L & TR 568; [1999] 2 EGLR 135.

term, so, unless the lease or guarantee expressly provides otherwise, the contractual liability of those liable on the tenant covenant expires on the contractual expiry date of the lease, even if statute continues the estate in favour of the ultimate assignee.[26]

Estate owner not in possession of the lease

The duality between the contractual and proprietary nature of a lease creates problems where the current tenant is not, in fact, in possession of the lease; in other words, where one person has a right to possess the lease, but another is in possession of it.

The first case to consider is that where the person in possession of the lease is a stranger to the tenant covenant, that is, someone who is liable to the landlord neither as a matter of contract nor as an assignee of the estate; in other words, a pure squatter.

The crucial point here is that the squatter may be in possession of the lease, but is not in possession as a contractual successor to the original tenant. There is no privity of contract or estate between the landlord and the squatter,[27] and consequently the only rights which may be enforced by or against the squatter are those which depend upon the bare fact of possession of the lease and nothing more. The squatter, like anyone else, has a right not to be dispossessed of the lease, except by someone who can show a better right to possess it, or to possess an estate free of the lease. So the landlord cannot evict the squatter simply on the ground that he or she is squatting on the lease, for the landlord has no title at all to the lease. In order to evict the squatter, the landlord must first do whatever might be necessary to determine the lease; for otherwise only the current tenant, as the person presently entitled to possess the estate in the lease, has a right to evict the squatter. Nor is the squatter at risk of being evicted by someone who is simply liable on the tenant covenant, for a mere contractual liability on the tenant covenant gives no right to possess the lease against third parties.

So far as the covenants in the lease are concerned, the squatter does not have any right to enforce the landlord's positive covenants contained in the lease, and nor can the positive tenant's covenants be enforced against

[26] *City of London* v. *Fell* [1994] 1 AC 458; [1993] 4 All ER 968; (1995) 69 P & CR 461.

[27] *O'Connor* v. *Foley* [1906] 1 IR 20, 26; *Ashe* v. *Hogan* [1920] 1 IR 104. See generally the Law Reform Commission in Ireland, 'Report on Title by Adverse Possession of Land' (LRC 67-2002).

a squatter (except indirectly by forfeiture[28] or distraint)[29] for the positive covenants in the lease are only enforceable where there is a relationship of privity of contract or estate. This is so even where the squatter has barred absolutely the true tenant's title by adverse possession[30] and been registered as proprietor of the lease. There is still neither privity of contract nor privity of estate between the landlord and the squatter, for privity of estate requires a contractual assignment of the benefit of the term.

The position is different so far as the negative covenants in the lease restrictive of user are concerned, however, because these are unregistrable restrictive covenants[31] enforceable by injunction against anyone in possession of the lease.[32]

The second situation is rather different. This is where the person in possession of the lease is someone who is liable as a matter of contract upon the tenant covenant, but is not entitled to be in possession of it as the current tenant. Whether the lease is an 'old' or 'new' lease, it often happens that, if the ultimate assignee becomes insolvent, and stops paying the rent, someone else who is liable on the tenant covenant informally reoccupies the property, so as to make some use of it, without formally reacquiring the lease.[33]

[28] If the landlord forfeits the lease, the squatter cannot apply for relief: *Tickner* v. *Buzzacot* [1965] Ch 426. In the case of registered land, where the true tenant's title was barred before 13 October 2003, it is possible that the squatter might have been able to compel the true tenant to apply for relief as trustee, but the better view is otherwise, because s.75 Land Registration Act 1925 did not create a true trust. See ch. 8.

[29] Distraint is a proprietary remedy in rem at common law. For its origins, see F. Pollock, *The Land Laws,* (3rd edn, London, MacMillan, 1896), p. 145. At common law there was no distinction between the goods of a tenant found on the premises and the goods of a sub-tenant, lodger or other third party. The landlord could distrain against the third party's goods, leaving the third party to claim over against the tenant. This was partly abrogated by the Law of Distress (Amendment) Act 1908. But the Act only protects the goods of third parties in a limited number of circumstances.

[30] See ch. 8.

[31] If the lease is unregistrable, then the restrictive covenant cannot be protected as a land charge: s.2(5) Land Charges Act 1972. If the lease is registered, then the restrictive covenant is not protectable by notice, unless it relates to other land: s.44(c) Land Registration Act 2002. If the lease is registrable, but is not registered, then anyone who subsequently takes free of the lease takes free of the covenant too.

[32] *Hemingway Securities* v. *Dunraven* [1995] 1 EGLR 61; *Mander* v. *Falcke* [1891] 2 Ch 554. See also ch. 8.

[33] Sometimes, the estate can be reacquired without any formal reassignment or overriding lease. If it was disposed of by an assignment which contained an equitable right of re-entry on breach, then the assignor can determine the assignment and reacquire the lease: *Shilo Spinners* v. *Harding* [1973] AC 691.

Occupiers with contractual liability but who have conveyed away the estate in the lease are in a difficult position.

If the lease is an 'old' lease, the landlord can enforce all the covenants in the lease directly against them subject only to service of any necessary notice under s.17 Landlord and Tenant (Covenants) Act 1995, notwithstanding that the lease is not currently vested in them, because a landlord who can sue in contract does not need to sue on the estate. But it does not follow that such an occupier can enforce the landlord's covenants directly against the landlord. The landlord is entitled to say that the benefit of the landlord's covenants has been assigned on to the ultimate assignee, in whom the estate is currently vested, so that the landlord's only liability is to the ultimate assignee.

If, however, the lease is a 'new' lease, the landlord will not normally be able to enforce the positive covenants directly against the occupier, for the contractual liability of the occupier will have been discharged on the first lawful assignment over, and the occupier will be in the same position as a simple trespasser upon the term.[34]

Possession and forfeiture

A lease is never forfeited automatically, even though the forfeiture clause might appear to say so in terms. Otherwise, tenants would be able to take advantage of their own breaches. Tenants would be able to force their landlords to treat their leases as forfeit, by deliberately breaching them, thereby determining their future liability under them. Consequently, a forfeiture clause is always construed as giving the landlord an option or 'election' whether to forfeit or not.[35]

The doctrine of election at common law requires a person, who has more than one remedy for a wrong, to choose between those remedies, if they are inconsistent.[36] Someone who brings an action claiming inconsistent remedies, is forced to make the choice when the judgment comes to be drawn, for the court cannot give judgment for conflicting remedies.[37] No one can be forced to choose until then, but he or she is free to make

[34] The penultimate assignee might still be liable as a matter of contract pursuant to the terms of an authorised guarantee agreement.

[35] *Alghussein* v. *Eton College* [1988] 1 WLR 587. A right to forfeit may therefore be waived, even if the lease purports to contain an 'anti-waiver' provision, because waiver, in this context, simply refers to the doctrine of election, and the doctrine of election is something that operates outside the contractual agreement between the parties.

[36] See per Lord Blackburn in *Scarf* v. *Jardine* (1882) 7 App Cas 345, 360; [1881–5] All ER Rep 651, 658.

[37] *Tang Man Sit* v. *Capacious Investments* [1996] 1 All ER 193.

the choice at any time after the wrong has been done. Once the choice has been communicated[38] to the wrongdoer, whether by words or conduct, it is irrevocable, even though the wrongdoer might not have relied on it or changed position in any way.[39]

If a landlord, therefore, does something by words or conduct which informs the tenant that the landlord has decided to affirm the lease (for instance, if the landlord, with knowledge of the breach, accepts rent which fell due at a time when the landlord could have exercised the right to forfeit instead) the landlord thereby waives the right to forfeit for that breach,[40] although not for any breach which might be committed or continue subsequently. Likewise, if a landlord chooses to forfeit a lease, the landlord cannot later affirm it.

Before the landlord can be said to have made a choice between affirmation and forfeiture, the landlord needs to know not merely that a breach has been committed, but also that there is a right to choose whether to forfeit or affirm.[41] The landlord does not, however, need to know that the choice is irrevocable.

Making an election in favour of forfeiture does not, in itself, end the lease. The lease ends by an entry, either actual or notional. Simply writing to the tenant saying 'I hereby elect to forfeit your lease' is, therefore, not sufficient to forfeit it, because that does not amount to an entry. But it does amount to an election to forfeit, which prevents the landlord affirming the lease subsequently. Having chosen to forfeit, the tenant could force the landlord to do so.

It is important to know when the entry was made, because the tenant's estate in and right to possess the lease determines at the moment when the entry is made; and the landlord's reversion free of the lease is accelerated with effect from then. Subject only to the possibility of relief, the landlord becomes entitled to possess the reversion upon the lease free from the

[38] *China National Foreign Trade Transportation Corp.* v. *Evlogia Shipping Co. SA of Panama, The Mihalios Xilas* [1979] 2 All ER 1044, 1049–1050; [1979] 1 WLR 1018, 1024 per Lord Diplock: 'It is trite law that in such circumstances to constitute an election to pursue one remedy so as to preclude the person making the election from subsequently resorting to the other remedy there must be an unequivocal act or statement by him communicated to the person against whom the two mutually exclusive remedies are available and showing that he intends to pursue one of them.'

[39] *Payman* v. *Lanjani* [1985] Ch 457.

[40] The burden of proof is on the tenant: *Fuller's Theatre and Vaudeville Co. Ltd* v. *Rofe* [1923] AC 435.

[41] Per Stephenson LJ in *Peyman* v. *Lanjani* [1985] Ch 457, 487; per May LJ (*ibid.*) 495; per Slade LJ (*ibid.*) 500; per Lord Atkin in *Evans* v. *Bartlam* [1937] AC 473, 479; [1937] 2 All ER 646, 649; per Lord Wright (*ibid.*) [1937] AC 473, 485; [1937] 2 All ER 646, 653.

burden of the lease with effect from that exact moment. When the court makes an order for possession in a forfeiture claim, it is deciding that the lease ended when the entry took place, and not later. Consequently, if the tenant remains in possession in the meantime, the landlord's claim for mesne profits runs from that date.

Usually the entry and the election to forfeit are made at the same time.

The election and entry may be made by peaceable re-entry (i.e. physical re-entry without a court order; it does not also need to be 'peaceful', and, usually, it is not). The rule here is simple. Peaceable re-entry is necessarily both an actual re-entry upon the lease and an election to forfeit, communicated by the act of re-entering. For this reason, re-entry onto only part of the premises is effective to forfeit the whole lease. A re-entry on a part is just as effective a communication of an election to determine the whole lease as a re-entry on the whole, unless the landlord has a right to forfeit a part separately.

Alternatively, the entry and election may be made by issue and service of an originating process[42] seeking relief solely on the footing that the lease has come to an end, electing immediately and unequivocally to forfeit it and claim possession; that is, to be put into possession of the reversion upon the lease free of the burden of the lease. Service of those proceedings is a notional re-entry on the land (because that is how it was treated in the action of ejectment)[43] and it is also a communication of the election to forfeit. Consequently, the lease determines as soon as the originating process is served.[44] If the claim for forfeiture is made by counterclaim against the tenant, rather than by original action, then the lease determines on service of the counterclaim.[45]

If the landlord instead re-lets the property to a new occupational tenant, the election and entry are made when the new tenant physically enters, or when proceedings are served against the former tenant seeking to recover possession, for the same reasons.[46]

[42] Formerly a 'writ' in the High Court, or a 'possession summons' in the county court; now, in either court, an 'N.5 claim form'.

[43] See ch. 2.

[44] *Canas Property Co.* v. *KL Television Services* [1970] 2 QB 433; [1970] 2 All ER 795.

[45] The right to make a counterclaim was first created by the Judicature Act 1873. For limitation purposes, the counterclaim relates back to the date of issue of the originating process, unless the court severs it (*Ernst & Young* v. *Butte Mining (No. 2)* [1997] 1 WLR 1485) but the rules applicable to limitation have nothing to do with the question of when the entry and election are made.

[46] *Redleaf* v. *Talbot* [1995] BCC 1091.

The landlord might, however, bring a claim seeking both forfeiture and enforcement of the terms of the lease in the alternative. In that event, the landlord does not make an election, and does not re-enter, until something is done to make the choice clear, or until judgment, when the landlord is forced to chose whether to take a possession order or not.[47]

Relief from forfeiture

Where a court grants relief from forfeiture,[48] relief may either take the form of a retrospective reinstatement of the original lease, or it may take the form of the grant of a new lease taking effect from the date of the order granting relief. It depends on whether the application is made by or in the name of the tenant, or is made by a sub-tenant or mortgagee as such.

If relief is granted on an application made by the tenant, or on an application made by a sub-tenant or mortgagee in the name of the tenant,[49] the order reinstates the original lease with retrospective effect.

In the meantime there is inevitably a twilight period of some uncertainty. During this period the landlord cannot enforce the terms of the lease against the tenant, but the tenant, who has not elected to determine the lease, can seek to enforce the covenants in the lease against the

[47] *Tang Man Sit* v. *Capicious Investments* [1996] 1 All ER 193; *Calabar Properties* v. *Seagull Autos* [1981] QB 202; [1980] 1 All ER 839.

[48] The equitable jurisdiction to grant relief against forfeiture for non-payment of rent was well established before the seventeenth century. The first statutory intervention was the Crown Lands Act 1623 (which is still in force, and which was necessary because the inherent jurisdiction could not be exercised against the Crown) and provided for automatic relief if the rent was paid before proceedings were issued. If the landlord was anyone else, automatic relief did not come until the enactment of the Landlord and Tenant Act 1730 (now, s.212 Common Law Procedure Act 1852). Before the enactment of s.14 Conveyancing Act 1881, the court could not, in general, grant relief against forfeiture for non-rental breaches: *Hill* v. *Barclay* (1811) 18 Ves 56. The first case where relief was granted following a peaceable re-entry was *Howard* v. *Fanshawe* [1895] 2 Ch 581. The jurisdiction today, in the High Court, is a mixture of the old inherent jurisdiction of the Court of Chancery, and the statutory jurisdiction contained in ss.211–212 Common Law Procedure Act 1852 and s.146 Law of Property Act 1925. In the county court the jurisdiction is exclusively statutory, and is to be found in ss.138–140 County Courts Act 1984.

[49] Mortgages commonly contain a security power of attorney to allow the mortgagee to apply in the name of the tenant. Such a power survives the bankruptcy or liquidation of the tenant (*Sowman* v. *David Samuel Trust Ltd* [1978] 1 WLR 22), and the advantage for the mortgagee in making the application in the name of the tenant is that the mortgagee does not then become liable on the covenants in the lease. Even absent such a power, a sub-tenant or mortgagee often has a statutory right to make an application in the tenant's name; see s.146(2) Law of Property Act 1925; *Escalus Properties* v. *Robinson* [1996] QB 231; [1995] 2 EGLR 23.

landlord. So the tenant can obtain interim relief to enforce the covenants, but the landlord cannot.[50]

If, however, relief is given to a sub-tenant or a mortgagee as such, and not in the name of the tenant, then relief takes the form of the grant of a new lease to the applicant with effect from the date of the order.

It follows that, even when an application for relief by a sub-tenant or mortgagee as such is successful, there will nonetheless be a gap between the date when the forfeiture was effected, and the date upon which relief is granted, during which time the landlord will be treated as having been entitled to possess the property free from the forfeited lease (for it has been forfeited, and is not reinstated by an order for relief) and also free of the relieved lease, for it has not been granted yet, and, when it is granted, that will not have retrospective effect.

Terms for the grant of relief

Where the forfeiture is by proceedings in the county court and is only for non-payment of rent, the tenant may obtain relief automatically by paying the arrears of rent and the costs of the action five clear days before the first return day specified on the front of the claim form.[51] Similarly, in High Court proceedings for forfeiture for non-payment of rent, where at least six months' rent is in arrears,[52] relief can be obtained automatically by paying all the arrears and the costs of the action before the trial.[53] In either case, contractual (but not statutory) interest will be payable as well.

In other cases, the terms of relief are in the discretion of the court, but there are six general principles to be applied.

[50] *Peninsular Maritime Ltd* v. *Padseal* (1981) 259 EG 860, 866; *Associated Deliveries Ltd* v. *Harrison* (1984) 272 EG 321. In fact, the position is not as simple as that. A landlord can obtain interim relief to enforce a covenant, if the right given by the covenant is a right that the landlord would have in any event, even on the premise that the lease had been forfeited; e.g. entry to repair (*Wheeler* v. *Keeble* [1920] 1 Ch 57): and, even if the right is not such a right, the landlord ought to be able to strike the application for relief out, as an abuse of process, if the tenant will not voluntarily perform the covenant; for the tenant cannot, on the one hand, be willing to perform the covenants in order to obtain relief, and on the other, refuse to do so pending the hearing of the application.

[51] Section 138(2) County Courts Act 1984. The 'return' day means the date specified on the front of the claim form: *Swordheath* v. *Bolt* [1992] 2 EGLR 68.

[52] *Standard Pattern* v. *Ivey* [1962] Ch 432; [1962] 2 WLR 656; [1962] 1 All ER 452. Where six months' rent is not in arrears, then relief can be sought on the same terms pursuant to s.38 Supreme Court Act 1981 on an application made to the court.

[53] Section 212 Common Law Procedure Act 1852.

First general principle

First, relief cannot be granted so as to prejudice the rights of any person who, between forfeiture and relief, has been granted a legal interest in the property for value without notice[54] of the tenant's right to relief.

This poses a particular problem where the third party interest not to be prejudiced is itself a legal lease; that is, where the landlord has granted a third party without notice a new legal lease of the property between the date of forfeiture and the date when relief is granted. If the applicant has delayed unreasonably in applying for relief, the court might refuse to grant relief at all.[55] If relief is granted, it has to be granted so as to take effect subject to all the rights of the new tenant. The only way in which that can be done is to grant relief in the form of a concurrent lease of the reversion,[56] for otherwise a subsequent forfeiture of the relieved lease would also forfeit the new lease. There is no conceptual difficulty in doing this where relief is to be granted to a sub-tenant or mortgagee by way of vesting order, for the lease granted by way of vesting order does not have retrospective effect, and so takes effect as a concurrent lease in any event. The difficulty arises where relief is granted on an application made by or in the name of the tenant, for that does have retrospective effect. So the court must ensure that the applicant agrees to subordinate the priority of the relieved lease to the new lease, as a condition of granting relief to the applicant at all. It must be subordinated not only so as to take effect in reversion upon the new lease, but also so as to take effect as a concurrent lease, rather than as a headlease; for otherwise a further forfeiture of the relieved lease would also forfeit the new lease.

Second general principle

The second principle is that the person applying for relief must do whatever is necessary to remedy the breaches of covenant for which the landlord

[54] In the case of an unregistered reversion, notice will depend upon a variety of factors. In unregistered conveyancing, a right to relief is an equitable right that can be neither protected as a land charge nor overreached, the validity of which therefore depends upon the pure doctrine of notice. The pure doctrine of notice is wholly irrelevant in registered conveyancing. Dispositions instead take effect subject to entries on the register (a form of statutory notice) and overriding interests. So relief cannot be granted so as to prejudice the priority obtained by a new tenant whose lease was granted out of a registered reversion at a time when the relieved lease was itself not registered and when the right to relief was not an overriding interest.

[55] *Silverman* v. *AFCO* [1988] 1 EGLR 51; (1988) 56 P & CR 185.

[56] *Fuller* v. *Judy Properties* [1992] 1 EGLR 75; (1992) 64 P & CR 176.

forfeited, in so far as they are capable of being remedied; and, if they are not capable of being remedied, then the applicant must pay the landlord appropriate compensation for the breaches. There is, however, generally no obligation on the tenant to remedy other breaches of covenant for which the landlord did not forfeit. So a landlord cannot forfeit for non-payment of rent, and then demand as a term of relief that the tenant remedy a pre-forfeiture non-rental breach.[57]

Third general principle

The third principle is that, in the case of a retrospective relief from forfeiture (relief claimed by or in the name of the tenant), the applicant must do whatever is necessary to put the landlord in the same position as if all the tenant's covenants had been performed between the date of forfeiture and the date upon which relief is granted.

Fourth general principle

Relief can be granted for both remediable and irremediable breaches. There is no rule that an irremediable breach is also an irrelievable breach. But in the case of a deliberate rather than an inadvertent breach of covenant, the fourth general principle requires that the landlord be given appropriate security for the tenant's future conduct.[58] In a rental case, this might include entering into a rent deposit deed. In a non-rental case, the tenant might be required to give undertakings to the court.

Fifth general principle

The fifth principle is that there must be an account taken between the landlord and the person applying for relief for the use which has been made of the property since the forfeiture. The rules for who has to give credit for what differ, depending on whether the application for relief is made by or in the name of the tenant, in order retrospectively to reinstate the lease, or whether the application is made by a sub-tenant or mortgagee in his or her own name, for a vesting order.

[57] *Gill* v. *Lewis* [1956] 2 QB 1; [1956] 1 All ER 844; cf. *Essex Furniture plc* v. *National Provident Institution* [2001] L & TR 32.

[58] There is no longer an absolute rule that relief will only be granted for a deliberate breach in exceptional circumstances: *Mount Cook Land* v. *Hartley* [2000] EGCS 26.

If the application is made by a sub-tenant or mortgagee as such for a vesting order, then the landlord will be treated, when taking the account, as having been entitled to possess the reversionary estate free of both the forfeited lease and the relieved lease during the period between the entry and the granting of relief.[59] If the applying sub-tenant or mortgagee has, itself, kept the landlord out of possession during that period, then it will have to pay the landlord mesne profits for that period as a condition of obtaining relief.[60] But the applicant ought not to have to pay if the tenant, or some third party, has kept the landlord out of possession, for then there could be double recovery. The landlord is entitled to bring an action for mesne profits against that person directly, for the vesting order does not have retrospective effect. It does not invalidate the original forfeiture, nor affect the landlord's accrued rights for the period prior to the grant of relief. So, if the sub-tenant or mortgagee had to pay mesne profits for that period in order to obtain relief, then the landlord could recover twice for the same wrong.[61]

Needless to say, if the landlord has, in fact, been enjoying the reversionary estate as if there were no lease, there is no question of the applicant for relief having to pay mesne profits for that period, because mesne profits are compensation for wrongly being kept out of possession. If the landlord has not been kept out of possession, there is no compensation to be paid.

Where relief is granted on an application made by or in the name of the tenant, then different problems are posed on the taking of the account because then relief is granted with retrospective effect. The basic principle is that, on the one side of the coin, the tenant must pay to the landlord all sums which would have been due under the lease, as if it had never been forfeited, and, on the other, the landlord must account to the tenant for the benefits received by reason of having forfeited the lease.

The simplest circumstance in which to apply this principle is where the tenant has remained in possession at all times since and notwithstanding the forfeiture. This will usually be the case where the forfeiture is effected by service of proceedings which are subsequently contested. Relief being retrospective, the effect of the grant of relief is that the tenant is treated as having always been entitled to possess under the terms of the lease, and the forfeiture is deemed never to have occurred. It follows that there are no mesne profits to be paid; instead the tenant must pay the rent (and

59 See above.

60 *Leeds Permanent BS* v. *Manyfield* Dyson J, QB, 16 June 1993, unreported.

61 The court, in its discretion, however, could require the applicant to pay if the landlord offered to assign any rights against the tenant or third party possessor to the applicant.

other sums) falling due under the lease down to the date on which relief is given.

If, however, the landlord has been in possession of the retrospectively relieved lease then, when relief is granted, in order to reinstate matters to how they would have stood if the forfeiture had never happened, the landlord will have to pay the tenant mesne profits, and the tenant pay the landlord whatever sums would have fallen due under the lease. Whether this will result in a net payment to the landlord or the tenant will, naturally, depend upon whether the rent due under the lease exceeds the open market rent for the premises, for the mesne profits are calculated on an open market rental value basis.[62] Where the lease is at a rack rent, in practice rough and ready justice can be done by simply setting off the two claims in extinction of each other. Where the forfeiture is for non-payment of rent, however, the landlord may only be charged with as much as 'he really and bona fide, without fraud, deceit or wilful neglect', made from the premises from the time the landlord took possession.[63]

If a third party has been in possession between the forfeiture and the grant of relief, then the position on taking the account where relief is retrospective is more complicated. Again, because relief is retrospective, as a condition of the grant of relief, the tenant must pay the rent and all other sums due under the lease from the date of forfeiture down to the date upon which relief is granted. Further, again because relief is retrospective, the landlord must account for any benefit received as a result of the forfeiture for the same period. So if, for instance, the third party has been in possession with the landlord's consent, the landlord must, at the tenant's election, either account for any payments received from the third party, or pay mesne profits at the open market letting value. If, however, the third party was simply a squatter who has not made any payment to the landlord, then there will be nothing for the landlord to account for, and, relief being retrospective, the tenant can bring an action against the squatter for mesne profits later.

Sixth (and last) general principle

The sixth principle is that as a condition of obtaining relief the person applying for relief normally[64] has to pay the costs of the action. This is

[62] *Inverugie Investments* v. *Hackett* [1995] 1 WLR 713.

[63] Section 211 Common Law Procedure Act 1852.

[64] The rule is not absolute. Where a landlord has forfeited oppressively, or unreasonably refused an offer made by the tenant, then the landlord may be deprived of costs, or even be made to pay the tenant's costs: *Mount Cook Land* v. *Hartley* [2000] EGCS 26.

true even if that person has the benefit of a public funding certificate (legal aid), for requiring someone to pay costs as a condition of granting relief does not, of itself, force anyone to pay those costs;[65] it just makes payment a condition of relief.[66] Where the lease contains a covenant to pay costs on an indemnity basis, then that will normally be the appropriate basis of assessment.[67] Otherwise, the appropriate basis of assessment is the standard basis.[68]

Contractual licences

If history recurs, then legal history is no exception. Lawyers dealing with contractual licences at the turn of the twenty-first century face precisely the same conceptual problem as their forebears who dealt with leases in the twelfth to fourteenth centuries[69] – namely, the extent to which an essentially contractual right also creates a property interest in land good against third parties – and the problem will probably take just as long to resolve.[70]

A lease or tenancy was originally seen purely as a contract. An evicted tenant might have a remedy in damages against the other party for wrongful termination of the contract, but that was all. Yet gradually they came to be enforceable against both the grantor and third parties as 'chattels real'. The intellectual dishonesty of the process by which this was done is apparent in the very name.

The position of licences today is, unhappily, less clear. The law has reached the reluctant compromise that the licensee can often make the licensor perform the contract, but does not have any status to enforce the contracted-for rights against anyone else.

Whether the parties have created a licence or a leasehold estate creating a tenancy is, therefore, a question of some practical importance. A tenancy

65 Section 11 Access to Justice Act 1999.

66 *Factors (Sundries) Ltd* v. *Miller* [1952] 2 All ER 630; [1952] 2 TLR 194; *Three Stars Property Holdings* v. *Driscoll* [1988] CLY 2795.

67 *Church Commissioners* v. *Ibrahim* [1997] 1 EGLR 13.

68 *Billson* v. *Residential Apartments* [1992] 1 AC 494; [1992] 2 WLR 15; [1992] 1 All ER 141; *Billson* v. *Residential Apartments (No. 3)* [1995] EGCS 155.

69 See F. Pollock and F. Maitland, *History of English Law* (2nd edn, Cambridge, Cambridge University Press, 1911), vol. 2, p. 106 et seq.; B. Simpson, *Introduction to the History of Land Law* (2nd edn, Oxford, Oxford University Press, 1961), p. 71.

70 By 1389, a tenant could recover possession from a third party: see M. Arnold, 'Fourteenth Century Promises', [1976] CLJ 321, 323–30. The law of covenants did not catch up until the Grantees of Reversions Act 1540 and the decision in *Spencer's Case* ((1583) 5 Co Rep 16a) in the sixteenth century.

is enforceable against the world. A licence is enforceable only against the grantor. That is the difference in effect. What though is the difference in character, that enables us to distinguish between the two, and to say, in the one case, that the grantor has created a tenancy, and, in the other, that the grantor has created only a licence?[71]

Both are contractual rights to use or enjoy land. Even a gratuitous licence is essentially contractual, though it may be unenforceable as a contract for want of consideration if it is not under seal. But one is turned into a piece of property, binding on third parties, and the other is not. What is it about the contract that has this effect?

The 'touchstone' that is supposed to distinguish a lease from a licence is the concept of 'exclusive possession':[72] a right to enter upon land which grants exclusive possession creates a leasehold estate and therefore a tenancy; any lesser permission is necessarily no more than a licence.

If, by exclusive possession, what is meant is possession of a legal estate, as explained in chapter 1, then this statement is certainly true, but it does not provide any assistance in distinguishing a lease from a licence. All it does is restate the problem in a tautologous way. It is tautologous because possession of an estate is necessarily exclusive and indivisible.[73] It restates the problem, rather than solving it, because it does not provide any information about what ingredients a contract must contain if it is to create such an estate.

If, on the other hand, what is meant by exclusive possession is exclusive occupation, then the 'touchstone' is quite simply wrong. It is quite possible for a tenant to be obliged by the lease to share occupation with the landlord, to a greater or lesser degree, and still be a tenant. Likewise, it is quite possible for a licensee to have a right of exclusive occupation, including a contractual right to exclude the licensor, and still be merely a licensee.[74]

If the term 'exclusive possession' is unhelpful as a way of distinguishing a lease from a licence, is there any better way? Plainly, it is not simply a question of labels. Admittedly, the labels used may say something about

[71] Originally, the rule was simple. If the 'licence' was for a fixed term, then it was a 'lease': *Hall* v. *Sebright* (1669) 1 Mod 14.

[72] Per Windeyer J in *Radaich* v. *Smith* (1959) 101 CLR 209, 223, approved by the House of Lords in *Street* v. *Mountford* [1985] AC 809.

[73] Per Denning LJ in *Hills (Patents) Ltd* v. *University College Hospital* [1956] 1 QB 90; *Akici* v. *LR Butlin Ltd* [2006] 1 WLR 201.

[74] *Marchant* v. *Charters* [1977] 1 WLR 1181; *Luganda* v. *Service Hotels Ltd* [1969] 2 Ch 209; *Thompson* v. *Ward* (1871) LR 6 CP 327; *Bahamas International* v. *Threadgood* [1974] 1 WLR 1514.

the true intentions of the parties, but a lease is a lease, even if it is called a licence, in the same way that a mortgage is a mortgage, even if it is disguised as something else.[75] Nor is it necessarily a question of the expressed intentions of the parties or the express terms of the agreement. Sham terms can be used to mask the real nature of the transaction. Rather it is something about the substance of the agreement: some crucial ingredient that turns a licence into a tenancy.

That crucial ingredient is the extent to which the parties intend that control of the property should pass from the grantor to the grantee.[76] In particular, if the substance of the transaction is that the grantee shall have a general right to permit some strangers to enter upon the property, and to exclude others, then what has been created is a tenancy, rather than a licence. That is why a lodger is merely a licensee, but a bed-sitter is a tenant. It also explains why a licensee is denied the ability to bring actions against third parties who interfere with the licence, except through the licensor.[77] It is because the genuine intention of the parties, when the licence was granted, was that the licensor would retain a degree of control of the property inconsistent with that right.

Protection of licences

A licensee, as we have seen, has no estate in the land. He or she merely has a contractual right to occupy,[78] which (unlike a lease) does not pass any estate in the land, either at common law or in equity.[79]

It follows that, by definition, the licensee does not have a right to possess any estate, nor, by virtue of the licence, can the licensee be in possession of any estate. For this reason, the three common law possessory actions which protect possession simply ought not to be available to a licensee.

[75] *IDC* v. *Clark* [1992] 2 EGLR 184.

[76] *Governors of the National Maternity Hospital* v. *McGouran* [1994] 1 ILRM 521; *Bradley* v. *Baylis* (1881) 8 QBD 195.

[77] See below.

[78] A 'licence coupled with an interest' (that is, a right to enter upon land that is annexed to an incorporeal hereditament) is not a 'licence' at all, any more than an incorporeal hereditament is a 'licence'. If a right of way is attached to the fee simple in a field, no one would say that the exercise of the right was pursuant to a 'licence'. So too, if a right to enter upon land is attached to a profit à prendre (for instance, a right of fishery), it would be wholly misleading to describe that as a 'licence' coupled to an interest; for, in truth, it is not a licence at all, but a property right that is an incident of the profit.

[79] In *Thomas* v. *Sorrell* (1673) Vaugh 330, 351, Vaughn CJ said: 'A dispensation or licence properly passeth no interest, nor alters or transfers property in any thing, but only makes an action lawful, which without it had been unlawful.'

An evicted licensee cannot bring an action for recovery of land, for the action is an action to be put into possession of an estate in land, and the licensee has no right or title to be put into possession of any such estate. For a similar reason, the licensee cannot bring the actions of trespass or nuisance either, for the complaint in trespass is of wrongful intrusion upon possession of a fee simple, a lease or a profit à prendre, and the complaint in nuisance is of an interference with one of those estates, or with a right to a legal interest in land.[80]

The remedies available to a licensee therefore lie exclusively in the law of contract.[81] If the licensor terminates the licence in breach of contract, then, at common law, the licensee may obtain damages for breach of contract. The licensee may also be able to obtain damages against the licensor if a third party interferes with the licence, depending upon the extent to which the licensor has warranted the grant. In equity, the licensee may also be able to obtain an order for specific performance of the contract against the licensor (including perhaps an order that the licensor bring proceedings against a third party), or an injunction against the licensor to prevent termination in breach of contract.[82] But the licensee has no direct remedy against interference by a third party. Even if the third party has committed the tort of inducing the licensor to breach the contract, that cannot turn the licence into a binding property interest.

The inability of the licensee to enforce the licence against third parties is a corollary of the rule that the burden of a licence does not run with the land. Though the benefit of covenants contained in a licence can usually be assigned,[83] the burden cannot.[84] Neither the licensor nor the licensee can transfer the burden of performing the agreement contained in the licence to an assignee, save with the consent of the other party by way of novation. So, if the licensor transfers the land to someone else, the transferee takes free of the licence, precisely because it is only enforceable between the parties as a matter of contract.[85]

If a licence does not bind third parties, it necessarily follows that a licensee cannot protect the licence by bringing any of the possessory

80 *Hunter* v. *Canary Wharf* [1997] AC 655; [1997] 2 All ER 426; M. Wonnacott, 'Flawed Judgment' (1999) 11 EG 165; J. Hill, 'The Proprietary Character of Possession', in *Modern Studies in Property Law* (ed. E. Cooke, Oxford, Hart Publishing, 2001) vol. 1, pp. 21–40.

81 By statute, some licences have additional protection: s.2 Agricultural Holdings Act 1986, for example, converts some agricultural licences into tenancies.

82 *Great Yarmouth BC* v. *Verrall* [1969] 1 Ch 451; [1968] 1 All ER 1.

83 *Tolhurst* v. *Associated Portland Cement Manufacturers* [1903] AC 414, 424; *J. Miller Ltd* v. *Laurence and Bardsley* [1966] 1 Lloyds LR 90.

84 *Ashburn Anstalt* v. *Arnold* [1989] Ch 1.

85 *Ibid.*

actions against a third party; for the effect of allowing the licensee to do so would be to make the burden of the licence binding on third parties.

Denying the possessory remedies to a licensee, on the technical ground that there is no estate in land, hides this basic truth, and any rule which appears to be grounded on no more than technicality can seem unjust and arbitrary. It is not intuitively obvious that it is inherent in the nature of a licence, that the proper person to protect the licence is the licensor. On a practical level, it is true, the consequences of interfering with rights granted by a licence are often just as serious as interfering with rights granted by a lease. But 'property rights are determined by fixed rules and settled principles. They are not discretionary. They do not depend upon ideas of what is "fair, just and reasonable". Such concepts, which in reality mask decisions of legal policy, have no place in the law of property.'[86]

Nonetheless, the courts sometimes strain to allow licensees to sue third parties by pretending that they have possession of an estate. In order to justify this, judges sometimes refer to a special class of licensee, the 'licensee with exclusive possession of the land'.[87] But this kind of muddled thinking merely exacerbates the problem. If, on the one hand, what is meant by 'exclusive possession' is possession of an estate, then the 'licensee' is not a licensee at all; the 'licensee' must be a tenant. If, on the other hand, what is meant by 'exclusive possession' is a contractual right of exclusive occupation, then that, in itself, is not an estate in the land, and so is insufficient to enable the licensee to bring any of the possessory actions. The root of the problem with the concept of a 'licensee with exclusive possession' is that judges are instinctively applying the rule that a person whose exclusive occupation of land cannot otherwise be explained, is presumed to have seisin, and so can bring the possessory actions as a fee simple possessor,[88] to a case where the occupation is fully explained by the licence, with the consequence that the occupier cannot be said to be in possession of the fee simple, and so cannot have the necessary standing to bring those actions.

Nor, it might be added, does equity help. Undoubtedly, there are proprietary interests which are recognised in equity, and for which equity

[86] Per Lord Millett in *Foskett* v. *McKeown* [2000] 1 AC 102, 127.

[87] *Newcastle-under-Lyme Corp.* v. *Wolstanton Ltd* [1947] Ch 92, 106-8; [1946] 2 All ER 447, 455–6, per Evershed J. This should not be confused with a right to enter upon another's land as part of an incorporeal hereditament (for instance, to stand on a river bank whilst exercising a right to fish) which is sometimes called 'a licence coupled with an interest', but which is not, in fact, a licence at all.

[88] See ch. 3.

provides some protection against third parties. But what equity cannot do, and does not do, is enable someone who has even a proprietary equitable right to bring a common law claim, by virtue of that right alone.[89]

Nonetheless, in hard cases, the Court of Appeal is quite capable of being seduced into thinking that the rule is nothing more than a technicality. In *Manchester Airport* v. *Dutton*,[90] the issue of whether a licensee could bring an action for recovery of land was squarely before the court. Laws LJ (with whom Kennedy LJ agreed) said 'the true principle is that a licensee not in occupation may claim possession against a trespasser if that is a necessary remedy to vindicate and give effect to such rights of occupation as by the contract with his licensor he enjoys,' and that the 'spectre of history ... which ought to be a friendly ghost' did not prevent this conclusion.

Friendly or not, this ghost was certainly mute. What history might have been trying to say was that exactly the same point had been conclusively decided, the other way, by the Exchequer Chamber (equivalent to the Court of Appeal) as long ago as 1863, in a case called *Hill* v. *Tupper*.[91] That case concerned an exclusive licence to use pleasure boats on a canal. The point made by that court was that the licensee could not obtain an order to prevent third parties using the canal for that purpose, because he was only a licensee, and so did not have any estate in the canal that he could enforce against third parties. Only the licensor, who did have such an estate, could bring those proceedings, and so the proceedings could only be brought in the licensor's name.

The occupier in *Manchester Airport* v. *Dutton* did not have legal representation, and, although *Hill* v. *Tupper* is a well-known case – the leading land law text at the time devoted more than half a page to it[92] – it was not referred to in any of the judgments. Chadwick LJ, who was the only member of the panel with any chancery experience, dissented, on the ground that a licensee cannot obtain an order to be put in possession of land. If the decision of the majority were right, then there would no longer be any difference between a lease and licence, for, if a licensee can obtain an

[89] See ch. 6. [90] [2000] QB 133.

[91] (1863) 2 H & C 121. The ghost might equally well have pointed to the judgment of Abbott CJ in *Doe* v. *Wood* (1819) Barn & Ald 724, 737. The court had the opportunity to put this right in *Alamo Housing* v. *Meredith* ([2003] EWCA Civ 495) but did not take it. See also *Countryside Residential* v. *Tugwell* [2000] 2 EGLR 59 and *McClymont* v. *Primecourt Property Management* [2000] EGCS 192.

[92] R. Megarry and W. Wade, *The Law of Real Property* (5th edn, London, Stevens, 1984), p. 837.

order to recover possession of the licence, then a licence has become an estate in land, identical to a lease.[93] Furthermore, if the decision of the majority were right, then it would follow that the decision of the House of Lords in *Hunter* v. *Canary Wharf*[94] must be wrong, for if a dispossessed licensee can recover possession of the whole licence, a licensee must be able to complain about lesser disturbances and interference. The decision must be, simply, *per incuriam.*

93 See also J. Hill, 'The Proprietary Character of Possession', in *Modern Studies in Property Law* (ed. E Cooke, Oxford, Hart Publishing, 2001) vol. 1, pp. 34–5.

94 [1997] AC 655.

5

Mortgages and charges

Introduction

If land is power, then mortgage lending is the means by which power may be obtained on credit.[1]

This chapter is about untangling the relationships between the debtor who has created the security over the land, the creditor who owns the security for the debt, and third parties who have some estate, right or interest in that land.

It is about who has the right to possess what, and who is 'in' possession of what, both before the credit runs out, and afterwards, when the secured creditor takes steps to enforce the security.

In order to untangle those relationships, it is necessary to untangle some of the legal history first; for, as in so much of land law, it is impossible to say where we are, without knowing how we got here.

Legal mortgages

The Law of Property Act 1925 reduced the number of legal estates in land to two; the 'fee simple absolute in possession',[2] and the lease for 'a term of years absolute'.[3]

Both expressions are potentially misleading. A fee simple is 'in possession' even if it is subject to a lease, for 'in possession' here means 'vested in possession',[4] and so includes the right to receive rents and profits;[5] and periodic tenancies and tenancies for fixed terms of less than a year are deemed to be for a 'term of years absolute'.[6]

[1] Britain is a 'real-property mortgaged to a building society owning democracy': per Lord Diplock in *Pettit* v. *Pettit* [1970] AC 777, 824.

[2] Section 1(1)(a) Law of Property Act 1925.

[3] Section 1(1)(b) Law of Property Act 1925.

[4] The meaning of 'vested in possession' is explained, and contrasted with 'vested in interest', in ch. 1.

[5] Section 205(1)(xix) Law of Property Act 1925.

[6] Section 205(1)(xxvii) Law of Property Act 1925.

Old form legal mortgages

These two estates, registered or unregistered, are the only estates in land which may now be mortgaged or charged by a legal security.[7]

Before 1926, if someone wished to raise money upon the security of an otherwise unencumbered fee simple,[8] that would normally be done by conveying it to the lender, reserving a right of reconveyance upon repayment of the debt.[9] The right to redeem the mortgage was recognised in equity,[10] and so equity would enforce the lender's obligation to convey the property back to the debtor on repayment of the secured debt; but, in the meantime, at common law, the lender was treated as having become the absolute owner of the fee simple.

Similarly, in order to mortgage a lease, the tenant would have assigned it to the lender, reserving a right of reassignment on repayment: equity recognised the right to redeem the mortgage and require the lease to be assigned back; but in the meantime the common law treated the lender as having become the absolute owner of the lease.

This form of mortgage had one substantial disadvantage (or advantage, depending upon your viewpoint). It was hard to raise additional money upon the security of second or subsequent mortgages. Those securities could only take effect in equity, for the debtor had no legal estate to offer whilst the first mortgage was still extant: all that could be offered by way

[7] A profit à prendre is technically a legal interest, rather than an estate (s.1(2) Law of Property Act 1925). A profit in gross may now be registered as if it were an estate, and such a profit may be charged by way of legal mortgage (s.51 Land Registration Act 2002). Otherwise, a profit cannot be mortgaged or charged by a legal security in its own right. But, if a profit is attached to a fee simple or a legal lease, it will be caught by any legal mortgage or charge of that estate.

[8] Copyhold land was mortgaged by conditional surrender, but all copyholds were converted into fees simple immediately before the Law of Property Act 1925 came into force on 1 January 1926 (s.202 Law of Property Act 1925).

[9] The statutory form of mortgage authorised by s.26 Conveyancing Act 1881 was in the following terms (Part 1 Sch. 3 Conveyancing Act 1881): 'This indenture made by way of statutory mortgage on the ... of ... 1882 between *A.* of [etc.] of the one part and *M.* of [etc.] of the other part WITNESSETH that in consideration of the sum of £ ... now paid to *A.* by *M.* of which sum *A.* hereby acknowledges the receipt *A.* as mortgagor and beneficial owner hereby conveys to *M.* All that [etc.] To hold to and to the use of *M.* in fee simple for securing payment on the ... day of ... 1883 of the principal sum of £ ... as the mortgage money with interest thereon at the rate of [four] per cent per annum. In witness etc.'

[10] For the development of the doctrine, see D Sugarman and R Warrington, 'Land Law, Citizenship, and the Invention of "Englishness": The Strange World of the Equity of Redemption', in *Early Modern Conceptions of Property* (ed. J. Brewer and S. Staves, London, Routledge, 1996), pp. 111–43.

of further security was the equity of redemption (the right in equity to require the property to be reconveyed on payment of the existing mortgage debt), and that was not very satisfactory.[11]

There was, however, an alternative way of creating a first legal mortgage which did not suffer from this problem. The debtor could grant the lender a lease (or a sub-lease) containing a proviso for cesser upon payment of the secured debt. The idea was that the lender's security would take the form of a lease which would last only until the debt was repaid, and this was called a 'mortgage term'.[12] The debtor retained the reversion upon the mortgage term, but in the meantime the lender had the right to possess the lease created by the mortgage. This meant that the debtor could create any number of subsequent legal mortgages by granting one or more concurrent mortgage terms out of the retained reversion, or the debtor could at least grant one more by transfer of the whole legal estate in the reversion to the subsequent lender in the traditional way.

This alternative method waxed and waned in popularity over the centuries, and had largely[13] fallen into disuse by the end of the nineteenth because of the practical disadvantages of leaving even a nominal reversion vested in the debtor when realising the security. The debtor, as landlord of the mortgage term, could make that very awkward if he or she wished, and many did.

Whatever method was used, however, a lender with a legal security in unregistered land granted before 1926 necessarily acquired an immediate right to possess an actual legal estate in his or her own name; for the debtor had either conveyed or assigned the legal estate to the lender by creating the mortgage in the traditional way, or the debtor had

[11] F. Maitland, *Equity* (Cambridge, Cambridge University Press, 1909), p. 283.

[12] The Law Commission, in the course of recommending that it should no longer be possible to create a mortgage over registered land in this way, expressed the view that 'the mortgage by demise or sub-demise was as much a creation of the Law of Property Act 1925 as was the charge expressed to be by way of legal mortgage' and that the charge over registered land introduced by the Land Transfer Act 1875 'had the longest pedigree' (Law Com No. 271, para. 7.2). But a mortgage by demise was known to Bracton in the thirteenth century (Bracton F.20) was often used in the seventeenth (W. Holdsworth, *Historical Introduction to Land Law* (Oxford, Oxford University Press, 1927), p. 264) had become 'usual' by the eighteenth (Blackstone, *Commentaries on the Laws of England* (11th edn, London, Strahan & Woodfall, 1791), vol. 2, p. 158) and was the 'almost universal' practice at the beginning of the nineteenth (J. Stuart, *The Practice of Conveyancing* (London, Butterworths, 1827), p. 154).

[13] Even at the end of the nineteenth century, mortgages were still sometimes created in this way; see eg. *Bonner* v. *Tottenham and Edmonton BS* [1899] 1 QB 161.

granted the lender an actual lease or sub-lease of it by way of mortgage term.

On 1 January 1926, everything changed. Thenceforth, it became impossible to create a legal mortgage by outright conveyance or assignment.[14] If the parties attempted it, they would find that they had automatically created a mortgage term instead.[15] Now, for registered land, even this is prohibited.[16]

A charge by way of legal mortgage

These, however, are securities for the conveyancer's curiosity cupboard. Since 1926, legal mortgages of both freeholds and leaseholds have almost invariably been created as 'charges by way of legal mortgage'; the radical new method was introduced, for registered land by the Land Transfer Act 1875, and for unregistered land by the Law of Property Act 1925.[17]

A charge by way of legal mortgage does not convey the debtor's fee simple nor does it assign the debtor's lease to the lender. The debtor retains the legal estate in both.[18] But the effect of a first legal charge of freehold land is to grant the lender the same rights and powers as if the debtor had created a mortgage term for 3,000 years,[19] and the effect of a first legal charge of a lease is to grant the lender the same rights and powers as if the debtor had created a mortgage sub-term for one day shorter than the lease.[20]

Although a charge by way of legal mortgage gives the lender all the advantages of an actual mortgage term, it does not go further than that. It does not actually create a mortgage term, nor deem the lender to be subject to the liabilities of a tenant under such a lease.[21] It simply gives

[14] Section 85(1) Law of Property Act 1925 (freeholds); s.86(1) Law of Property Act 1925 (leaseholds).

[15] Section 85(2) Law of Property Act 1925 (freeholds); s.86(2) Law of Property Act 1925 (leaseholds).

[16] An attempt to create a mortgage term automatically creates a legal charge: ss.23 and 51 Land Registration Act 2002.

[17] In the case of unregistered land, it must be 'expressed' to be by way of legal mortgage. It has already been noted that, in the case of registered land, a profit à prendre in gross which has been registered in its own right may be charged in this way too (s.51 Land Registration Act 2002).

[18] Section 95(4) Law of Property Act 1925.

[19] Section 87(1)(a) Law of Property Act 1925.

[20] Section 87(1) Law of Property Act 1925.

[21] See below.

the lender the same 'protection, powers and remedies' as if he or she were such a tenant.[22]

Since, when the debtor grants a first charge by way of legal mortgage, the debtor retains a legal estate in the property, there is nothing to stop the debtor creating second or subsequent securities as legal charges too. The lender secured by a second or subsequent legal charge has the same rights and powers as the holder of a concurrent mortgage term, that is, a mortgage term granted by the debtor subject to, and in reversion upon, the rights of prior chargees.

A legal mortgagee's right to possession

At common law, it is often said, a legal mortgagee is entitled to possession 'before the ink is dry on the mortgage.'[23] Formerly, as we have seen, legal mortgages were often created by way of outright conveyance or assignment, and where the mortgage was created in this way, the lender was, in truth, entitled to take possession whilst the ink was still wet; for, by delivering the deed the debtor transferred the land to the lender absolutely, until such time as the debt was repaid. The lender was entitled to take possession of the whole of the debtor's estate, because, by executing the mortgage deed, the debtor had transferred that estate to the lender.

Nowadays, when legal mortgages are almost invariably created as charges by way of legal mortgage, the lender does not acquire title to the whole of the debtor's estate. So, to say simply that the lender has an immediate right to possession, whilst true, conceals an important point. The lender does not take or recover possession of the whole mortgaged estate as would have been the case under a conventional mortgage granted before 1926. When a lender 'takes' or 'goes into' possession of the security, what the lender does is exercise those rights which the lender would have had, if the debtor had actually granted the lender a long lease (or sub-lease) by way of mortgage term. But the basic point is the same. If an actual lease (or sub-lease) had been granted to the lender, then the lender would have been entitled to take possession of it immediately, and to confine the debtor to the use and enjoyment of the reversion upon that

22 *Weg Motors* v. *Hales* [1962] Ch 49, 73, 74, 77. There being no actual mortgage term, it follows that it is not a breach of a covenant against underletting to charge a lease by way of legal mortgage.

23 Per Harman J in *Fourmaids Ltd* v. *Dudley Marshall (Properties) Ltd* [1957] Ch 317, 320; [1957] 2 All ER 35, 36.

lease; and a legal charge grants the lender the right to do exactly the same thing, even though it does not create an actual lease.

The rule was perhaps best summarised by Nourse LJ in *National Westminster Bank plc* v. *Skelton*:[24]

> The general rule established by long-standing authority is that, except in so far as his rights are limited by contract or statute, a mortgagee by way of legal charge is entitled to seek possession of the mortgaged property at any time after the mortgage is executed: see e.g. *Mobil Oil Co. Ltd* v. *Rawlinson* (1981) 43 P & CR 221, *Barclays Bank plc* v. *Tennet* [1984] CA Transcript 242 and *Citibank Trust Ltd* v. *Ayivor* [1987] 3 All ER 241, [1987] 1 WLR 1157. In *Birmingham Citizens Permanent Building Society* v. *Caunt* [1962] 1 All ER 163 at 168, [1962] Ch 883 at 890 Russell J cited with approval a passage from the judgment of Harman J in *Fourmaids Ltd* v. *Dudley Marshall (Properties) Ltd* [1957] Ch 317 at 320 in which he put the matter thus:
>
> 'I said [in an earlier case] and I repeat, that the right of the mortgagee to possession in the absence of some specific contract has nothing to do with default on the part of the debtor. The mortgagee may go into possession before the ink is dry on the mortgage unless by a term expressed or necessarily implied in the contract he has contracted himself out of that right. He has the right because he has a legal term of years in the property. If there is an attornment clause, he must give notice. If there is a provision express or to be implied that, so long as certain payments are made he will not go into possession, then he has contracted himself out of his rights. Apart from that, possession is a matter of course.'

That said, although a lender with a legal security is entitled to take possession at any time, any institutional lender which did so as a matter of course would not be in the mortgage lending business for very long. The whole point of the immediate right to take possession is that it is a threat, held *in terrorem* over the head of the debtor, to encourage punctual repayment of the mortgage debt and interest. In the meantime, the debtor is not strictly a tenant at will of the lender, for the debtor is not a 'tenant' at all, but for all practical purposes the debtor's rights (or lack of them) and obligations are the same as if he or she were.[25] The debtor has no additional estate in the property by reason of his being left in possession, and so a contract to

[24] [1993] 1 All ER 242, 248. See also *Marquis of Cholmondeley* v. *Clonton* (1817) 2 Mer 171; *Hughes* v. *Waite* [1957] 1 WLR 713, 715; *Midland Bank* v. *McGrath* [1996] EGCS 61.

[25] *Ex parte Calwell* (1828) 1 Mod 259; *Patterson* v. *Reilly* (1882) 10 LR Ir 304; *Campion* v. *Palmer* [1896] 2 IR 445.

allow the debtor to remain in possession does not need to comply with any formalities.[26]

There are, nonetheless, six circumstances where even a debtor whose estate is subject to a legal security will be able to keep the lender out of possession of it.

The first is where every penny of the secured debt has been repaid. If the whole secured debt has been repaid, so that the debtor has an immediate right to redeem the security, then, notwithstanding that redemption does not actually take place until delivery up of the mortgage deed or delivery of the notification of redemption to the Land Registry, in equity the security is treated as having been redeemed already, and the debtor will be entitled to an injunction to keep the lender out of possession.

This principle is, however, a very narrow one.[27] The courts have frequently stressed that a debtor is not entitled unilaterally to appropriate or to set off the value of a cross-claim against the secured debt. Even a cross-claim that, in any other action, could be pleaded as an equitable set-off is not sufficient.[28] If the cross-claim does not impugn the validity of the original grant of the security, then the debtor must allow the lender to take possession first, and litigate out the cross-claim later.

The second is where the debtor has attorned to the lender otherwise than as tenant at will,[29] and the lender has not given the requisite notice. This, however, was never more than a formality, and modern securities do not contain attornment clauses.[30]

The third is where the lender has expressly or impliedly agreed not to take possession. But securities which expressly limit the lender's right to take possession are extremely rare, and the courts are reluctant to say that any like term can arise by implication. As Buckley LJ said in *Western Bank Ltd* v. *Schindler*:[31]

> A legal mortgagee's right to possession is a common law right which is an incident of his estate in the land. It should not, in my opinion, be lightly treated as abrogated or restricted.

[26] *Kumah* v. *Osbornes (a firm)* [1997] 1 EGCS 1.

[27] For a historical explanation, see F. Maitland, *Equity* (Cambridge, Cambridge University Press, 1909), p. 273.

[28] *Samuel Keller* [1971] 1 WLR 43; [1970] 3 All ER 950; *Mobil Oil* v. *Rawlinson* (1981) 43 P & CR 221; *National Westminster Bank plc* v. *Skelton* [1993] 1 All ER 242.

[29] *Woolwich Equitable BS* v. *Preston* [1938] Ch 129.

[30] Formerly, an attornment clause was included because it made it easier for the mortgagee to recover possession by bringing summary possession proceedings in the Queen's Bench Division. That advantage has long since gone.

[31] [1977] Ch 1, 9; [1976] 2 All ER 393, 396.

The fourth is where the loan falls within the terms of the Consumer Credit Act 1974. Then the lender is not entitled to take possession before obtaining an order of the court, and the court has a wide discretion to make a 'time order' allowing the debtor to reschedule repayment of the debt according to means, without having to allow the lender to take possession of its security in the meantime. Most securities, however, fall outside the provisions of the Act, either because of the status of the lender or because the debt exceeds its relatively modest financial limits.[32]

The fifth, and by far the most common, circumstance is where the property is residential. In those circumstances, the court has power[33] to reschedule any arrears due under an instalment mortgage or charge[34] over the whole of the remaining term of the loan,[35] disregarding any provision in the mortgage requiring earlier repayment[36] and to stay or suspend any possession order, for so long as the arrears are paid on those terms.

Finally, even where the security is repayable on demand, and not in instalments, or the property is non-residential, the court has a residual discretion to postpone the date for giving up possession for a short time, to enable the debtor to attempt to repay the whole debt.[37]

The legal mortgagee in possession

It is important to know if and precisely when a lender has taken possession of the security against the debtor, because it matters in terms of both the lender's rights against third parties[38] and the lender's obligations to the debtor. As soon as the lender takes possession of the security, the lender becomes strictly liable to account to the debtor, not only for every benefit thereafter received from the estate, but also for every benefit that might, with reasonable diligence, have been obtained from it. For this reason, as Maitland said: 'On the whole it is not a pleasant thing to be a mortgagee in possession. In general a mortgagee is very loath to take possession, and only does so when he is forced into doing it.'[39]

32 Currently £25,000, but this will go, except for business loans, when the Consumer Credit Act 2006 is brought into force.

33 Section 36 Adminstration of Justice Act 1970. 34 Section 39(1).

35 *Cheltenham & Gloucester BS* v. *Norgan* [1996] 1 WLR 343; [1996] 1 All ER 449.

36 Section 8 Administration of Justice Act 1973.

37 *Royal Trust Co. of Canada* v. *Markham* [1975] 1 WLR 1416; *Birmingham Citizens Permanent Building Society* v. *Caunt* [1962] Ch 883, 912; [1962] 1 All ER 163, 182.

38 See below.

39 F. Maitland, *Equity* (Cambridge, Cambridge University Press, 1909), p. 274.

So what is the test of whether the lender has, or has not, gone into or taken possession of the security?

If the security consists of an actual mortgage term, then the lender is 'in' possession of the security if, as a matter of observable fact, the lender is using or enjoying the property as a tenant might be expected to, and the debtor has been excluded from dominion and control of it, so that all the debtor is enjoying now is the reversion upon that lease. So, if the debtor has been left in occupation of the property, then the lender takes possession by evicting the debtor, and either letting the property to an occupational tenant, or leaving it empty, or going into occupation itself. 'But in a case where an estate is let to tenants, of course the mortgagee [taking possession] does not enter upon actual occupation of the demised premises. He may fall under the principle as a person who enters and takes possession of the rent and profits; but only . . . if he does something which goes beyond the mere receipt of sums of money to which the rents and profits may amount, and reaches a point at which he displaces, for the purpose of realising the security, the debtor from control and dominion of the reversion of the estate which is demised.'[40]

Although it creates no actual mortgage term, the same principles apply to a charge by way of legal mortgage. The lender under such a security has the same rights and powers as if the security had created a mortgage term, and so the principles for determining whether such a lender has taken possession of the security are the same. Essentially, the question is: 'Is the lender using and enjoying the property in the same way as might be expected of a tenant under a long lease (or sub-lease) granted by the debtor?'

Having taken possession of the security, the lender may, however, go out of possession again by ceasing to use and enjoy it in that way and by giving dominion and control back to the debtor. This requires a positive act, but it can usually be achieved relatively simply by appointing a receiver. A receiver is deemed to be the agent of a solvent debtor,[41] and so the appointment of a receiver restores possession to that debtor.[42]

[40] Per Bowen LJ in *Noyes* v. *Pollock* (1886) 32 ChD 53, 64. By 'the reversion of the estate which is demised' Bowen LJ was, of course, referring to the reversion upon the occupational lease, and not the reversion upon the mortgage term.

[41] See ch. 7.

[42] By s.67 Landlord and Tenant Act 1954, a mortgagee is deemed to be the competent landlord for the purpose of that Act if the mortgagee is in possession or has appointed a receiver.

Equitable securities

An equitable mortgage or charge, as the name suggests, is a security that takes effect only in equity, and so is not recognised at common law. It is one that, prior to the Judicature Acts, could have been enforced only in a court of equity.

In practice, there are three reasons why a security might take effect only in equity.

The first is that it might be the unintended consequence of the failure of a legal security. Equity saves failed legal securities in a wide variety of circumstances. A legal security, for instance, might fail because the parties have not executed it as a deed. Equity will enforce it as a contract to grant a legal security, if they have executed it under hand.[43] Or it might fail as a legal security because the debtor has a right to avoid it for undue influence or misrepresentation or some other wrong. It might even be a forgery. But equity can again rescue the lender, for, if the mortgage advance was used to redeem a previous valid legal security, equity will subrogate the lender to the previous security, which is treated as having been assigned to the lender instead of discharged.[44] Or, if the security was a purchase monies mortgage, equity will subrogate the lender to the equitable lien which the vendor would have retained, if the purchase had been completed but the vendor had not been paid the balance of the purchase price out of the mortgage advance.[45] Similarly, where one of two co-owners has a right to avoid a mortgage granted by both of them, but the other does not, then notwithstanding that the mortgage will fail as a mortgage of the legal estate, it will nonetheless take effect as an equitable charge over the second owner's beneficial share, severing any beneficial joint tenancy for that purpose.[46]

Secondly, the nature of the property might be such that it would be impossible to create a legal security over it. The property itself might be property that only exists in equity. It might for instance consist of a

[43] *Matadeen* v. *Caribean Insurance Co Ltd* [2002] UKPC 69.

[44] *Ghana Commercial Bank* v. *Chandiram* [1960] AC 745; *Castle Phillips Finance* v. *Piddington* [1995] 1 FLR 783. See generally M. Dixon, 'Consenting away Proprietary Rights: Mortgagees and Co-owners: Subordination or Subrogation', in *Modern Studies in Property Law* (ed. E. Cooke, Oxford, Hart, 2001), vol. 1, pp. 181–200.

[45] *UCB* v. *Hedworth (No. 2)* [2003] EWCA Civ 1717.

[46] *Williams & Glyn's Bank* v. *Boland* [1981] AC 487, 507; *Bowers* v. *Bowers* (Hoffmann J, Chancery Division, 3 February 1987, unreported); *Ahmed* v. *Kendrick* (1987) 56 P & CR 120: *Penn* v. *Bristol & West Building Society* [1995] 2 FLR 938 (appealed on other grounds at [1997] 3 All ER 470), so far as it holds to the contrary, is *per incuriam.*

beneficial interest under a trust. That cannot be mortgaged by way of legal mortgage, because the common law is blind to all equitable rights. The common law cannot even enforce the trust in favour of the beneficiary; far less can it recognise the transfer of the beneficiary's rights to the lender. So, if the property only exists in equity, it can only be mortgaged or charged in equity too.

The third is that, even if the property secured consists of a legal estate, the parties or parliament[47] might have intended to create an equitable security, because equity allows the creation of more flexible securities by way of charge than the common law. The only charge that takes effect at law is a charge by way of legal mortgage. All other charges,[48] including that most flexible of all securities, the floating charge, are recognised only in equity.[49] Or the parties might have intended to create an equitable security in order to avoid the inconvenience and transaction costs involved in creating a formal legal mortgage. Until recently, for instance, it was standard practice for banks to secure short-term borrowings informally by requiring the debtor to hand over the title deeds or the land certificate, which was sufficient to create an equitable mortgage, and which gave the lender the practical security of knowing that, without the deeds or the certificate, the debtor would find it difficult to dispose of the land to anyone else.[50]

In exceptional cases, the lender under an equitable security will have an immediate right, in equity, to possess the debtor's legal estate, or at least to be put in the same position as if the security had been created as a charge by way of legal mortgage. This right might be granted expressly

[47] The Charging Orders Act 1979 makes it possible for a judgment creditor to obtain an equitable charge over the debtor's land: s.3(4).

[48] The conceptual difference between a mortgage and a charge is that a mortgage is a contractual, proprietary estate in land, defeasible on repayment of the secured debt, whereas a charge is an appropriation of property towards a debt, without giving the creditor either a general or special property in the security (W. Fisher and J. Lightwood, *Law of Mortgages* (11th edn, London, Butterworths, 2002), p. 5). The practical differences are much less significant than formerly, not least because a legal chargee has all the rights and remedies of the tenant of a legal mortgage term.

[49] An individual cannot charge assets by way of floating charge, for this is prohibited by the Bills of Sale Acts 1878 and 1882.

[50] This was stopped by the the decision in *United Bank of Kuwait* v. *Sahib* [1997] Ch 107, in which the Court of Appeal held that s.2 Law of Property (Miscellaneous Provisions) Act 1989 prevented the creation of equitable securities in this way; a wholly unforeseen and unintended consequence of a well-meant but botched reform by the Law Commission ('Formalities for Contracts for Sale of Land' (Law Com No. 164, 1987)).

as a term of the equitable charge.[51] Or it might be inherent in the nature of the security, as when the security is a specifically enforceable contract to create a legal charge,[52] or an equitable right to be subrogated to a legal security.[53] In each of these cases, the holder of an equitable security will have an equitable interest in possession in a legal estate (a legal mortgage term), or the same rights in equity as if he or she had such an interest in possession in such a legal estate. So the lender has an immediate right in equity against the debtor to take possession of the security, and may also bring any of the possessory actions against third parties, by joining the debtor as defendant if the debtor will not or cannot be joined as co-claimant.[54]

These, however, are relatively rare cases. Most equitable securities do not carry with them any immediate right to possess an actual mortgage term, nor to be put into the same position as if the equitable security had taken the form of a charge by way of legal mortgage. So, in order to enforce the security, an equitable chargee or mortgagee must normally apply to the court for a declaration of charge,[55] and ask the court in its discretion to order a sale of the property to realise the security, and to make an order for possession in aid of that order for sale. In practice, the court usually directs that the security shall take effect as if a charge by way of legal mortgage had been created, and rolls that up in the same order. The order for sale, and the order for possession in aid of that order, in these cases are, however, ultimately a matter of discretion. Unless and until the court makes an order, the lender is not entitled to enter into possession of the security as against the debtor. Consequently, until the order is made, the lender does not have the necessary status to bring any of the possessory actions against third parties. If the lender holds a

51 *Ocean Accident and Guarantee* v. *Ilford Gas Co.* [1905] 2 KB 493.

52 *Re Gordon* (1889) 61 LT 299. See, generally, H. Wade, 'An Equitable Mortgagee's Right to Possession' (1955) 71 LQR 204.

53 *UCB* v. *Hedworth (No. 2)* [2003] EWCA Civ 1717.

54 See ch. 6. Generally, a person cannot be joined as co-claimant to an action without written consent (CPR Part 19A PD 2.1). But securities often contain an irrevocable security power of attorney, authorising the lender, or any receiver appointed by the lender, to bring proceedings in the name of the debtor.

55 *Barclays Bank* v. *Bird* [1954] 1 All ER 449, 452 per Harman J: 'The only limitation on an equitable mortgagee in that respect is that he has no right to possession until the court gives it to him, and the equitable mortgagee could always apply to the court to foreclose and have a receiver appointed to receive the rents and profits. Indeed, the practice of the Court of Chancery, back to the time of Lord Eldon at least, was to allow the equitable mortgagee to have the rents and profits from the date of the petition and not merely from the date of the decree of foreclosure.' See also *Fink* v. *Tranter* [1905] 1 KB 427.

security power of attorney, then it can make the claim in the debtor's name. Otherwise, unless the debtor is willing to be joined as co-claimant, the lender must wait until a possession order is made.

A mortgaged lease: covenants

Until 1926, as we have already seen, if a tenant wanted to create a legal mortgage of the lease (or, more accurately, if the lender would not lend the money otherwise) the tenant would usually do so by assigning the lease to the lender until the debt was repaid.

When a tenant assigns a lease, the assignee normally steps into the shoes of the former tenant immediately.[56] For so long as the lease remains vested in the assignee thereafter, that assignee can enforce the covenants given by the landlord, and the landlord can enforce the tenant's covenants against that assignee, for there is privity of estate between them.[57] If the lease which has been assigned is, itself, the immediate reversion upon a sub-lease, the assignee normally similarly becomes the landlord of the sub-lease at the same moment, with the result that the covenants in the sub-lease become enforceable by and against him or her as landlord of the sub-lease from that moment too.

But a mortgage is a more subtle entity than a pure assignment, and even when it was possible to mortgage a lease by assignment, there was always a special rule. If the mortgage lender left the debtor-tenant in possession of the mortgaged lease, then the debtor was treated as still being the tenant of it, notwithstanding that the mortgage took effect by assignment. The lender only became the tenant of the mortgaged lease once the lender took possession of it as against the debtor.[58]

Of course, as we have already noted several times, legal mortgages have not been created in this way since 1926. If the lease is mortgaged in the now conventional way (a charge by way of legal mortgage), then the lender has the same rights and remedies as if the tenant had granted the lender a sub-lease.[59] As such, the lender is not an assignee of the term, with the consequence that there is neither privity of contract nor privity of estate between the mortgage lender and the landlord of the lease, even when the lender is in possession as against the debtor.[60]

[56] If the lease is a registered lease, then the assignment is not completed until a subsequently successful application to register the transfer has been lodged.

[57] See ch. 4. [58] *Eaton* v. *Jaques* (1780) 2 Doug 456.

[59] Section 87(1)(b) Law of Property Act 1925.

[60] *Smith* v. *Spaul* [2003] QB 983; [2003] 2 WLR 495.

Consequently, apart from statute, a mortgage lender relying on the security of a lease cannot directly enforce the covenants contained in it against the landlord.[61] Nor can the landlord directly[62] enforce the tenant's covenants against the lender. The only exception is a covenant restrictive of user, which may be enforced directly even against a stranger with notice of the covenant.[63]

Since an equitable security over a lease cannot be created by outright assignment either, the same principles apply where the security is purely equitable.[64]

By statute, however, where the lease is a 'new' lease – generally meaning one made on or after 1 January 1996 – a mortgagee or chargee[65] in possession of the security[66] may enforce the landlord's covenants directly against the landlord.[67] Likewise, the landlord may enforce the tenant's covenants in a 'new' lease against a mortgagee or chargee in possession.[68]

For new leases, the law has accordingly turned full circle. The position is restored to that which it would have been before 1926, had the lease been mortgaged by outright assignment in the traditional way.

A mortgaged reversion: covenants

The relationship between a tenant and the landlord's mortgage lender is very different from the relationship between a landlord and the tenant's mortgage lender.

[61] A well-drawn mortgage will contain a security power of attorney, enabling the mortgagee to bring proceedings in the name of the mortgagor.

[62] The covenants can be enforced indirectly, by forfeiture or distraint.

[63] *Mander* v. *Falke* [1891] 2 Ch 554.

[64] Even an oral lease may only be assigned by deed: *Crago* v. *Julien* [1992] 1 EGLR 84. A mortgage of an unregistered lease, created by deed of assignment takes effect as a mortgage term: ss.85(2) and 86(2) Law of Property Act 1925. Likewise, for a registered lease, if the deed of assignment was delivered before 13 October 2003. Afterwards, it could only take effect as a legal charge.

[65] Section 15(6) Landlord and Tenant (Covenants) Act 1995.

[66] It is at least arguable that this includes an equitable mortgagee or chargee. The words 'those premises' in s.15(3)–(4) cannot refer to the tenant's legal estate in the tenancy, because it is impossible now to create a mortgage by way of assignment. Even a legal mortgagee or chargee cannot take possession of the tenant's legal estate in the tenancy. So those words must be referring, instead, to the corporeal land held under the tenancy; and, if that is what they mean, then those holding equitable securities might be included too.

[67] Section 15(3) Landlord and Tenant (Covenants) Act 1995.

[68] Section 15(4).

In order to explain the difference, it is best first to focus on the paradigm of a reversion mortgaged by way of actual mortgage term,[69] and then go on to consider the much more usual ways in which securities are now created.

Lease then mortgage term

If the reversion upon an existing lease is mortgaged by creating a mortgage term, the mortgage term will take effect as a concurrent lease. So, if the tenant of the existing lease wants to surrender, the surrender must be to the mortgagee, as the person in whom the immediate reversion is vested as concurrent tenant, rather than to the debtor.[70] Similarly, at least at common law,[71] only the mortgagee could forfeit the existing lease, for, as a concurrent tenant, the mortgagee was the immediate reversioner upon the term.[72]

But the rule is different so far as enforcement of the covenants is concerned. The concurrent term is treated as suspended for this purpose until the lender takes possession of it. In the meantime, the debtor is treated as still being the immediate reversioner upon the existing lease, and covenants in the lease are not enforceable between the debtor and the mortgagee. As soon as the mortgagee enters into possession of the security the lender becomes an actual concurrent tenant of the property for all purposes. The result is that taking possession of the mortgage creates a full relationship of privity of estate between the lender and the tenant of the pre-existing lease, so that the covenants in that lease may be enforced by and against the lender from that point onwards.

If, however, the lender subsequently goes out of possession, the relationship ends, for going out of possession has the same effect on the relationship, so far as the covenants are concerned, but not otherwise, as

[69] This is only possible now for unregistered land, and, in practice, it is never done.

[70] A mortgagor has a limited statutory power to accept surrenders (s.100 Law of Property Act 1925) but that right is usually excluded by the mortgage deed. If the tenant purports to surrender to the mortgagor, when there is no power to do so, that actually takes effect as an assignment of the term to the mortgagor; s.63 Law of Property Act 1925; *Thellusson* v. *Liddard* [1902] 2 Ch 635.

[71] The inconvenience of this rule was such that, in equity, the defendant could sometimes be enjoined from taking the point: *Scott* v. *Scott* (1854) 4 HLC 1065; 10 ER 779.

[72] A mortgagor in possession now has a statutory right to forfeit: s.141(2) Law of Property Act 1925; *Turner* v. *Walsh* [1909] 2 KB 484 ('old' tenancies); s.15 Landlord and Tenant (Covenants) Act 1995 ('new' tenancies).

if the lender had transferred the reversion upon the existing lease back to the debtor.

Mortgage term then lease

Of course, the order of events may be different. The debtor might first mortgage the estate by way of a mortgage term, and then grant someone else an occupational lease (or sub-lease) of it. The position then depends upon whether the debtor has been given authority to make subsequent leases binding on the lender, either under the terms of the security or by statute.[73]

If the debtor had that authority, and the lender afterwards takes possession of the mortgage term, then the mortgage will take effect from that moment as a headlease, and not a concurrent lease; for the mortgage was granted first, and the lease therefore takes effect as if granted out of the mortgage term. Practically, however, this makes little difference, for the rights and liabilities of the lender, who enters into possession of the security and who is bound by a lease created afterwards, are the same, irrespective of whether the reason is internal or external to the security. For so long as the lender remains in possession of the security, there is a full relationship of privity of estate between the lender and the tenant, which means that the covenants in the occupational lease can be enforced by and against them both.

The debtor could, by this means, create 'poison pill' occupational leases in order to discourage the lender from taking possession. So standard mortgage conditions always attempt[74] to exclude the debtor's leasing powers. Where those powers have been effectively excluded, the mortgage term takes priority to any lease created afterwards,[75] and the lender is entitled to take possession of the security free of that lease. Consequently, as soon as the lender takes possession of the security, the lender may evict the tenant. The lender has a right to enjoy the mortgage term free of the tenancy by title paramount.

73 Section 99 Law of Property Act 1925.

74 The attempt was not always successful; see eg. Sch.14 Agricultural Holdings Act 1986.

75 This assumes that the mortgage has been properly protected, as against the subsequent lease, by registration. If the lease takes priority to the mortgage because the mortgage has not been protected, then the mortgage term will take effect as a concurrent term upon the reversion of the lease: *Barclays Bank* v. *Zaroovabili* [1997] Ch 321; [1997] 2 All ER 19.

Other securities

So much for the paradigm. The rules are essentially the same where the security does not take the form of an actual mortgage term but is instead a charge by way of legal mortgage. There is, however, one difference. Because the charge grants the lender the same powers, rights and remedies as if a mortgage term had been created, but without creating an actual term, the tenant of a lease granted by the debtor cannot enforce any of the covenants in the lease against the lender, even where the lender is bound by the lease and has taken possession. A chargee by way of legal mortgage gets all the benefits of a mortgage term, without any of the burdens.

If, however, the actual lease is a 'new' lease for the purpose of the Landlord and Tenant (Covenants) Act 1995, then, by statute, the position is restored to what it would have been had the charge been created by way of actual mortgage term. If the lender is bound by the lease, and so is not entitled to evict the tenant by title paramount, then both the tenant and the lender may enforce the covenants contained in that new lease against each other for the period during which the lender is in possession.[76]

If the landlord's security is equitable instead of legal, then, until the lender takes possession of the security, the lender has no rights against or liabilities to third parties, and the lender normally cannot take possession until the court makes an order. Even if the lender does so, that does not bring about a relationship of privity of contract or estate with the debtor's tenant, for a lender in possession of an equitable security cannot be the legal reversioner upon the lease created by the debtor. When the court makes an order granting the lender possession, the lender's rights against third parties thereafter will depend upon the terms of the order. If the court makes the usual order that the security shall take effect as if a charge by way of legal mortgage had been created, then the lender, from that moment onwards, has all the rights and liabilities of such a chargee.

But there is, of course, a greater risk with equitable securities that a subsequently created legal lease will take priority to the security, either because the security does not expressly exclude the debtor's statutory power of leasing, or because the security has not been protected by registration, with the result that the lender will not then be able to evict the tenant under a subsequent lease by title paramount.[77]

[76] Section 15 Landlord and Tenant (Covenants) Act 1995.

[77] *Barclays Bank* v. *Zaroovabili* [1997] Ch 321; [1997] 2 All ER 19.

6

Equity and trusts

Introduction

This chapter is about the impact and effect of equitable rights on the common law of possession: the ways in which equity alters and restricts the common law, in favour of some, but not others.

It might seem old-fashioned to deal with this subject separately. But, where land is concerned, the difference between a legal right and an equitable right is still of critical importance.[1]

Equitable rights in land can be divided into three types. The first is a right, recognised in equity, to possess the whole of a common law estate. The second is a right to some lesser equitable interest in a common law estate. The third is an equitable right to do something, in relation to land, that has no counterpart at common law at all.

This chapter explains why those distinctions are still important, and the remedies available to vindicate each type of equitable right.

The relationship between common law and equity

No one sitting down with a blank piece of paper, attempting to produce a rational and coherent property-law code, would produce that which the forces of history and the ingenuity of conveyancers have produced in England and Wales. It is possible that someone might decide that there should be a partial statutory code, and that judges should otherwise be permitted to develop the principles. But what no one could imagine would be a partial statutory code, supplemented by two inconsistent and competing systems of judge-made law, one to qualify and contradict the other.

That, nonetheless, is what we have.

[1] 'An equitable right is not equivalent to a legal right. Between the contracting parties an agreement for a lease may be as good as a lease, just so between the contracting parties an agreement for the sale of land may serve as well as a completed sale and conveyance. But introduce a third party and then you will see the difference.' F. Maitland, *Equity* (Cambridge, Cambridge University Press, 1909), p. 161.

The common law is a system of rules which provide a limited number of rather crude remedies (generally payment of a sum of money or delivery up of a corporeal thing) to a narrow class of persons for a series of closely defined wrongs.

Equity is a separate system of principles providing different and more subtle remedies (e.g. injunctions, rectification, rescission) not only for wrongs recognised by the common law, but also for its own wrongs which have no counterpart at common law. But equity also has another aspect too, which is particularly important in the common law of possession. Sometimes it prevents people relying upon or enforcing their common law rights at all.[2]

On occasion, lawyers and judges express the view that none of this matters any more: that the effect of the Judicature Acts 1873 to 1875 has not so much been to fuse as to blend the common law and equity; that unified principles are somehow fermenting in the soup; and that we no longer need to worry about the individual ingredients.[3] The fiercest champion of this view in recent times was Lord Diplock, who in *United Scientific Holdings* v. *Burnley Borough Council*[4] said:

> Your Lordships have been referred to the vivid phrase traceable to the first edition of Ashburner's Principles of Equity where, in speaking in 1902 of the effect of the Judicature Act, he says 'the two streams of jurisdiction [i.e. law and equity], though they run in the same channel, run side by side and do not mingle their waters'. My Lords, by 1977 this metaphor has in my view become both mischievous and deceptive. The innate conservatism of English lawyers may have made them slow to recognise that by the Judicature Act 1873 the two systems of substantive and adjectival law formerly administered by courts of law and courts of chancery (as well as those administered by courts of admiralty, probate and matrimonial causes), were fused. As at the confluence of the Rhone and Soane, it may be possible for a short distance to discern the source from which each part of the combined stream came, but there comes a point at which this ceases to be possible. If Professor Ashburner's fluvial metaphor is to be retained at all, the waters of the confluent streams of law and equity have surely mingled now.

[2] Before the Judicature Acts, it did this by 'common injunction', that is, an injunction to prevent a litigant proceeding in, or enforcing the judgment of, a common law court.

[3] When it suited his purposes, Lord Denning was a strong proponent of this view: *Letang* v. *Cooper* [1965] 2 QB 232, 239. See also Nourse LJ in *Gafford* v. *Graham* [1998] EWCA Civ 666; cf. *Shaw* v. *Applegate* [1977] 1 WLR 970.

[4] [1978] AC 904, 924.

But that is simply not what the Judicature Acts did, and nor is it what they were intended to do.[5] For, as Lindley LJ explained in *Joseph* v. *Lyons*:[6]

> Reliance was placed upon the provisions of the Judicature Acts, and it was contended that the effect of them was to abolish the distinction between law and equity. Certainly, that is not the effect of these statutes, otherwise they would abolish the distinction between a trustee and a cestui que trust.

The Acts, it is true, did make some, very small, changes to the substantive law, but those changes were all made expressly.[7] Otherwise, the effect of the Acts was entirely procedural, as Brett LJ explained in *Britain* v. *Rossiter*:[8]

> I think that the true construction of the Judicature Acts is that they confer no new rights; they only confirm rights which previously were to be found existing in the Courts either of Law or of Equity; if they did more, they would alter the rights of parties, whereas in truth they only change the procedure. Before the passing of the Judicature Acts no one could be charged on this contract either at law or in equity; and if the plaintiff could now enforce this contract, it would be an alteration of the law.

Maitland elegantly illustrated the procedural effect of the Acts[9] by pointing out that before the Acts there was a visible, physical distinction between the common law and equity. You could have gone to Westminster Hall, and seen a common law court grant judgment in a common law action begun by writ. Then you could have gone to the Old Hall in Lincoln's Inn and seen the Vice–Chancellor grant a decree in an equity suit begun by bill. The bill might even have been for a 'common injunction' to prevent the successful litigant in the Westminster action enforcing the common law judgment. Afterwards, everything happened at one and the same time before the same judge in the same court, called 'the High Court

5 See A. Mason, 'The Place of Equity and Equitable Remedies in the Common Law World' (1994) 110 LQR 238, 240–2; R. Meagher, W. Gummow and J. Lehane, *Equity, Doctrines and Remedies* (4th edn, Sydney, Butterworths, 2002), pp. 45–83; *Lanecrest* v. *Asiwaju* [2005] EWCA Civ 117; [2005] 1 EGLR 40, 41.

6 (1884) 15 QBD 280, 287.

7 Section 25 Judicature Act 1873, s.10 Judicature Act 1875. One of those changes was to the rules about when time was to be treated as being of the essence of a contract (now s.41 Law of Property Act 1925) which was what was actually in issue in *United Scientific Holdings* v. *Burnley Borough Council* [1978] AC 904.

8 (1882) 11 QBD 123, 129. See also *British South Africa Company* v. *Companhia de Mocambique* [1893] AC 602.

9 F. Maitland, *Equity* (Cambridge, Cambridge University Press, 1909), p. 150.

of Justice';[10] and, although the court was divided into different divisions, it did not matter in which division a judge sat. The same judge was required to administer the whole of the common law and the whole of equity, just as it would have been administered by two separate judges in the two separate courts beforehand, so as to produce the same net result.[11]

The differences between the common law and equity do, therefore, still matter. They matter not simply because the principles are different, but also because the available remedies depend on the nature of the wrong, and, in particular, whether it is a wrong of a type that would have been recognised at common law, or in equity, or by both, before 1875.[12]

In short, it remains the law that common law remedies are not available at all for wrongs that are recognised only in equity; and equitable remedies are only available as additional remedies for a common law wrong (for instance, an injunction to prevent a continuing nuisance) or to vindicate a purely equitable right in accordance with equitable principles.

So, if a property right is recognised only in equity, then only equitable remedies are available to protect it; and, if the right exists at common law, equity may provide an additional remedy but only in accordance with equitable principles.

Personal and proprietary equitable rights

Some common law rights are plainly proprietary in character, meaning that they create rights in things, enforceable against third parties (rights 'in rem') whereas others are purely personal, creating only rights enforceable against a particular person (rights 'in personam'). So, for example, a right to possess a fee simple, or a legal lease, is a common law proprietary right,

[10] The county courts are a separate creature of statute. They were created by the County Courts Act 1846, as successors to the courts of requests, as a cheap alternative for low value claims. From their inception, they had a limited, but combined, common law and equity jurisdiction. Since 1990, the common law jurisdiction of the county courts has been unlimited, but the equity jurisdiction is generally still limited to claims involving property worth less than £30,000 (s.23 County Courts Act 1984).

[11] 'Every judge in whatever division he may be sitting is bound to apply every rule whether of common law or equity that is applicable to the case before him. He cannot stop short and say, that is a question of common law which I am incompetent to decide, or, that is merely an equitable right and I can take no notice of it.' F. Maitland, *Equity* (Cambridge, Cambridge University Press, 1909), p. 151. See also *The Nile Rhapsody* [1992] 2 Lloyds LR 399.

[12] See per Lord Greene MR in *Re Diplock: Diplock* v. *Wintle* [1948] Ch 465, 481–2.

whereas a right to recover an unsecured debt or a right to damages for breach of contract is a common law personal right.

But some rights which are personal at common law are made proprietary in equity. The burden of a restrictive covenant, for instance, is only enforceable against the original contracting party at common law. In equity, however, this is turned into a proprietary right, enforceable against anyone except a bona fide purchaser of a legal estate for value without notice of it.[13] Similarly, a purchaser under a contract to buy land has a personal right to require the vendor to perform the contract at common law, but a proprietary right in equity by virtue of the constructive trust which exists between contract and completion.[14]

It does not follow, however, from the fact that equity treats some rights which are personal at common law as proprietary, that all the rights recognised by equity are proprietary in character. The same dichotomy between proprietary and personal rights which exist at common law also exists in equity. Nor does it follow that all the rights which equity recognises have a personal counterpart at common law. There are personal and proprietary rights which exist in equity but have no counterpart at common law at all.

Some examples will help to make the distinctions clear. A life tenant under a voluntary trust has no right at all recognised by the common law. The common law simply cannot see the trust, because the trust obligations exist only in equity.[15] But, in equity, the life tenant has a proprietary right: he or she has an interest in the property itself, which is held under the trust, and which can be enforced directly against third parties. Make the life tenant a beneficiary of a discretionary trust instead, however, and that changes. There is still no right recognised by the common law, but now there is only a personal right in equity. The beneficiary can compel the trustee (the legal owner of the trust property) to perform the trust, but cannot point to any property and say: 'In equity, that is mine.' There is a personal right, in equity, to require the trustee to do something, but no

13 Of course, there are now rules about registration, and it is a rare case where the proprietary force of an equitable right depends upon the doctrine of notice in its pure form.

14 T. Williams, *Vendor and Purchaser* (4th edn, London, Sweet & Maxwell, 1936), p. 546. If the purchaser has paid a deposit, there will also be an equitable purchaser's lien (*ibid.*, p. 1006).

15 So, at common law, a trustee can recover possession against a beneficiary of the trust, even if the beneficiary is absolutely entitled to the trust property in equity: *Roe* v. *Read* (1799) 8 TR 118.

right to any particular property capable of being enforced directly against third parties before it had been done.

Similarly, a specific legatee is treated in equity as having a proprietary interest in the property of the legacy, even before the estate has been fully administered, subject only to the possibility of disfeasence to pay the deceased's debts; whereas a general or residuary legatee only has a personal right to require the estate to be duly administered.[16]

Equity and an action to recover land

An action to recover land is a common law action. In it, the claimant alleges that he or she is entitled to possess a legal estate. By this what is meant is that the claimant has a legal, fixed and vested right to enjoy the whole of a common law estate in the land (a fee simple, a lease or, notwithstanding that it is technically an interest rather than an estate, a profit à prendre). The complaint is that the defendant is wrongly keeping the claimant out of possession of it, and the claimant seeks, as a remedy, an order that he or she be put into possession of that legal estate, and compensation in money (mesne profits) for having been wrongly kept out of possession of it in the meantime. It follows that to succeed the claimant must show a better title to the legal estate claimed than the defendant, or, as the case may be, a better title than any one under whom the defendant holds.[17]

So a claimant who has an equitable interest in that estate, albeit a proprietary one, can never recover on the strength of that interest alone,[18] any more than someone with a purely equitable interest can recover mesne profits; that is, common law damages for wrongly having been kept out of possession of a legal estate. Even if the claimant is the absolute beneficial owner, with an immediate right to collapse the trust and call for a conveyance from the legal owner,[19] the claimant will not be able to show any legal title to the estate until the trustee has actually conveyed it.[20] The same applies if the claimant is the purchaser of that estate

[16] *Re Neeld, Carpenter* v. *Inigo-Jones* [1960] Ch 455. [17] See ch. 2.

[18] W. Holdsworth, *History of English Law* (2nd edn, London, Sweet & Maxwell, 1925), vol. VII, p. 19; *Doe* v. *Staple* (1788) 2 TR 684; *Butler* v. *Kensington* (1846) 8 QB 429.

[19] *Saunders* v. *Vautier* (1841) 4 Beav 115; 41 ER 482.

[20] *Chudleigh's Case* (1589–95) 1 Co Rep 114, 140. It is sometimes said that the Judicature Acts have changed this; that a person may recover possession on the strength of an equitable title alone. In 1955, H. Wade wrote: 'Would anyone today argue that an equitable tenant, i.e. a tenant entitled under an agreement for lease, is not entitled to possession because he has no legal estate? Or that a purchaser of an equity of redemption has no means for suing

under a specifically enforceable, but uncompleted, contract to purchase land.[21]

Nonetheless, a person who has an equitable interest in a common law estate, which the common law cannot see, but which is 'vested in possession'[22] in equity, is allowed to bring the action by joining the legal owner; if the legal owner will not agree to be joined as a co-claimant, he or she may be joined as a defendant,[23] but the legal owner must be joined.[24]

This is simply an application of a more general rule. Whenever a person has an equitable right immediately to possess the whole of a thing which exists at common law, that person is allowed to bring common law actions to protect that right, provided that the legal owner of the thing is joined

for possession of the land?' See H. Wade, 'An Equitable Mortgagee's Right to Possession' (1955) 71 LQR 204, 215. The answer to the first question is, no, if that person has already entered and paid rent, and thereby become a legal periodic tenant; otherwise, yes, for until the lease is completed, that person has no legal estate. The answer to the second question is, no, but only because the Judicature Acts expressly made a few, small, changes to the substantive law, and that was one of them. Before those Acts, the defendant could be enjoined from pleading 'temporary bars' to a legal estate, such as an unsatisfied mortgage term (*Scott* v. *Scott* (1854) 4 HLC 1065; 10 ER 779) Afterwards, by s.25(5) Judicature Act 1873 (now s.98 Law of Property Act 1925), an unsatisfied mortgage, where the mortgagee has not taken possession, is not to be a bar to 'recovery of possession or trespass or any other wrong relative thereto'.

21 It follows that during the registration gap – the period between completion of a registrable disposition and the lodging of the application to register it at the Land Registry – it is the transferor, and not the transferee, who has the right at common law to bring an action for recovery of the land, or for trespass or nuisance. This is subject to one exception. Where the registered estate is the reversion upon an 'old' lease for the purpose of the Landlord and Tenant (Covenants) Act 1995, then the transferee can bring a possession action against the tenant even before being registered: *Scribes West* v. *Relsa Anstalt (No. 3)* [2005] 1 EGLR 22.

22 For the meaning of 'vested in possession' see ch. 1.

23 '[N]o action for ejectment or, as it is now called, an action for recovery of land, can be defeated for want of the legal estate where the plaintiff has the title to possession': per Jessell MR in *General Finance* v. *Liberation Permanent BS* (1878) 10 Ch.D 15, 24.

24 *Allen* v. *Woods* (1893) 68 LT 143; *Matthews* v. *Usher* [1900] 2 QB 535. In *Dearman* v. *Simpletest* (CCRTF/99/0473/2), Henry LJ said this was 'good practice and guidance, rather than black letter law'. But that remark was made without reference to *Allen* v. *Woods* (1893) 68 LT 143 which was directly on point, and was based on a misunderstanding of a note which appeared in the 1999 Supreme Court Practice. The reference there ought to have been to s.169 Common Law Procedure Act 1852, which required the writ in ejectment to be brought in 'the names of all the persons in whom title is alleged to be', and to s.19 Common Law Procedure Act 1860, which required every action to be brought 'in the name of all persons in whom the legal right may be supposed to exist'. The solution to the problem would have been to join the legal owner to the appeal; see *Midtown* v. *City of London Real Pty Co.* [2005] 1 EGLR 65, 67.

as a party to the action. So an equitable assignee of a common law debt may sue in debt (a common law action) provided that the assignor, who is the legal owner of the debt, is joined.[25] The conceptual reason why this is possible is that the equitable owner could instead bring an action against the legal owner of the thing, requiring the owner to bring the action as trustee, and provided that an appropriate indemnity as to costs was given to the trustee, there could be no defence to that claim. So there is no hardship to the real defendant in allowing that to be rolled up in the same action, by joining the legal owner as a wholly nominal party. But the legal owner must be joined, partly as a formality, for the action is a common law action, but mostly to protect the real defendant from the risk of being sued twice.[26]

This right only applies where the claimant has a right to an equitable interest in possession in the property, or where the claimants, as a class, have that right. The same privilege is not afforded to a claimant who has an equitable, albeit proprietary, interest in the property which is less than that. This is fair and logical, for the action is an action in which the claimant asserts an immediate right to possess a legal estate; if a person with a common law interest less than that cannot bring the action, there is no reason why the action should be available to someone with a lesser interest in equity. So a person with a one-half beneficial share in a common law estate cannot bring an action to recover the estate by virtue of that entitlement alone, even by joining the trustee as a defendant. Of course, if the trustee consents to be joined as co-claimant, that solves the problem, because then the trustee can recover on the strength of the legal title. Indeed, in that circumstance, the owner of the beneficial half share does not need to be a party at all. Similarly, if the owner of the other half share is willing to be joined as a co-claimant, that solves the problem too, for then the claimants as a class will have an equitable interest in possession in the whole of the common law estate, and they can join the trustee as a defendant if he or she will not agree to be joined as claimant. But, if the owner of the other half share is not willing or able to be joined as

[25] *Weddell* v. *Pearce & Major* [1988] 1 Ch 26, 40.

[26] Per Viscount Cave LC in *Performing Right Society Ltd* v. *London Theatre of Varieties Ltd* [1924] AC 1, 14: 'In general, when a plaintiff has only an equitable right in the thing demanded, the person having the legal right to demand it must in due course be made a party to the action. If this were not so, a defendant after defeating the claim of an equitable claimant might have to resist like proceedings by the legal owner, or by persons claiming under him as assignees for value without notice of any prior equity, and proceedings might be indefinitely and oppressively multiplied.'

co-claimant, then the beneficiary cannot bring the action. The beneficiary's proper remedy is to bring an adminstration action against the trustee instead, enforcing the trust so as to require the trustee to bring the claim against the third party.[27]

There are, however, two exceptional cases where the owner of an equitable interest that is less than an interest in possession of a common law estate may bring an action for recovery of land without joining the legal owner.

First, a person who has an equitable interest in possession in an estate which is the legal reversion upon an 'old' lease[28] has a statutory right to bring a possession action against the tenant without joining the legal owner of the reversion.[29]

Secondly, it occasionally happens that a person who has an equitable interest was formerly, in fact, in possession of the legal estate too. The legal estate may be 'dry', meaning that the legal owner has allowed someone to take possession and act, in all respects, as if he or she were the legal owner. This sometimes occurs with unadministered estates. The legal owner dies, those entitled under the will or the intestacy rules take possession of the property as if it had been duly assented to them, but nobody ever bothers to take out a grant of probate.

Whatever the reason for it, a person who has, in fact, previously been in possession of the legal estate, does not need to prove the lawfulness of that possession as against a subsequent dispossessor, by relying on an equitable title, or, indeed, any title at all.[30] A person who has formerly been in possession of a legal estate is, as we have seen,[31] allowed to bring an action to recover it on the basis of prior possession alone. That person may plead the bare fact of his or her prior possession only, and will succeed

[27] *Sharp* v. *San Paulo Rly Co.* (1873) LR 8 Ch App 597, 609–10; *Wily* v. *Fuller* [2000] FCA 1512.

[28] Section 1 Landlord and Tenant (Covenants) Act 1995.

[29] Section 141(2) Law of Property Act 1925; *Scribes West* v. *Relsa Anstalt (No. 3)* [2005] 1 EGLR 22; cf. s.15(1) Landlord and Tenant (Covenants) Act 1995 for 'new' tenancies.

[30] In *Roe* v. *Read* (1799) 8 TR 118, 122-3, Lord Kenyon CJ said: '[W]here the beneficial occupation of an estate by the possessor has given reason to suppose that possibly there may have been conveyance of the legal estate to the person who is equitably entitled to it, a jury may be advised to presume a conveyance of the legal estate; but if it appears in a special verdict on a special case that the legal estate is outstanding in another person, the party not clothed with that legal estate cannot recover in a court of law; and in this respect I cannot distinguish between the case of ejectment brought by a trustee against his cestui que trust, and an ejectment brought by another person.'

[31] See ch. 2.

against a subsequent dispossessor, unless that person can show a better title or right to remain in possession.[32]

The same complications do not apply where a person with an equitable right is a defendant to an action to recover land. Even a person with no proprietary right in the land at all, such as a bare licensee, is entitled to defend an action for recovery of land on the basis that he or she has some lawful authority to keep the claimant out of possession of the estate claimed.[33] So it is irrelevant that the authority consists of an equitable proprietary right. The authority could just as well be an equitable personal right or even a bare permission given by the legal owner conferring no proprietary right at all.

Equity, trespass and nuisance

Subject to one important qualification, the same basic principles apply to the actions of trespass and nuisance. The actions are both common law actions, so someone with an equitable right cannot bring those actions unless the legal owner is willing to be joined as co-claimant, except where the equitable right is a beneficial interest in possession in the whole of the legal estate, in which event the actions can be brought by joining the legal owner as an additional defendant; and, if either of those claims is brought against a person claiming an equitable right, that person may rely on the equitable right as the basis of the defence, in the same way as an equitable right may be relied upon as a defence to a claim for recovery of land.

The important qualification is as follows. In an action for recovery of land, the owner of an equitable right can never assert that he or she is, in fact, already in possession of the relevant legal estate. The whole point of the action is to recover possession of that estate. If the claimant were

[32] The rule was explained as follows by Lord Brandon in *Leigh and Sillivan* v. *Aliakmon Shipping* [1986] 1 AC 785, 812: 'There may be cases where a person who is the equitable owner of certain goods has also a possessory title to them. In such a case he is entitled, by virtue of his possessory title rather than his equitable ownership, to sue in tort for negligence anyone whose want of care has caused loss of or damage to the goods without joining the legal owner as a party to the action: see, for instance, *Healey* v. *Healey* [1915] 1 KB 938. If, however, the person is the equitable owner of the goods and no more, then he must join the legal owner as a party to the action, either as co-plaintiff if he is willing or as co-defendant if he is not. This has always been the law in the field of equitable ownership of land and I see no reason why it should not also be so in the field of equitable ownership of goods.'

[33] See ch. 2.

already in possession, it would not be necessary to bring the action at all. There might be some cases where the claimant is able to assert that he or she was formerly in possession of the legal estate, and be able to bring the action in that way, but, as has been observed, those cases are relatively rare.

In the actions of trespass and nuisance, however, the claimant will often currently be 'in' possession of the relevant legal estate, and so will be able to bring those actions, even absent any title to the legal estate, and absent any right to possess it at all; for the bare fact of possession of a legal estate is sufficient to maintain the action against anyone except someone who has a better right to possess that estate than the claimant, or someone who claims through or under such a person.[34] That is why a pure squatter is entitled to bring those claims. Someone with an equitable right is in no worse position than a pure squatter. If he or she is in fact in possession of the legal estate, it is irrelevant to the action that someone else has a better right to it, unless that person is the defendant, or someone through whom the defendant claims.

Equity, trusts and injunctions

The owner of an equitable interest in possession in the whole of a common law estate is unusually privileged in having the power to bring an action for recovery of land. The owners of lesser equitable rights must, at best, persuade the probably reluctant legal owner to join with them in making the claim: a well-advised legal owner will insist on an indemnity for costs, as the price for consent, and may require it to be backed by security, or might refuse consent altogether, in which event they can only attempt to force the legal owner to make the claim by an administration action.

Sometimes the difficulty will be worse than that. It may be impossible for the owner of the equitable right to persuade or compel a legal owner of the right to bring a common law action, for not every equitable right has a legal owner.

This particular problem cannot arise where what is claimed is an equitable right to a share of a freehold estate, for that can only subsist behind a trust of the legal estate, and, where there is a trust, there must be a trustee or someone who can be appointed as trustee.[35]

[34] See ch. 3. See also *MCC Proceeds Inc.* v. *Lehman Bros International* [1998] 4 All ER 675.

[35] Section 44 Trustee Act 1925.

Nor does it tend to be a problem with equitable leases. An equitable tenant, who enters and pays rent, becomes a legal periodic tenant on the terms of the equitable lease, in so far as those terms are consistent with a periodic tenancy, whilst retaining any additional equitable rights. So the claimant can bring common law actions as a legal periodic tenant, without worrying about joining anyone else.[36]

But incorporeal hereditaments, such as easements and profits à prendre, are different. A right to an incorporeal hereditament can exist in equity only, without there being any equivalent legal right, and without anyone being under an obligation to create one. Even if the right is annexed to a legal estate, the owner of the legal estate cannot use common law remedies to protect the right. So, if, for example, a purely equitable easement is attached to a legal estate, the owner of that estate cannot sue in nuisance for interference with the easement; any more than that owner could recover common law damages for breach of a restrictive covenant against a successor in title to the original covenantor. In both cases, although the estate injured is a legal estate, the property right infringed is one that exists only in equity, and so only equitable remedies are available to protect it.

Yet the owner of a purely equitable proprietary interest of this character is not necessarily disadvantaged. The full panoply of equitable remedies, including injunctions, specific performance and the taking of accounts, are available, for a right that exists only in equity may be enforced in equity by the equitable owner without reference to anyone else.[37]

Of course, these remedies are available to owners of equitable proprietary interests in a common law estate too; the only difference is that they must join the legal owner of the right to the action, as a defendant if necessary, in order to obtain a final remedy.[38]

So, whilst someone who owns an equitable interest in a common law estate, which is less than an equitable interest in possession, needs the active assistance of the legal owner in order to protect it by one of the possessory actions; that person does not need any help from the legal owner in order to bring an equitable action to obtain an equitable remedy. All that needs to be done is to join the legal owner as a defendant.

Why then go to all the trouble of trying to persuade the legal owner to bring a common law possessory action at all? Why, indeed, do absolute

36 *Chan* v. *Cresdon Pty Ltd* [1989] HCA 63; (1989) 168 CLR 242.

37 *Earl of Leicester* v. *Wells-next-the-Sea UDC* [1973] Ch 110.

38 *Performing Rights Society* v. *London Theatre of Varieties* [1924] AC 1; s.25(8) Judicature Act 1873 (now s.49 Supreme Court Act 1981).

legal owners still bring common law claims, instead of simply claiming equitable remedies as beneficial owners of the estate? Essentially, there are three reasons for this.

First, all equitable rights, including the right to an injunction, are ultimately discretionary, and thus may be defeated on grounds which are, in practice if not in theory,[39] somewhat unpredictable, and which may have nothing to do with the conduct of the claimant. By contrast, the court cannot refuse to grant the relief sought in a common law action if the right is otherwise made out. At common law, if the right is made out, then the relief follows automatically.

Secondly, as Lord Nicholls observed in *Attorney-General* v. *Blake*,[40] it is generally accepted that Lord Cairns' Act[41] had two effects. It empowered 'the court of chancery, sitting in Lincoln's Inn, to award damages when declining to grant equitable relief rather than, as had been the practice since Lord Eldon's decision in *Todd* v. *Gee*,[42] sending suitors across London to the common law courts at Westminster Hall'. That aspect of the power, of course, became redundant on the creation of the High Court in 1875, after which there was only one court. Additionally, it changed the measure of damages recoverable when an injunction was refused, or granted only in part, as a matter of discretion, so as to enable the court to compensate for future losses; in effect, for the expropriation of the right.[43] But what it did not do was empower the court to grant damages for breach of an equitable right in a case where the court, as a matter of jurisdiction, could not have granted an injunction.[44] If, however, the legal owner is joined, then damages can be awarded at common law, even if there is no power to do so under Lord Cairns' Act.

Finally, injunctions are complicated and expensive to enforce. The usual method of enforcement is committal: in essence, the person who has breached the injunction is threatened with prison. A further hearing is required for this, the application must be served personally, and any formal

[39] *Shelfer* v. *City of London Electric Lighting* [1895] 1 Ch 287; *Cowper* v. *Laidler* [1903] 2 Ch 337; *Harrow LBC* v. *Donohue* [1995] 1 EGLR 257; *Bloor* v. *Calcott* [2001] EWHC Ch 467.

[40] [2001] 1 AC 268, 281; [2000] 3 WLR 625, 634.

[41] Section 2 Chancery Amendment Act 1858, now s.50 Supreme Court Act 1981.

[42] (1810) 10 Ves 273.

[43] *Leeds Industrial Co-op* v. *Slack* [1924] AC 851; *Amec* v. *Jury's Hotels* [2001] 1 EGLR 81; *Gafford* v. *Graham* [1998] EWCA Civ 666.

[44] T. Ingram and T. Wakefield, 'Equitable Damages under Lord Cairns' Act' [1981] Conv 286, J. Jolowicz, 'Damages in Equity – A Study of Lord Cairns' Act' [1975] CLJ 224; P. Petitt, 'Lord Cairns' Act in the County Court' [1977] CLJ 369. See also per Hoffmann LJ in *Sindall* v. *Cambridgeshire County Council* [1994] 1 WLR 1016, 1037.

defect is likely to be fatal to the application.[45] A judgment in one of the possessory actions is likely to be much easier to enforce,[46] and so it is usually a false economy to refrain from joining the legal owner at the outset.

Of course, if the equitable right is personal rather than proprietary, then there is no right which, as a matter of substantive law, may be enforced directly against third parties. The right, in so far as it may be enforced at all, may only be enforced indirectly, in an administration action against the legal owner, requiring the legal owner to bring proceedings against the third party.

Equity and leases to minors

A minor, being an individual under eighteen years of age, cannot hold a legal estate in land. A minor can neither have the right to possess, nor be 'in' possession of, a legal estate. If an attempt is made to convey a legal estate to a minor, the conveyance takes effect as if it were a declaration of trust by the conveying party in favour of the minor.[47] So the rights of the minor are necessarily equitable only, subsisting, as they do, behind a declaration of trust. As soon as the minor attains the age of eighteen years, he or she may call for a transfer of the legal estate, but in the meantime all he or she has is a beneficial interest subsisting behind a trust of land.

That is simple enough to apply where the legal estate is a freehold or a profit à prendre. Nor is there any difficulty when a lease is assigned to a minor. In each case, the transferor simply becomes an involuntary bare trustee of what he or she has purported to convey or assign, and otherwise retains no further interest in it.

The position is much more complicated where a lease is granted to a minor as original tenant, for a lease is already a dangerous combination of contract and estate, and adding a trust to the mix is bound to make things worse. Nor is this simply an academic problem. Local authorities and housing associations often grant short-term leases to vulnerable young people. When they do, how does the existence of the trust affect the relationship between the landlord and the tenant?

The existence of the trust has no impact on the tenant's contractual liability on the covenants. The usual rule applies. The covenants may be

[45] CCR Ord.29 r.1; CPR PD 29 para. 3.1. [46] See ch. 9.

[47] Para. 1(1) Sch. 1 Trusts of Land and Appointment of Trustees Act 1996.

enforced against the minor as a matter of contract in so far as they can be said to have been made as of necessity, but not otherwise.

But the trust does make a difference to those parts of the relationship which are governed by the law of property, such as the right to determine the tenancy.

This does not make any practical difference where the landlord has no power to determine the tenancy without the assistance of the court, and the court has a discretion whether to determine it or not, which is the case when the minor is, in equity, a secure tenant within the Housing Act 1985, or if the minor is an equitable assured tenant within the Housing Act 1988, and the landlord is seeking possession on one of the discretionary grounds provided for in those Acts.

It does make a difference, however, if the tenancy is a pure, common law, periodic tenancy, as is often the case where a local authority provides temporary accommodation for the vulnerable. The explanation for this is that a person cannot grant a legal lease to himself or herself alone, even if the lease is to be held in some other capacity.[48] So the 'land' held on the statutory trust for the minor cannot be the lease. The land must be the estate out of which the lease is to be granted. That land is held upon trust to grant the lease to the minor, and, whilst that trust is subsisting, the minor has a statutory right to occupy the land.[49]

That trust cannot be terminated by a common law notice to quit served by the trustee for three reasons.

First, the lease does not yet exist, so there is no lease which is capable of termination by notice to quit; there is merely an obligation under the law of trusts to create it. What is required is something to terminate the trust.

Secondly, if it did exist, the trustee could not, as a matter of mechanics, terminate it by notice to quit served on the minor, because the legal estate in the lease would not be vested in the minor, and a notice to quit must be served on the person in whom the legal estate is vested.[50]

Thirdly, as a matter of substance, it would be a breach of trust for the landlord to serve the notice to quit on himself or herself, for a trustee owes the beneficiary a duty to preserve the trust property, and not to deal with it so as to acquire it for his or her own benefit; this is the rule

[48] *Rye* v. *Rye* [1962] AC 496; [1962] 1 All ER 146.

[49] Section 12 Trusts of Land and Appointment of Trustees Act 1996.

[50] *Brown & Root* v. *Sun Alliance* [1996] Ch 51.

in *Keech* v. *Sandford*.[51] If a landlord wishes to do so, the landlord must obtain permission from the court. Otherwise, the landlord will simply hold the property upon a remedial constructive trust for the minor.

This third point applies with equal force to assured tenancies, where the landlord is relying on a mandatory ground for possession; for then it is the landlord who is making the decision to terminate the tenancy, rather than the court.

Consequently, in these cases, the landlord cannot exercise a right to terminate the tenancy, and then recover possession using the normal route. The landlord must, instead, apply to the court for an order under s.14 Trusts of Land and Appointment of Trustees Act 1996.

[51] (1726) Cas temp King 61.

7

Birth and death, dissolution and insolvency

Introduction

This chapter is about changes in status and involuntary dispositions. It is about the circumstances in which a person may acquire a right to possess an estate simply as a result of a change in that person's status, or the status of someone else; and the consequences for the person who is in fact in possession of the estate when that happens.

Birth

An individual does not have any legal personality unless and until he or she is born alive. All of the rights which might be acquired and enforced subsequently are necessarily contingent on being born alive, and no one can be sure that will happen before the event.

So before then, an individual cannot have a vested right to possess any estate, whether at common law or in equity. The right cannot be 'vested in possession', because the vesting is necessarily contingent on the birth, and contingent rights are not even 'vested'; far less are they 'vested in possession'.[1]

It follows that nor can anyone be 'in' possession of any estate before he or she is born, for, until then, that individual cannot 'be' anything.

At the moment of birth, that changes. An estate may vest in an individual for a interest in possession at the very moment when he or she is born alive, without the need for any further intervention.

For instance, property may be held upon trust for 'A' until the birth of 'A's' first daughter, remainder over to her. As soon as the first female child is born, 'A' is automatically divested of any interest under the trust, and the child becomes absolutely entitled to the trust property. If the property is land, the child cannot immediately call for the legal estate, for it must be held upon trust during his or her minority,[2] but that does not affect

[1] See ch. 1. [2] Para. 1(1) Sch. 1 Trusts of Land and Appointment of Trustees Act 1996.

the principle that the entire beneficial interest vests in her automatically simply by reason of the birth. She has a right to a vested beneficial interest in possession in the property, and for so long as the trustees are, in fact, administering the trust for her benefit, she is 'in' possession of that beneficial interest; though it is the trustees who are in possession of, and retain the right to possess, the legal estate during her minority.[3]

It does not follow, however, from the fact that the rights of a child are contingent on birth, that the courts will do nothing to preserve those rights before that child is born, or even conceived. The courts will act to preserve contingent rights on behalf of a class, or members of a class, subject only to the rules against perpetuities and accumulations, in precisely the same way as they will act to protect present vested rights on an application made by an individual. So, even before someone is born, the courts may require the trustees to preserve the trust property to which he or she will become entitled, should such a person subsequently be born alive; and, if that happens, and the trustees have failed to do so in the meantime, they will be liable for the breach of trust which they committed before the birth. But, in order to have the status to hold property in his or her own right, the child must be born alive.

Death

Afterwards is death. At the moment of his or her death, an individual automatically ceases to have the legal personality that was acquired at birth, and, for that reason, death automatically and irreversibly divests an individual of all property. Property is vested in individuals only for so long as they live and they automatically cease to be in possession of it at the very moment of their deaths.

The exact moment of someone's death may be in doubt. Normally, this does not matter very much (except, of course, to the deceased). But it can matter when two or more members of the same family are killed by the same event, for the doctrine of lapse normally means that legacies are conditional upon the legatee being alive when the testator dies. So whether the family property passes to one branch or another may depend entirely on who died first. In an immobile agrarian economy, this rarely causes problems. But it became a problem in England after the Industrial Revolution, when whole families were drowned, burned or eaten together in distant parts of the world, and there was no means of telling who had

[3] See ch. 6.

drowned or been consumed first.[4] The practical solution imposed by statute was to assume, in the absence of evidence to the contrary, that the youngest were the strongest, and so endured the longest.[5]

Some property expires automatically along with the deceased. Examples are a tenancy at will, a gratuitous licence, and a life interest in a trust. No right ever passes to anyone else, for there is no *scintilla temporis* between the death and the determination of the estate or interest. The property and the life end together, at exactly the same moment.

Otherwise, all of the property which was vested in the deceased at the moment of death passes automatically, at that moment, to the deceased's personal representatives.[6]

The deceased might, or might not, have had the foresight to make a valid will appointing an executor. If an executor named in the will proves it by taking a grant of representation in the Probate Registry, then the executor's title to the property relates back to the moment of the death; the property is deemed for all purposes to have vested in the proving executor at that moment without any gap. So, if the executor has dealt with the property between the death and the grant, that dealing is retrospectively validated.

The rule is different where the deceased dies without leaving a valid will, or where none of the appointed executors is willing or able to prove the will and take a grant of probate.[7] In that event, the deceased's estate is deemed to have vested in the Public Trustee[8] at the moment of death, and only passes to the administrators appointed to wind up the estate on the date upon which a grant of representation is subsequently made to them by the Probate Registry.

Whether the personal representative is an executor appointed by the deceased or an administrator appointed by the Probate Registry, the representative does not enter into or take possession of any estate in land

4 *Re Alston* [1892] P 143; *Re Beynon* [1901] P 141.

5 Section 184 Law of Property Act 1925. But see s. 46(3) Administration of Estates Act 1925.

6 Until 1 January 1898, when the Land Transfer Act 1897 came into force, real property did not pass to the testator's personal representatives, unless specifically bequeathed: it passed straight to the legatee, or the heir-at-law, on an intestacy. A will of land was viewed as a form of conveyance, taking effect on death; see W. Holdsworth and C. Vickers, *The Law of Succession* (Oxford, Blackwell & Stevens, 1899), pp. 28–9.

7 They might all renounce, or have died before the testator.

8 Section 14(1) Law of Property (Miscellaneous Provisions) Act 1994. Formerly, it vested in the Probate Judge (s.9 Administration of Estates Act 1925) who, since 1971, has been the President of the Family Division. The law was changed when some probate lawyers, with dry wit, started serving notices on the President personally at his home address, notwithstanding a Practice Direction requiring notices to be sent to the Treasury Solicitor.

forming part of the deceased's property merely by virtue of that vesting. The representative has a right to possess it, but neither the death nor the taking of a grant, in itself, puts the representative 'in' possession of it.

The liability of a personal representative who never enters into possession is purely representative. This means that he or she must ensure that any debts and liabilities are discharged out of the assets of the estate before any of those assets are distributed or applied towards the legacies, and the representative will be liable personally to the creditors in the tort of devastavit if he or she fails to apply the available assets towards the debts and liabilities of the estate. But the liability is limited to the value of the assets which should have been applied from the deceased's property to pay those debts. Provided that the representative does not enter into or take possession of the particular estate in land to which the debt or liability attaches, the representative cannot be made to pay more than ought to have been paid out of the assets of the deceased in the course of the due administration of the estate.

If, however, the representative actually enters into possession of it, by using and enjoying the estate (even if it was necessary to do so for the benefit and protection of the creditors, and even though the representative might not have received any personal benefit at all) then the representative becomes personally liable in respect of any obligation attaching to that estate to the same extent as if it had been his or her own personal property.

Suppose, for instance, that the property is a lease. At the moment of the tenant's death, the lease vests in those executors who subsequently prove the will. If there is no will, or no executor proves it, then the lease vests in the Public Trustee until letters of administration are granted, whereupon it vests in the administrator of the estate. But, in either event, the representatives are not personally liable to pay the rent nor to perform the covenants simply by virtue of the vesting. They must treat the rent due under the lease, and any liability on the covenants contained in it, as a debt of the estate, and must apply the assets of the estate in or towards satisfaction of those liabilities.[9] But, if a representative actually enters into possession – if, for instance, the representative moves into the property or evicts squatters or receives rents from a sub-tenant or does anything else amounting to use or enjoyment of the estate – then the representative becomes personally liable on the covenants contained in the

[9] There might also be contingent liabilities under the lease, but the personal representative is normally permitted to wind up the estate without regard to these, and the representative's liability is excluded by statute if that is done (s.26 Trustee Act 1925).

lease,[10] precisely as if he or she had personally taken an assignment of it.[11]

Of course, if possession was taken for the benefit of the creditors and legatees, the representative will have right of recourse against the deceased's assets, for a representative has an indemnity for anything properly done for the protection of the assets of the estate. But as between the representative and the landlord, the liability is personal. The representative must personally pay any shortfall between the amount due to the landlord and the amount that the representative recovers from the estate.

The position is essentially the same even if the estate is insolvent. In that event, there will be no question of paying or distributing legacies. The representative will not even be able to pay all of the deceased's debts. So he or she must instead apply the deceased's property in part payment of those debts, in the same priority after payment of the funeral expenses as would have been the case if winding up the estate of a living bankrupt. In those circumstances, the representative's personal right of recourse against the estate might well be valueless. But, in one respect, a personal representative of an insolvent estate is in a better position than a solvent counterpart. The representative of an insolvent estate, or an estate that becomes insolvent in the course of administration, may obtain an insolvency administration order. In effect, this is a bankruptcy order against the estate. It is retrospective to the date of the death of the deceased,[12] with the result that the estate is deemed never to have vested in the personal representative, and the representative is treated as never having acquired any personal liability in respect of it.[13]

Dispositions to the non-extant

A non-existent person cannot dispose of land, or any interest in land, because a non-existent person cannot hold it in the first place. But what happens if someone purports to transfer land, or an interest in land, to a non-existent person?

[10] *Re Owers* [1941] Ch 389.

[11] It is possible that the liability on the covenant to pay rent is limited to the letting value of the land: *Rendall* v. *Andreae* (1892) 8 TLR 615. If the representative is an executor, then the liability relates back to the death; the same applies to an administrator (s.21 Administration of Estates Act 1925).

[12] Para. 12 Sch. 1 Administration of Insolvent Estates of Deceased Persons Order (SI 1986 No. 1999).

[13] *Re Bradley* [1956] Ch. 615.

The principles are different, depending upon whether the disposition is to someone who once existed, but who does not exist any more, or to someone who has never existed; and depending upon whether the disposition is to an individual or a corporation.

If the disposition is to an individual who has died, then the rule is relatively simple: the property vests in that individual's personal representatives, for they represent the deceased.[14]

If the disposition is to an individual who has not yet been born, and who might consequently never have any legal personality at all, then the rule is different. Normally, a legal estate or interest in land can only be created by deed,[15] and the deed takes effect from the moment when it is delivered. So, a deed which purports to convey something to a person who was not in existence when the deed is delivered is simply void.[16] It conveys nothing. But it may be saved by redelivery. Although a deed may only be delivered once, an attempt to deliver it to a non-existent person is not a delivery at all. So, if, after that person comes into existence, the deed is redelivered, then it may take effect from that redelivery.[17]

In those exceptional cases where a legal estate or interest can be conveyed without a deed (the most important of which is the grant of a short lease)[18] the rule ought to be the same. The grant can only be made if there is a competent grantee. A non-existent person is not a competent grantee. It follows that, unless the grant is re-made, after that person has come into existence, nothing passes.

Equity does not alter this, unless the transfer is for value to a non-existent person as trustee. In that circumstance, the trust could be enforced against the grantor. But, where the intention is simply to vest the property to the non-existent person as beneficial owner, equity will not enforce the transfer, even if that person subsequently comes into existence, for equity does not complete a transfer except to someone who has given value for it.

[14] A gift made by will to someone who has died before the testator lapses. But the rule is easy to avoid. Whilst a legacy to 'X, whether he should predecease me or not' would lapse, a legacy to 'X or his personal representatives, should he predecease me' would be valid, and, if 'X' died first, the assent would be to 'X's' personal representatives; see H. Ford, 'Lapse of Devises and Bequests' (1962) 78 LQR 89, 90–5.

[15] Section 54 Law of Property Act 1925.

[16] *Sheppard's Touchstones* (7th edn, London, Clarke, 1820), vol. 1, p. 56.

[17] *Sheppard's Touchstones* (7th edn, London, Clarke, 1820) vol. I, p. 60; *Norton on Deeds* (2nd edn, London, Sweet & Maxwell, 1928), p. 14.

[18] Section 54(2) Law of Property Act 1925.

A disposition to a corporation which once existed, but has been dissolved, fails for the same reason. The Crown does not take as *bona vacantia*, for the Crown is not the representative of the dissolved corporation. The Crown simply takes anything that had been effectively transferred to the dissolved corporation whilst it was extant, and was still vested in the corporation when it was dissolved.

The same rules as for individuals apply at common law to corporations which have never existed. There is, however, a statutory exception for companies which have never existed. Subject to any agreement to the contrary, any contract or deed takes effect as if made with any person purporting to act for the company or act as agent for it.[19]

Private receivership

Receivership is the process by which a secured creditor seizes control of the land usually as the first step towards selling it for the purpose of recovering the secured debt. The debtor may be a company or an individual. It does not matter. The principle is the same.

A secured creditor does not enter into possession of the security simply by appointing a receiver over the secured estate.[20] Although there could hardly be any greater displacement of the debtor's dominion and control over the secured estate than the appointment of a receiver, appointed to end the debtor's enjoyment of it and to pass whatever benefit can be obtained to the secured lender, nonetheless a receiver is deemed to be and to act as the agent of the debtor. This is provided for by statute[21] and is normally reinforced by the terms of the mortgage deed or debenture. Although in reality the receiver acts almost exclusively for the benefit of the secured lender, in law everything the receiver does is deemed to have been done in right and on behalf of the debtor.

It follows that, if a secured lender who has already taken possession of the security wishes to go out of possession again, all that the lender need do is appoint a receiver to act as agent for the debtor. The appointment of the receiver restores possession of the secured estate to the debtor, and the lender's mortgage term or equivalent rights are once again held

[19] Section 36C Companies Act 1985.

[20] So, if the mortgaged estate consists of a lease, the mortgagee does not, by appointing a receiver, become liable on the covenants contained in the lease. See ch. 5.

[21] Section 109(2) Law of Property Act 1925; s.44 Insolvency Act 1986.

in suspension,[22] because the receiver is deemed to be the agent of the debtor.[23]

In some circumstances, however, a receiver simply cannot act as agent for the debtor. When a bankruptcy order is made against a debtor, all existing agency relationships are extinguished, and thereafter, pending the appointment of a trustee in bankruptcy, only the Official Receiver may appoint new agents to deal with the bankrupt's property. The exclusive right to appoint agents then passes to the trustee in bankruptcy, once appointed. Similarly, if a winding-up order is made against a company, or a company passes a resolution for voluntary winding up, all existing agency relationships are extinguished, and thereafter only the liquidator may appoint agents on behalf of the company.[24]

The fact that the receiver cannot act as agent for the debtor, in these circumstances, does not discharge the appointment, nor, indeed, prevent a receiver being appointed. Whether the receiver can act as agent for the debtor or not, a secured lender has a right to appoint a receiver to receive rents and profits from the secured estate. Furthermore, when dealing with third parties, the receiver still has authority to deal with the property in the name of the debtor,[25] including even authority to bring proceedings in the debtor's name;[26] but, as between the lender and the debtor, if the receiver cannot act as agent for the debtor, the receiver normally becomes the agent of the lender, with the consequence that the secured lender will then be treated as having entered into possession of the security.[27]

The receiver does not, however, invariably become the agent of the secured lender in these circumstances. There is another possibility, which is that the receiver has taken possession as principal in his or her own right, albeit subject to an obligation to account to the lender for the rents and profits. Whether the receiver has taken possession as agent for the lender or as a principal is a pure question of fact, depending upon the terms of the appointment[28] and the degree of autonomy given to the receiver.

[22] See ch. 5.

[23] *Refuge Assurance* v. *Pearlberg* [1938] Ch 687. The lender is, however, deemed to remain the competent landlord for the purposes of Part II of the Landlord and Tenant Act 1954 (s.67).

[24] *Gosling* v. *Gaskell* [1897] AC 575.

[25] *Sowman* v. *David Samuel Trust Ltd* [1978] 1 WLR 22; s.4 Powers of Attorney Act 1971.

[26] *Goughs Garages* v. *Pugsley* [1930] 1 KB 615.

[27] For the consequences, see ch. 5.

[28] The standard terms upon which lenders appoint receivers often provide that the receiver shall in no circumstances become the agent of the lender.

It is important to determine precisely who is in possession of what when a receiver has been appointed because, as we saw in chapter 2, possession of an estate, or a right to possess an estate, is the essence of the various possessory actions. So, if, for example, a lender has appointed a receiver, and the receiver is acting as agent for the debtor, the receiver cannot bring a possession action against the debtor. Similarly, if the lender brings a possession action against the debtor (that is, an action to be put into possession of the mortgage term, or rights equivalent to a mortgage term),[29] the lender will thereby dismiss the receiver; for, if the lender is to be put into possession of the security, the receiver cannot collect the rent and profits as if the lender were not in possession. Likewise, if the lender wishes to bring a trespass or nuisance action against a third party, the receiver must be dismissed first; for the actions cannot be brought by someone who is out of possession until that person has attempted to take possession.[30]

It is also important because, as we saw in chapter 5, the liability of a secured lender on the covenants contained in a lease often depends upon whether the lender has taken possession.

Finally, it is important because the liability of a secured lender in possession to account to a debtor is limited to the period during which the lender is in possession of the security.

Court-appointed receivers

The authority of a court-appointed receiver comes directly from the court, rather than from either of the parties. So, if the court appoints a receiver over an estate, the receiver does not act as agent for either party,[31] but rather takes possession as principal in his or her own right. Consequently, although a court-appointed receiver is not a statutory assignee of the property, he or she does have the rights and liabilities of a person in possession.[32] So, a court-appointed receiver, who is dispossessed by a third party, may bring an action to recover possession of the estate, and may also sue in trespass and nuisance. But, as an officer of the court, the receiver also has an additional remedy; for, if the court appoints an officer to take possession of an estate, it is a contempt to interfere with that, unless the receiver or the court gives permission first.[33] So, in the absence

[29] See ch. 5. [30] See ch. 2. [31] *Re Newdigate Colliery Ltd* [1912] 1 Ch 468.
[32] *Re Sacker* (1889) 22 QBD 179. [33] *Angel* v. *Smith* (1804) 9 Ves 335.

of permission, the receiver may apply to commit the offender to prison or to sequestrate its assets.

A court may require a party to deliver up possession to a receiver, even on an interim basis and in defiance of a claimed proprietary right to remain in possession.[34]

Bankruptcy and winding up

Bankruptcy is the process by which unsecured creditors may use the machinery of the state to seize and sell the assets of individual debtors, and then apply the net proceeds towards their debts.

Liquidation (or 'winding up') is the equivalent process for companies.

Although the objects of bankruptcy and liquidation are generally the same, the processes are very different.

Bankruptcy begins with the presentation of a bankruptcy petition.[35] The petition is usually presented by a creditor, though sometimes debtors who wish to be rid of their debts present their own petitions.[36] If the court makes a bankruptcy order, then the Official Receiver acquires the exclusive right to manage and control most of the bankrupt's property (called 'the bankrupt's estate') with effect retrospectively to the date of presentation of the petition.[37]

The Official Receiver continues to have that right until a trustee in bankruptcy is appointed at the creditors' meeting.[38] The property comprised within the bankrupt's estate automatically vests in the trustee in bankruptcy on appointment without any further formality or conveyance. The Official Receiver thereafter no longer has any power to manage or control the estate.

As a result, if the bankrupt's estate includes an estate in land, it is the bankrupt who is normally 'in' possession of it down to the point when the trustee in bankruptcy is appointed; the Official Receiver manages and controls the estate, but does so in the name of and in right of the bankrupt, in the same way as a private receiver would. For that reason, until a trustee in bankruptcy is appointed, any action concerning the land is brought by or against the bankrupt, in the bankrupt's own name, and not against the Official Receiver, albeit that the Official Receiver is the only person

[34] *Marshall* v. *Charteris* [1920] 1 Ch 520.
[35] Rule 6.10 Insolvency Rules 1986.
[36] Rule 6.40 Insolvency Rules 1986.
[37] Section 284 Insolvency Act 1986.
[38] *Heath* v. *Tang* [1993] 1 WLR 1421; [1993] 4 All ER 694; *Royal Bank of Scotland plc* v. *Farley* [1996] BPIR 638.

who has authority to give instructions about the conduct of the action.[39] Nonetheless, in *Razzaq* v. *Pala*,[40] Lightman J. suggested that the Official Receiver, in fact, obtains possession, by analogy with the position of a receiver appointed by the court,[41] with the result that it is a contempt of court to exercise any self-help remedy, or to enforce a judgment, against the bankrupt's land before the trustee in bankruptcy has been appointed. But this cannot be right, for, if the Official Receiver were in possession of any estate in the bankrupt's land, he or she personally would be a proper defendant in an action to recover it, and would be personally liable in costs and for mesne profits if the bankrupt wrongly remained in occupation. The correct analysis is that a receiver appointed by the court does obtain possession, but only because he or she is put into possession by the court. The Official Receiver, however, only has the right to manage the bankrupt's estate, and so does not obtain possession in his or her own right.

A trustee in bankruptcy is a statutory assignee of the bankrupt's estate. The assignment takes effect on the day on which the trustee is appointed.[42] The same applies, in low value bankruptcies, when the Official Receiver becomes an ex officio trustee.[43] Consequently, the trustee is personally liable to perform covenants attached to the bankrupt's estate in the same way, and to the same extent, as a voluntary assignee would be liable, unless the trustee exercises the statutory power to disclaim the property to which the covenant is attached (see below). So, if the bankrupt's estate includes a lease, then, absent any disclaimer, the trustee is personally liable to pay the rent falling due for payment after the trustee's appointment, and is likewise personally liable to perform the other tenant's covenants contained in the lease, accruing due for performance after that date.

Some land, exceptionally, is deemed not to form part of the bankrupt's estate, is therefore not subject to the control of the Official Receiver,

[39] *Heath* v. *Tang* [1993] 1 WLR 1421; [1993] 4 All ER 694; *Royal Bank of Scotland plc* v. *Farley* [1996] BPIR 638; *Ord* v. *Upton* [2000] 1 All ER 193. Once a trustee in bankruptcy has been appointed, as Hoffmann LJ explained in *Heath* v. *Tang* [1993] 1 WLR 1421, 1423: 'The bankrupt cannot commence any proceedings based upon such a cause of action and, if the proceedings have already been commenced, he ceases to have sufficient interest to continue them. Under the old system of pleadings, the defendant was entitled to plead the plaintiff's supervening bankruptcy as a plea in abatement. Since the Supreme Court of Judicature Act 1875, the cause of action does not abate but the action will be stayed or dismissed unless the trustee is willing to be substituted as plaintiff: see *Jackson* v. *North Eastern Rly Co.* (1877) 5 ChD 844.' See also s.49 County Courts Act 1984.

[40] [1997] 1 WLR 1336; [1997] 2 EGLR 53.

[41] Section 287 Insolvency Act 1986.

[42] Section 306 Insolvency Act 1986.

[43] Section 306(1) Insolvency Act 1986.

and does not automatically vest in the trustee in bankruptcy. Assured tenancies, Rent Act protected and statutory tenancies, their agricultural equivalents, and secure tenancies fall into this category.[44] Accordingly, unless the trustee elects to call in the tenancy,[45] the trustee does not acquire any right to possess those estates, and any action to enforce the terms of the tenancy will be an action by, or against, the bankrupt, and not the trustee.

A bankruptcy order has no effect on property held by the bankrupt upon trust for any other person.[46] Nor does it prevent the bankrupt becoming a trustee. In either event, the bankrupt continues to hold the property as trustee. Of course, if the bankrupt has a beneficial interest in the trust property too, then that beneficial interest does form part of the bankrupt's estate, and so vests in the trustee in bankruptcy as part of the bankrupt's estate.

If the court decides that the bankruptcy order should never have been made, it may annul the order.[47] In that event, the bankrupt's estate re-vests in the bankrupt, but subject to the rights of third parties who might have acquired an interest in the property in the meantime. Otherwise, the bankrupt is normally discharged from the bankruptcy after one year.[48] But the bankrupt does not reacquire anything on discharge.

Liquidation is somewhat different. It starts either with a resolution to wind the company up, or with the making by the court of a compulsory winding-up order. A liquidator is then appointed, to take control of and realise the company's assets, pay those creditors who can be paid in the required statutory order, distribute any surplus amongst the shareholders, and finally dissolve the company.

The crucial difference between the bankruptcy of an individual and the liquidation of a company (apart, of course, from the obvious one that the final duty of the trustee is not to kill the debtor) is this: the company's property never vests in the liquidator. Throughout the process, the property of the company remains vested in the company, and the liquidator simply has power to deal with it on behalf of the company. The liquidator, in effect, acts as agent for the company, never as principal. So, whilst a liquidator who authorises or commits a tort is personally liable (for it is never a defence to the personal liability of the actor that the tort was committed in some representative capacity), a liquidator does

[44] Section 283(3A) Insolvency Act 1986.
[45] Section 308A Insolvency Act 1986.
[46] Section 283(3)(a) Insolvency Act 1986.
[47] Section 282(1) Insolvency Act 1986.
[48] Section 279 Insolvency Act 1986.

not acquire personally any contractual liability which is attached to the company's property or which depends upon having taken possession of that property.

Disclaimer

The power to disclaim property is a statutory power, which may be exercised in three circumstances only.

First, a trustee in bankruptcy may disclaim property comprised within the bankrupt's estate,[49] including leaseholds.[50] If the trustee does so, then the property is deemed never to have vested in the trustee in bankruptcy at all.[51] The result is that the trustee is retrospectively released from the personal liability which otherwise attaches by virtue of the statutory vesting of that property in the trustee. The trustee does, however, remain liable to administer the bankrupt's estate as if that property had continued to exist down to the date of disclaimer, and as if liabilities had continued to accrue under it down to that date. Furthermore, anyone suffering loss consequent upon the disclaimer may prove for it in the bankruptcy as an unsecured creditor.

So, if the property is a lease, the effect of the disclaimer is that the trustee is retrospectively discharged from personal liability to pay the rent and to perform the other covenants in the lease. But the landlord may prove in the bankruptcy for any unpaid rent up to the date of the disclaimer, and may also prove for any future loss caused by the disclaimer, credit being given for the likelihood of reletting.[52] Furthermore, if, in the meantime, the trustee has entered into possession of the lease, he or she must treat the unpaid rent for that period as an expense of the bankruptcy, rather than simply as an unsecured debt, so that it must be paid in full before anything is paid to the general body of unsecured creditors.

Secondly, where a company is in the course of being wound up, the liquidator may disclaim property belonging to it,[53] including leaseholds,[54]

[49] Section 315 Insolvency Act 1986. [50] Section 317 Insolvency Act 1986.

[51] Section 315(3) Insolvency Act 1986. Before a trustee had statutory power to disclaim, he was treated as an involuntary assignee. Unless the trustee actually joined in the assignment of the lease made to him by the commissioners in bankruptcy (*Copeland* v. *Stephens* (1818) 1 Barn & Ald 593, 601), he could reject the assignment as *damnosa haereditas*, but, if he accepted the assignment by entering into possession of the property or otherwise, he became liable upon the covenants contained in the lease as if he were an ordinary assignee: *Hanson* v. *Stephenson* (1818) 1 Barn & Ald 308.

[52] *Re Park Air Services* [2000] 2 AC 172. [53] Section 178(2) Insolvency Act 1986.

[54] Section 179 Insolvency Act 1986.

on behalf of the company, whether the winding up is compulsory or voluntary. The disclaimer is made on behalf of the company, there being no equivalent in liquidation of the statutory vesting of the bankrupt's estate in a trustee in bankruptcy. Consequently, the liquidator never acquires any personal liability, and so the disclaimer makes no difference to the liquidator's personal position. Otherwise, the effect of the disclaimer so far as it concerns the administration of the company's property in the liquidation is the same as the effect on a bankrupt's estate of a disclaimer by a trustee in bankruptcy.

Thirdly, where property is still vested in a company on its dissolution, and so would otherwise vest in the Crown as *bona vacantia*,[55] the Crown may subsequently disclaim it,[56] with the result that it is deemed never to have vested in the Crown at all,[57] and is otherwise treated as if a liquidator had disclaimed the property immediately before the dissolution.[58]

A disclaimer only ever affects the rights and liabilities of the disclaiming party directly. It has no effect on the rights and obligations of third parties as between themselves. So, if an estate is disclaimed, the obligations attached to the estate can no longer be enforced against the disclaiming party, and nor can the disclaiming party any longer enforce the rights attached to the estate against anyone else; for, so far as the disclaiming party is concerned, the disclaimer has destroyed the estate. But the disclaimer does not have any wider effect. In so far as the rights and obligations of third parties, as between themselves, depend upon the continued existence of the estate, it is treated as if it were still extant; and, similarly, in so far as the rights and obligations of third parties, as between themselves, depend on the continuing liability of the disclaiming party, that liability is treated as continuing. So a disclaimer acts entirely in personam between the disclaiming party and anyone else. It does not have any effect in rem.

An example will help to make this clear. Suppose that the disclaimed property consists of a lease. As between the landlord and the disclaiming tenant, the effect is the same as if the estate in the lease had been destroyed by a surrender at the moment when the disclaimer took effect. So existing rights and liabilities are preserved, but contingent and future rights and

[55] Section 654 Companies Act 1985. [56] Section 656 Companies Act 1985.

[57] Section 657 Companies Act 1985.

[58] It is not so treated for the purpose of a contractual covenant to take a new lease following a disclaimer by a liquidator or trustee in bankruptcy: *Re Yarmarine* [1992] BCLC 276.

liabilities are extinguished.[59] So too, as between the disclaiming tenant and any sub-tenant, the sub-lease is treated as if it had been surrendered on that date, for the lease is the reversion upon the sub-term, and the lease, as between the disclaiming tenant and anyone else, is treated as having been extinguished by the disclaimer.

Yet, as between the head-landlord and the sub-tenant (as third parties), the disclaimed head-lease and the disclaimed sub-lease are both treated as if they were still extant,[60] with the result that the head-landlord cannot evict the sub-tenant except by going through the charade of doing whatever would have been necessary to determine those leases if they had not been disclaimed.[61]

Similarly, as between a disclaiming tenant and any surety for that tenant, the guarantee is treated as having been discharged on the date of the disclaimer, with the result that the surety's implied right of indemnity against the disclaiming tenant is discharged too. Likewise, as between the disclaiming tenant and the penultimate assignee, any indemnity covenant in the transfer is treated as having been discharged, for these are all direct liabilities of the disclaiming party to someone else. But, as between third parties, the disclaimer is disregarded. So, subject to the ordinary statutory restrictions contained in the Landlord and Tenant (Covenants) Act 1995, the landlord can continue to enforce the original tenant's contractual liability, the liability of any intermediate assignee contained in a licence to assign or other contractual instrument, and the liability of any surety, including a surety for the ultimate, disclaiming assignee.[62]

If the Crown disclaims a freehold estate, that brings about an escheat.

[59] If the disclaimer is by a trustee in bankruptcy, it also has the effect of releasing the trustee from any personal liability (see above).

[60] *Re A E Realisations* [1988] 1 WLR 200; *Re Thompson and Cottrell's Contract* [1943] 1 All ER 169.

[61] The same point applies where a liquidator or the Crown disclaims property held on trust (the issue does not arise with a trustee in bankruptcy, because trust property does not form part of the bankrupt's estate). As between the trustee and the beneficiary, the trust relationship is destroyed. But, as between the beneficiary and everyone else, the beneficiary is still treated as having all the rights of a beneficiary of that trust.

[62] *Hindcastle* v. *Barbara Attenborough Associates* [1997] AC 70; [1996] 1 All ER 737; [1996] 1 EGLR 94. A sub-tenant, affected by a forfeiture following a disclaimer, is entitled to apply for relief from forfeiture by way of vesting order under the statutory (but not, apparently, the inherent) jurisdiction of the court to grant relief to a sub-tenant: *Pelicano* v. *MEPC* [1994] 1 EGLR 104; *Hill* v. *Griffin* [1987] 1 EGLR 81; *Barclays Bank* v. *Prudential Assurance* [1998] BPIR 427; [1998] 1 EGLR 44. A sub-tenant may also apply for a vesting order pursuant to s.320 Insolvency Act 1986; r.6.186 Insolvency Rules 1986.

Escheat

Escheat is part of the doctrine of tenures, which still underpins the whole of English land law.[63] Just as there is a reversion to every lease, so there is a reversion to every freehold. The difference is that it has not been possible to create new sub-freeholds since the practice was outlawed by the Statute of Quia Emptores in 1290. Yet it remained common in Ireland until relatively recent times, and there are many English manors (intermediate freehold interests) which cannot be shown to have a provenance that pre-dates the Civil War.

Formerly an escheat happened whenever an owner died intestate without an heir or committed a felony. Both of these forms of escheat have been abolished by statute.[64] But an escheat does still occur whenever the Crown disclaims a freehold estate.[65]

An escheat is not the same thing as a Crown acquisition of unowned property by *bona vacantia*. There are two differences.

The first is that an escheat is not necessarily to the Crown. There may still be some mesne lord of the manor to whom the property will escheat. A surprising amount of freehold land is still held of some manor, or reputed manor, rather than directly of the Crown.[66]

The second is that an acquisition by *bona vacantia* is equivalent to an assignment. The Crown acquires the title and estate that was previously vested in someone else. But the process of escheat is more like a forfeiture; for, on an escheat, the previous title simply ceases to exist, and the immediate reversion is automatically accelerated.[67] The immediate reversioner might be the Crown, if the escheating freehold was held in tenant in chief *ut de corona* or it might be the owner of an intermediate seigniorial manor, but, whoever it is, that person will be entitled to enjoy that land free from the previous freehold, but subject to any derivative estates.

[63] 'Escheat is a sort of interruption to the course of descent, by which the original lord gets his estate back into his own hands, by an escheat or cheat – the former being merely the long and the latter the short of it. The law of escheat is founded on the supposition that the blood of the last tenant is extinct and gone, so that, as Coke says, "ye tenant failing in bloodde ye lordde walketh in and bones ye property" ': G. A. Beckett, revised and extended by A. A. Beckett, *The Comic Blackstone* (London, Bradbury, Agnew & Co., 1887), p. 146.

[64] Section 45 Administration of Estates Act 1925; s.1 Forfeiture Act 1870.

[65] Other forfeitures to the Crown are possible (for instance, under s.3(8) Crown Estates Act 1961) but a forfeiture that can *only* be to the Crown is not strictly an escheat.

[66] For a different view, see *Re Lowe's W.T.* [1973] 1 WLR 882, 886.

[67] See F. Enever, *Bona Vacantia* (London, HM Stationery Office, 1927), p. 52; *Scmlla Properties Ltd* v. *Gesso Properties (BVI) Ltd* [1995] BCC 793.

Dissolution

Dissolution is corporate death. A company is dissolved as the final act in the course of its liquidation, whether as the result of a compulsory or voluntary winding up.[68] Or it may be dissolved summarily, without being wound up, by being struck off the register of companies as defunct, for failing to carry on any business or to be in operation.[69] That normally happens when it fails to lodge accounts or an annual return.

Any property which still belongs beneficially to the company when it is dissolved passes to the Crown as *bona vacantia.*[70] The Crown, as we have already seen, may then either accept that property or disclaim it.

A company, unlike an individual, may be revived. If it has been dissolved after being wound up, the application to revive it must be made within two years of the dissolution,[71] but if it has been administratively dissolved as defunct, then the application can be made as late as twenty years afterwards.[72] Even a contingent creditor may make the application.[73]

Where a company is revived, any property which passed to the Crown as *bona vacantia* re-vests in the company, with retrospective effect, just as if the company had always owned the property, but subject to any disposition that might have been made by the Crown in the meantime;[74] as compensation, the Crown has to pay the company whatever consideration was received on the disposition. So the Crown, in effect, has a statutory power of overreaching. A Crown disclaimer, however, is not a disposition for this purpose.[75] So, if the Crown disclaims, then anyone else into whose hands that property later comes runs the risk that he or she will be divested of it without compensation if an application is made to revive the company.

Not all corporations are companies regulated by the Companies Act 1985. Ecclesiastical corporations are usually corporations sole or corporations aggregate, and there remain many ancient livery companies which owe their corporate status to a Crown grant. Corporations which are not regulated by the Companies Act may be dissolved by forfeiture, or for internal failure, or by revocation of their charters, or on an application made by the Crown to the administrative court.

[68] Sections 201–205 Insolvency Act 1986. [69] Section 652 Companies Act 1985.
[70] Section 654 Companies Act 1985. [71] Section 651 Companies Act 1985.
[72] Section 653(2) Companies Act 1985.
[73] *Re Harvest Lane Motor Bodies Ltd* [1969] 1 Ch 457.
[74] Section 655 Companies Act 1985. [75] *Allied Dunbar* v. *Fowle* [1994] 1 EGLR 122.

Where such a corporation is dissolved, its property (including land) vests in the Crown as *bona vacantia* at common law.[76] For a long time, this was in doubt. Sir Edward Coke took the view that every conveyance of land to a corporation was subject to an implied condition for reverter in the event of its dissolution.[77] Blackstone agreed,[78] and it was not until 1933 that this was held to be wrong for leasehold land,[79] and 1948 for freehold land.[80] Parliament has not yet caught up,[81] so there is still no statutory power to disclaim, but the Crown, as an involuntary assignee, probably has a right to reject the property entirely as *damnosa haereditas*, for no one, not even the Crown, can be compelled to accept an onerous and unwanted gift.

76 *Re Strathblaine Estates* [1948] Ch 228. Possibly, the decision ought to have been that there had been an escheat; for according to Lord Brougham in *Henchman v. A-G* (1834) 3 My & K 485, 492, the Crown cannot take freehold land as bona vacantia.

77 Co Litt 13b.

78 Blackstone, *Commentaries on the Laws of England* (11th edn, London, Strahan & Woodfall, 1791), vol. I, p. 472; vol. II, p. 256.

79 *Re Wells, Swinburne–Hanham* v. *Howard* [1933] 1 Ch 29.

80 *Re Strathblaine Estates* [1948] Ch 228. Cf. s. 181 Law of Property Act 1925.

81 There is power to register old companies (s.680 Companies Act 1985) with a view to winding them up, and to wind up unregistered companies (but not other corporations) in a similar way (s.220 Insolvency Act 1986).

8

Adverse possession and prescription

Introduction

Adverse possession and prescription are both processes by which rights in land are barred by lapse of time.

The right to recover possession of an estate is barred by adverse possession.

The right to use and enjoy an estate in a particular way is barred by prescription. Prescription bars the estate owner's right to complain about trespasses and nuisances, and also bars the right to exploit the estate in particular ways. But it bars only those rights which a predecessor could have granted away from the estate as an incorporeal hereditament.[1]

So the difference, in effect, between the two is that adverse possession is the means by which the entire ownership of an estate is extinguished whereas prescription is the means by which lesser rights are acquired against it, without affecting the ownership of the estate itself.

This chapter explores the similarities and differences in these processes, and explains the reasons for them.

Conceptual similarities and differences

English land law, as we have already seen, is built on the rather shaky foundation that William the Conqueror extinguished all subsisting estates and interests in 1066, and carved the whole country up afresh. The buttress between this fiction and the firm ground of reality is the rule that the

[1] Blackstone said (*Commentaries on the Laws of England* 11th edn, London, Strahan & Woodfall, 1791, vol. 2, p. 17): 'Hereditaments then, to use the largest expression, are of two kinds, corporeal, and incorporeal. Corporeal consist of such as affect the senses; such as may be seen and handled by the body: incorporeal are not the object of sensation, can neither be seen nor handled, are creatures of the mind, and exist only in contemplation.' On the distinction between corporeal and incorporeal rights, and the Roman origin of the distinction, see J. Getzler, 'Roman Ideas of Land Ownership', in *Land Law Themes and Perspectives* (ed. S. Bright and J. Dewar, Oxford, Oxford University Press, 1998), p. 93.

legitimate enjoyment of any estate or interest is presumptively proved by prior enjoyment.[2]

So present possession of an estate is presumptive evidence of all the necessary links in the chain of title going back to an original, unimpeachable and probably wholly fictional, post-conquest Crown grant, which only those with an older, and therefore better, claim are permitted to rebut.

Similarly, if an estate owner has been prevented from enjoying the estate in a particular manner – if someone has been allowed to exercise some right over it – this is presumptive evidence that, at some point in the past, the owner of it granted away that right. Prior enjoyment of that interest (the right to do something that would otherwise be a trespass or nuisance, or to prevent the estate being exploited in a particular way) is presumptive evidence of its lawful creation, and the longer that interest has been enjoyed, the better that evidence.

The practical problem with this is that there might be very nearly a millennium of events available to be argued about for the purpose of proving or rebutting claims to ownership of an estate or an entitlement to exercise rights over it.[3]

Adverse possession and prescription are both entirely practical solutions to this particular problem. They are rules which restrict the amount of history that the law requires or allows to be proved. They both make proof of recent enjoyment of a right for a particular period conclusive of the entitlement, even in the face of contrary and older evidence. Yet they do so in slightly different ways.

Adverse possession works as a matter of substantive law. It starts from the premise that, in the absence of an actual Crown grant, the best title to an estate is the one with the oldest root, that is, the one founded on the oldest acts of possession.[4] The best title is therefore the one that can be traced back to the oldest conveyance, that being evidence of a transfer of possession at that time.[5] It then modifies that rule by positively extinguishing the claims to that title of all those who have not in fact enjoyed the estate in the recent past. It is not the estate itself which is extinguished. Rather it is the title to it of those persons whose rights are barred.[6] That is why an adverse possessor takes subject to all the burdens and incidents attached to the estate, such as rights of way and charges.[7]

[2] See ch. 3. [3] *Iveagh* v. *Martin* [1961] 1 QB 232. [4] See ch. 3.

[5] *Wiberley* v. *Insley* [1999] 1 WLR 894. [6] Section 17 Limitation Act 1980.

[7] A legal charge may itself be barred by adverse possession (s.20 Limitation Act 1980). It is treated in the same way as an estate, because the chargee has the same rights and remedies as if the charge had created a mortgage term (a legal lease).

Prescription, by contrast, is essentially a rule of evidence. It starts from the same premise as adverse possession; that long use is the evidential foundation from which the court is able to conclude that the use began with a lawful grant made at some time in the past, by the then owner of the estate.[8] The rule then shifts the evidential burden of rebutting the presumption to the current estate owner, instead of barring the estate owner's claim to take free of the interest as a matter of substantive law.

For common law prescription and the doctrine of lost modern grant, this means that, once the claimant has shown the requisite period of use, the burden then shifts to the owner to prove positively not simply that the use did not have a lawful origin, but also that there could not have been one.

Statutory prescription under the Prescription Act 1832 works similarly, but more strongly. It bars absolutely the right to adduce certain types of evidence in order to defeat the presumption of lawful origin, and the types of evidence which it prohibits generally depends on whether the use has been for twenty or forty years before the action was commenced.

So the rules of adverse possession and the rules of prescription are both designed to limit the amount of history that can be or need be proved; adverse possession does it as a matter of substantive law, while prescription does it by preventing the estate owner adducing relevant evidence about the origin of the use.

This difference in the way the two principles work explains why a title by adverse possession may be acquired by force or trick or secretly, whereas prescriptive rights cannot be acquired in that manner. An act done by force, trick or secretly is not something which is likely to have had a lawful origin, and consequently those acts cannot be the evidential foundation of a prescriptive right. By contrast, there is no supposedly lawful origin to acts of adverse possession. On the contrary, adverse possession is acknowledged to be the process by which an otherwise better, lawful title to an estate is barred by acts done without any lawful origin whatsoever. So it does not matter how the estate was taken.[9]

[8] *Bakewell Management* v. *Brandwood* [2004] 2 AC 519.

[9] The point was elegantly explained by Nourse LJ in *Buckinghamshire County Council* v. *Moran* [1990] Ch 623, 644; [1989] 2 All ER 225, 228, as follows: 'Under most systems of law a squatter who has been in long possession of land can acquire title to it in the place of the true owner. The Scots and continental systems, more faithful to the Roman law, have opted for prescription, a doctrine founded on the fiction that the land has been granted to the squatter. In England, prescription, although a shoot well favoured by the common law, was stunted in its lateral growth by the statutes of limitation, being confined in its maturity

The conceptual differences, however, cannot explain all the differences between the rules. Some of them are simply the accidents of history; for the rules applicable have developed separately, without reference to each other, and this can lead to curious results.

For instance, there is no good reason for the discrepancy between the period of possession necessary to obtain title by adverse possession and the generally longer period of user necessary to acquire an easement by prescription.[10] So someone squatting in part of an unregistered building generally acquires title to that part by adverse possession after twelve years, but has to wait another eight years before acquiring any prescriptive easement over the rest. In the meantime, he or she owns part of the property without any right of access to it, or of support for it, through the rest.

Touchstones of adverse possession

Most of the cases on adverse possession turn on the essentially factual question of whether the alleged possessor was or was not in adverse possession of the estate during the requisite period.

In order to answer that question, there are essentially ten principles which must be applied in turn.

1. *All estates may be possessed but there is not necessarily someone 'in' possession of every estate*

As we have already seen from chapter 3, there is no allodial land in England and Wales. If a particular parcel of land is not for the time being owned by the Crown absolutely as part of the residual royal demesne, then there is only one possible explanation: an estate must have been carved out of it and that estate must be owned by someone. Someone must have a good title to it, being a better title than anyone else. So there must necessarily

to the acquisition of easements and profits à prendre over another's land. Limitation, so far from being founded on some fictional grant, extinguishes the right of the true owner to recover the land, so that the squatter's possession becomes impregnable, giving him a title superior to all others. The essential difference between prescription and limitation is that in the former case title can be acquired only by possession as of right. That is the antithesis of what is required for limitation, which perhaps can be described as possession as of wrong.'

10 Until 1879, the period for adverse possession was generally twenty years too. It was reduced to twelve years by s.1 Real Property Limitation Act 1874.

be someone who is entitled to possess every such estate. In the last resort, the estate belongs to the Crown as *bona vacantia* rather than as part of the residual royal demesne.

It does not follow, however, from the fact that there must be someone who has a better title to it than anyone else, that there must be someone who is, in fact, 'in' possession of it. Someone must have a title to it, but no one need be enjoying the fruits of ownership. It might simply be unpossessed.[11] Indeed, there might be any number of rival claimants, one of whom necessarily has a better title and therefore a better right to possess it than any of the others, but it does not follow that any of them is actually 'in' possession of it. For a person retains possession of an estate only for so long as he or she is actually enjoying at least some of the fruits of it.

2. *Possession is indivisible (or exclusive)*

Possession is indivisible. Only one person can be in possession of a particular estate in land at any one time. This is true even when land is vested in two or more persons as joint tenants, for joint tenants are treated in law as one person. They hold *per my et per tout*, of the whole, but with a right to alienate an equal share.[12]

So, if, at any time, a particular person is in possession of an estate, it follows that there cannot be anyone with a rival claim who is also in possession of it.

The explanation for this is caught up in the forms of actions at common law. It rests on the distinction between an action in *ejectment* and the action of *trespass quare clausum fregit.*

[11] An individual who dies necessarily ceases to be in possession of any estate in land, and the personal representatives do not take possession, as such, until they enter. In the meantime, the estate is unpossessed. Formerly, this was called 'abatement': Blackstone, *Commentaries on the Laws of England* (11th edn, London, Strahan & Woodfall, 1791), vol. 3, p. 168. Similarly, a corporation sole cannot be in possession of any land whilst the office is vacant: see F. Maitland, 'The Corporation Sole' (1900) 16 LQR 335.

[12] Blackstone, *Commentaries on the Laws of England* (11th edn, London, Strahan & Woodfall, 1791), vol. 2, p. 182. 'Possession in law is, of course, single and exclusive; but occupation may be shared with others or had on behalf of others': per Lord Denning LJ in *Hills (Patents) Ltd* v. *University College Hospital* [1956] 1 QB 90, 99. Consequently, a covenant against 'sharing possession' is construed as allowing another to enjoy the property as if he or she were a joint tenant: *Akici* v. *L. R. Butlin Ltd* [2006] 1 WLR 201.

Ejectment was the action by which a person who was not in possession of an estate asserted a right to possess it. It is, as we have already seen,[13] now called an action for recovery of land.

Trespass quare clausum fregit was the action by which a person who was in possession could obtain damages for intrusions upon that possession. The complaint was that the defendant had broken into the claimant's actual or notional close. It is the basis of the modern action of trespass to land.

So to say that someone has acquired title by adverse possession is simply another way of saying that the previous owner's right to recover the land by ejectment has been barred by lapse of time.[14] The clock starts ticking on the first day on which the action could have been brought, but was not. But someone who is already in possession cannot bring the action; you cannot 'recover' possession from yourself. The remedy for intrusions upon the claimant's possession lies in trespass instead. So mere intrusions, no matter how persistent, are not sufficient to start the adverse possession clock ticking.

It follows that, where there is already someone in possession of an estate, a stranger will not obtain possession of it unless he or she first excludes or ousts the prior possessor.[15] If the intruder does not succeed in ousting the prior possessor entirely from the use and enjoyment of the estate, then the prior possessor retains possession, and the intruder is nothing more than that.[16] To retain possession is easy; to gain it is difficult.

If, therefore, two persons, who are not joint tenants, both appear to be in possession of the same estate, it follows that the appearance is deceptive. Either one of them is in possession of the estate (usually the one who began using the estate before the other) and the other is an intruder upon it. Or they are both intruders on someone else's possession. They cannot both be in possession of it, because possession is indivisible.

3. *Possession is a question of fact*

The crucial issue in adverse possession claims is always this: who was 'in' possession of the relevant estate at each moment during the relevant

[13] See ch. 2.

[14] W. Holdsworth, *History of English Law* (2nd edn, London, Sweet & Maxwell, 1925), vol. VII, p. 69.

[15] In *Rains* v. *Buxton* (1880) 14 ChD 537, 540, Fry J said that dispossession happens 'where a person comes in and drives out the others from possession' or 'where the person in possession goes out and is followed into possession by other persons'.

[16] Per Denning LJ in *Hills (Patents) Ltd* v. *University College Hospital* [1956] 1 QB 90, 99.

limitation period; in other words, who, as a matter of observable fact, has been 'in' possession of the estate, and not simply intruding upon it.

This, it must be stressed, is a pure question of fact. For the reasons explained above, there are only two possible answers to it. At any one time either no one is in possession of the estate in question or there is one person who is in possession of it. The answer to the question cannot be that more than one person is in possession of the estate, unless they are claiming in right of and through each other as joint tenants.

Where land has apparently been abandoned or where the previous possessor has died or been dissolved – where, in short, there is no one obviously 'in' possession of the estate – then it is relatively easy for a stranger to acquire possession of it. Insignificant use of the land (such as occasionally mowing grass) will be sufficient to give the stranger possession of it, for, in this circumstance, there is no alternative possibility that he or she is simply intruding on someone else's possession.[17]

Where, however, there is someone already in possession of the estate, then much more will be required before the stranger can acquire possession. To acquire possession he or she must physically exclude the prior possessor or else entirely prevent the previous possessor continuing to enjoy the estate, for otherwise he or she will have done no more than intrude upon that person's prior possession, and (for the reasons explained above) that is not sufficient.

In some cases, the contest may not simply be a two-handed one. There may be two or more protagonists, each of whom is attempting to wrest possession from a prior possessor. In this situation, whilst the acts done by any one of them, viewed in isolation, might have been sufficient to dispossess the prior possessor, it may be that, viewed in the context of the contest between them, neither of them ever obtains a sufficient degree of control of the land, as against the other, to enable either of them to say that the original possessor has been dispossessed.[18]

4. *Possession is necessarily 'adverse'*

If a person 'has' or is 'in' possession of an estate, then that possession is necessarily 'adverse' to anyone who claims a better right to possess that estate. Non-adverse possession would be a contradiction in terms.

[17] *Red House Farms* v. *Catchpole* [1977] 2 EGLR 125 (shooting fowl over abandoned, overgrown land).

[18] *Simpson* v. *Fergus* (2000) 69 P & CR 398.

A person in possession of an estate must hold in his or her own right. Someone who holds in right of another or subject to another's will or claim, is not in possession at all.[19]

5. *A person 'in' possession of an estate in land must intend to possess it*

There is a mental element to factual possession, for whether someone is enjoying an estate in his or her own right or is holding subject to the will of another depends, to a certain extent, on that person's own state of mind. This, however, is ultimately a factual question for 'the state of a man's mind is as much a question of fact as the state of his digestion'.[20]

So, if I believe that I am obliged to account for the entire benefit I have received from the land to a third party, or that I am holding because someone else has permitted me to do so, then it is the third party who possesses through me.[21] If on the other hand I voluntarily hand over those benefits to someone else, once I have received them in my own right, then I am in possession; for choosing to give someone else the benefit of what I have received from the land is as much an assertion that the benefit is mine as if I had decided to keep it for myself.

6. *A person is not in possession of an estate in land unless he or she has dealt with it as an owner might have been expected to deal with it*

Possession is evidenced by acts of use and enjoyment of the estate claimed. What is required is evidence that the possessor has dealt with the estate in the same way as an owner might have been expected to deal with it.

So, if a person does something that an owner positively would not do – for instance, seeking permission from a third party before using the land – then that conclusively demonstrates that he or she is not in possession of it.

If a person does something which is equivocal because it falls short of occupation or the receipt of rent – something which an owner of the estate

[19] For fiduciaries, see *Lyell* v. *Kennedy* (1989) 14 App Cas 437. Formerly, 'non-adverse' possession was highly technical term of art. It was sufficient to bar rights in an action of ejectment, but not in real actions. Real actions were abolished in 1833, and thereafter non-adverse possession became irrelevant: *Pye* v. *Graham* [2003] AC 1 419, 433.

[20] *Edgington* v. *Fitzmaurice* (1885) 29 ChD 459, 483 per Bowen LJ.

[21] There are statutory exceptions for some tenants, who believe that they are, and who in fact are, entitled to be in possession of a leasehold estate, but who are nonetheless deemed to be in possession of the reversion too; see paras. 5, 6 Sch. 1 Limitation Act 1980; *Lodge* v. *Wakefield* [1995] 2 EGLR 124.

might do, but which alternatively might be explained on the basis of an independent right (for instance, a public right or the exercise of a right of way attached to other land) – then that is not evidence of possession of the estate either.[22]

But someone who is in occupation or in receipt of rent is presumed to have seisin and to be in possession of the fee simple,[23] and so occupation is not treated as equivocal for this purpose, even though there could be some other explanation for it.

The ways in which an owner might be expected to deal with the land depend upon whether the estate is of a type that is capable of physical occupation, and, if so, upon the physical characteristics of the property.

If the estate is of a type which cannot be occupied, then the physical characteristics of the property are irrelevant. If, for example, the estate is a reversion upon a lease, then an owner might expect to enjoy it by receiving the rent from the tenant, and exercising any rights reserved out of the lease. The person who does those things is in possession of that estate. The person in occupation is in possession of the lease, not the reversion.

If, however, the estate is one that carries with it a right of physical occupation, then the owner might be expected to use and enjoy it by occupying it personally, or by authorising others to do so. So, in the ordinary course, someone is in possession of that type of estate if he or she is using it in that way and otherwise is not. But this is not necessarily so. The estate might be subject to legal burdens that would make enjoyment of it by exclusive physical occupation unlawful. It might, for instance, consist of the soil in a public highway or be land subject to a private right of way. Alternatively, there may be no legal objection to its occupation but its physical characteristics might make enjoyment by occupation impractical. It could be covered by water. In each of these cases, an estate owner would be expected to use it by doing acts amounting to something less than exclusive occupation, and a squatter can accordingly obtain possession by the same means. If the land is part of the highway, the squatter might deal with it as an owner would by taking steps to require the highway authority to maintain it. If it is subject to a private right of way, the squatter might install a gate, or mark out passing places or parking bays. If it is covered with water, the squatter might put a boat on it. All of these things, in those circumstances, would be acts consistent with taking or retaining possession even though falling short of exclusive occupation.

22 *Sindall* v. *Cambridgeshire County Council* [1994] 1 WLR 1016, 1024.

23 See ch. 3.

7. An intention to possess means an intention to exclude the world at large, including the paper title owner, so far as the process of law will allow

A person 'in' possession must intend to enjoy the fruits of the estate in his or her own right. That person must intend to deal with the entire benefit of the estate as if it were his or hers for the time being. If he or she intends to hold subject to the true owner's claim, then the true owner retains possession. However, he or she need only intend to retain and enjoy it in so far as the law allows. It is not necessary to intend to exclude the true owner forcefully. In *Powell* v. *McFarlane*,[24] Slade LJ explained the principle in this way:

> What is really meant, in my judgment, is that the *animus possidendi* involves the intention, in one's own name and on one's own behalf, to exclude the world at large, including the owner with the paper title if he be not the possessor, so far as is reasonably practicable and so far as the processes of the law will allow.

In *Lambeth LBC* v. *Blackburn*,[25] Clarke LJ explained that passage as follows:

> That is an important passage in the context of the present case because it emphasises the fact that trespassers are likely to be aware that they will in practice be unable to exclude the owner if he takes steps to recover possession of the property. It thus shows that in order to have the necessary intention the trespasser does not have to regard himself as entitled to exclude the lawful owner from the premises. It is to my mind sufficient if he intends to keep the true owner out for the time being until he is evicted.

8. An intention to possess is not an intention to own

It might be thought paradoxical that a person intending to possess an estate need not intend to own it. But, in fact, there is no paradox here, for to be in adverse possession is simply to be in possession of it for the time being. In order to possess something now, a person does not need to intend to possess it in the future, and, if it is not necessary to intend to possess it in the future, it must follow that it is not necessary to intend to own it either. The question of whether someone is 'in' possession now is not affected by events which might happen in the future.

[24] (1979) 38 P & CR 452, 471. [25] [2001] EWCA Civ 912.

9. A person intends to possess, even if he or she would be willing to take a licence from the paper title owner, if offered

The true owner might assert the right to possess an estate by bringing proceedings to recover possession from the squatter. Alternatively, the true owner might offer to allow the squatter to stay on terms, by granting a licence. It might be that, if such an offer were to be made, the squatter would be happy to accept it. But that does not prevent the squatter being in possession in the meantime. A squatter can have a present intention to possess even though he or she might not have any intention to possess in the future. So it cannot make any difference that, if, at some point in the future, the true owner were to offer a licence, the squatter would accept it. Of course, if that actually happens – if a squatter accepts a licence from the true owner – then at that point the squatter ceases to be in possession, and the true owner regains it, for by accepting the licence the squatter acknowledges the claim, and the title of, and restores possession to, the true owner.

10. The intentions of the paper title owner are irrelevant

This too follows from the fact that 'adverse' possession is simply possession. If a squatter is in fact enjoying the fruits of an estate, and intends to do so in his or her own right, it does not matter why the paper title owner is not doing so. The squatter is 'in' possession.

Adverse possession, prescription and consent

Adverse possession is normally made manifest by adverse occupation. But not all estates can be occupied and a person in occupation of land is not necessarily in possession of any estate in it. The owner of land can enjoy the estate, and therefore be in possession of it, just as well by permitting someone else to occupy the land as by occupying it himself or herself.

So, if a squatter is in occupation without the consent of the true owner, the squatter is the person in possession of the estate. But if the true owner grants the squatter a licence to occupy the land, which the squatter accepts, the squatter ceases to be in possession of the land; the true owner resumes possession of the estate by granting the licence to the squatter.[26] There

[26] *BP Properties* v. *Buckler* [1987] 2 EGLR 168; cf. *Allen* v. *Roughley* (1955) 94 CLR 98, 124 per Fullager J: 'It is enough if actual possession was taken and continued, even though it be with the consent of the true owner.'

must, however, be some manifest[27] granting of consent to the squatter's occupation. It is not enough that the squatter's use is simply tolerated by a true owner who has no immediate use for the land. In that situation, as between the true owner and the squatter, it is the squatter who is using and enjoying the estate in the land, and so it necessarily follows that the squatter, and not the true owner, is in possession.[28] Nor is it enough that the permission is granted unilaterally. The paper title owner might write to the squatter, granting the licence. But, if the squatter were to respond by rejecting it, the squatter would retain possession. A unilateral licence stops the clock and resets it to zero if the squatter fails to respond at all, for, by failing to do so, the squatter is treated as having accepted the licence, and thereby accepted the grant and acknowledged the title of the paper owner.

Consent works differently in prescription, though the effect is similar. Use that is referable to an actual known grant or permission can never be the evidential foundation of a prescriptive right, for if there is an actual grant or permission which authorises the use, that provides a complete explanation for the lawful origin of the use, and leaves no room for evidential presumptions about an alternative lawful origin, which is the basis of prescription. So, if a landowner gives permission for the use before it begins, no prescriptive user ever commences, and if the landowner does so during the prescription period, thereafter the user is referable to that permission, with the consequence that the prescriptive clock stops. Of course, the same qualification applies here too. If the permission is rejected, then there is no bar to claiming a prescriptive right, for rejecting the permission is consistent with the existence of an alternative prior grant authorising the use.

Adverse possession and leases

If all estates are founded on prior possession, why is it that there is no privity of estate between a landlord and a squatter upon the lease even after the true tenant's title has been barred by adverse possession? Why cannot the squatter, who has acquired an indefeasible title to the lease, enforce the covenants contained in it given by the landlord? Why

[27] The consent can be implied by conduct, if the conduct is clear enough: *R (Beresford)* v. *Sunderland City Council* [2004] 1 AC 889.

[28] *Buckinghamshire CC* v. *Moran* [1990] Ch 623.

is the landlord similarly barred from enforcing the tenant's covenants directly?[29]

The answer is that this is a consequence of the essential difference in character between an acquisition by prior possession and an acquisition by adverse possession. To recap, prior possession is essentially negative. It is the method by which a person may prove a presumptively good title to the estate claimed (notwithstanding that a Crown grant or all the necessary links in the chain of title onwards cannot be shown) because there is no one who can show a better title.[30] Adverse possession is positive. It is a method by which a person may extinguish what would otherwise be an older and better title to an estate.

In the same way as a presumptively lawful title to a fee simple may be established by prior possession, it would be possible to establish a presumptively lawful title to a lease, giving rise to a relationship of privity of estate.

This is not an entirely theoretical possibility. From the thirteenth century onwards, corporations often took peppercorn leases for terms of a thousand years or more because they were forbidden to acquire freeholds by the Statutes of Mortmain.[31] A person today may today be in occupation under such a lease, and may be able to show a root of title going back a century or more, but be unable to prove all the necessary assignments going back to the original tenant. In the absence of positive evidence that the lease is still vested in the original tenant or someone else, the possessor will establish title to the lease by prior possession, giving rise to a full relationship of landlord and tenant with privity of estate.

In the real world, however, this rarely happens.[32] If someone is holding a lease, unlike a freehold, we know in every case that there must once have been a genuine post-conquest grant, and we normally know the names of the parties to it (because they are recorded on the lease). So, when a squatter takes possession of a lease, there is usually a person who is known

[29] *Tichborne* v. *Weir* (1892) 67 LT 735. The landlord may enforce the covenants by indirect methods that do not depend upon privity of estate. The landlord may, for instance, forfeit the lease, or distrain, or enforce the covenants restrictive of user as restrictive covenants (see ch. 4).

[30] See ch. 3.

[31] The first was the statute De Viris Religiosis 1279.

[32] Most very long medieval leases, having been granted for fixed rents, were destroyed by inflation. When it was no longer worth collecting the rent, the lease was eventually forgotten, and the tenant was assumed to be the freeholder. Long leases granted before the modern period are, however, still relatively common in Yorkshire, memory of them having been preserved by the peculiar system of deeds registration that applied there from 1704 until as late as 1976. See s.16(1) Law of Property Act 1969.

by the landlord to have a better title to it than the squatter. In order to remain in possession of the lease, the squatter is driven to assert that he or she has barred the true tenant's title. Having done so, the squatter cannot then claim to be a contractual successor to the true tenant, and without contractual succession, there cannot be privity of estate between landlord and tenant.[33]

Adverse possession and restrictive covenants

As between landlord and tenant, covenants run with the legal term of the lease[34] and with the legal term of the reversion.[35] Landlord and tenant apart, however, covenants are not directly enforceable against successors in title at common law. Absent the relationship of privity of estate created by a lease, at common law the burden of the covenant may only be enforced against the original contracting party as a matter of contract.[36]

But, by a very late invention of the courts of equity,[37] the burden of a covenant restrictive of the use of land may be made to run with land even where there is no privity of estate. The covenant is treated not simply as a covenant but as an equitable incumbrance on the burdened estate analogous to an easement,[38] and so, subject to the rules about notice and registration explained below, may be enforced in precisely the same way as any other equitable incumbrance on that estate, even against a complete stranger.[39]

Acquisition of the burdened estate by adverse possession does not affect this. Adverse possession extinguishes the title to an estate, rather than the estate itself. So an adverse possessor takes the estate subject to all existing incumbrances, including the restrictive covenants. Consequently, restrictive covenants may be enforced against an adverse possessor, in precisely

[33] See ch. 4. In Ireland, the problem was sufficiently acute to prompt the Irish Law Commission to recommend that adverse possession of leaseholds should take effect by way of parliamentary conveyance: LRC 67-2002.

[34] *Spencer's Case* (1583) 5 Co Rep 16a. For 'new' tenancies, see s.3 Landlord and Tenant (Covenants) Act 1995.

[35] Section 142 Law of Property Act 1925, reproducing the amendments made to s.2 Grantees of Reversions Act 1540 by the Conveyancing Act 1881. For 'new' tenancies, see s.3 Landlord and Tenant (Covenants) Act 1995.

[36] *Rhone* v. *Stephens* [1994] 2 AC 310.

[37] *Mann* v. *Stephens* (1846) 15 Sim 377; *Tulk* v. *Moxhay* (1848) 2 Ph 774.

[38] *Re Nisbet and Potts Contract* [1906] 1 Ch 386; D. Hayton, 'Restrictive Covenants as Property Interests' (1971) 88 LQR 539, 541.

[39] *Mander* v. *Falcke* [1891] 2 Ch 554.

the same way as rights of way may be, notwithstanding the absence of any privity of contract or estate. If the land is unregistered, the covenant may be enforced whether or not it has been protected under the Land Charges Act 1972, for an adverse possessor will never be a purchaser 'for money or money's worth'.[40] If, however, the land is registered, and the restrictive covenant has not been protected by entry on the charges register, then the adverse possessor will take free of it under the old registration regime,[41] which is preserved where the adverse possessor had already barred the title of the registered proprietor on 13 October 2003, but not where title is acquired by adverse possession after that date.[42]

The benefit of a restrictive covenant attached to an estate may also be enforced by someone in adverse possession of that estate, unless the covenant was made before 1926. If it was made before 1926, then the benefit can only be enforced by successors in title, and an adverse possessor is not a successor in title of the original covenantee, for a squatter is not an heir nor an assignee.[43] If, however, the covenant was made subsequently, then the adverse possessor has a statutory right to enforce it, for s.78(1) Law of Property Act 1925 deems an 'owner' for the time being of an estate to be a successor in title of the original covenantee.[44]

Adverse possession and land registration

Where a person acquires an estate in unregistered land by adverse possession, the title of the previous owner is automatically extinguished. In registered conveyancing, however, the register itself is the title. The person who is the registered proprietor of the estate is the legal owner of it and has power to deal with it subject to any restrictions on the register, unless and until someone else is registered as proprietor instead.

Accordingly, the title of the previous owner cannot be extinguished automatically. Registered land must either be made immune to adverse possession, or there must be some procedure by which the register can be changed, so as to show the adverse possessor as the new owner, once the title of the registered proprietor has been barred.

40 Section 4(6). Pre-1926 restrictive covenants bind the squatter if they bound the barred paper title owner, for a squatter is not a 'purchaser' of the legal estate for value.
41 Section 75(3) Land Registration Act 1925.
42 Para. 9(2) Sch. 6 and s.29 Land Registration Act 2002.
43 Section 58 Conveyancing Act 1881.
44 *Federated Homes* v. *Mill Lodge Properties* [1980] 1 WLR 594.

Originally, registered land was immune. Between 1862 and 1897, registered land could not be acquired by adverse possession. But there was hardly any of it,[45] so it did not matter very much.

In 1897, that changed. All the rules of adverse possession were incorporated into the registered regime, and that remained the law until 2003. Once the point was reached at which the proprietor's title to the estate would have been extinguished, had the land been unregistered, then the adverse possessor acquired the right to be registered as proprietor instead;[46] and, in the meantime, the existing proprietor held the land as if it belonged to the adverse possessor.[47]

The mechanics of registration under the 1925 Act had an effect on the law of adverse possession of leases. If an unregistered lease is acquired by adverse possession, then, as we have seen,[48] that does not create any privity of estate between the adverse possessor and the landlord. The adverse possessor is not a contractual nor a statutory assignee of the term of the lease, with the consequence that an adverse possessor cannot enforce its terms against the landlord. So, if the lease is unregistered, the landlord may take a surrender from the tenant whose title to the lease has been barred, but who, as between the landlord and the tenant, remains the tenant bound by a relationship of privity of estate.[49]

For registered leases, however, the position was more complicated. In *Spectrum Investment Co.* v. *Holmes*,[50] the court held that, where a squatter had been registered as proprietor of a lease, the ousted previous proprietor could no longer surrender the lease, because the Land Registration Act 1925 gave the registered proprietor the exclusive power of disposition. In *Central London Commercial Estates* v. *Kato Kagaku*,[51] the court went further and held that, in the meantime, the proprietor could not surrender, because any surrender would take effect subject to the statutory trust in favour of the adverse possessor[52] which was an overriding interest.

[45] By 1897, fewer than 5,000 titles had been registered. For the reasons why the system failed, see J. Anderson, *Lawyers and the Making of English Land Law* (Oxford, Clarendon, 1992).

[46] Section 75(2) and (3) Land Registration Act 1925.

[47] Section 75(1) Land Registration Act 1925.

[48] See ch. 4.

[49] *Fairweather* v. *St. Marylebone Property Co.* [1963] AC 510; cf. *Chung Ping Kwan* v. *Lam Island Development. Co.* [1997] AC 38, 47; *Perry* v. *Woodfarm Homes Ltd* [1975] IR 104; M. Higgins, 'Adverse Possession – Surrender of Lease' [1962] CLJ 31; H. Wade, 'Landlord, Tenant and Squatter' (1962) 78 LQR 541.

[50] [1981] 1 WLR 221.

[51] [1998] 4 All ER 948.

[52] Section 75 Land Registration Act 1925. It was sometimes said that, until the adverse possessor applied to be registered under s.75(2), the existing proprietor owed the adverse possessor all the duties of a trustee by virtue of s.75(1). This, however, was doubted by

Both of those decisions were probably wrong. The ability of a tenant to surrender depends upon the existence of a subsisting relationship of privity of estate, nothing more. Even where a squatter has been registered as proprietor of a lease, the squatter is not a contractual or statutory assignee of the term, for registration does not, of itself, create any relationship of privity of estate. So the ousted tenant retains the power to surrender. Nor can this have been affected by the statutory trust, for, if the ousted tenant retained power to surrender after the trust had been fully executed (that is, after the squatter had been registered as proprietor) it cannot have been a breach of trust to surrender it in the meantime. The point is that the benefit of the right to surrender was never part of the property held upon trust for the adverse possessor at all, because it was an incident of the relationship of privity of estate, which the adverse possessor never acquired.

The rules all changed again on 13 October 2003, when the Land Registration Act 2002 came into force.[53] The general principle of that Act is that, except where the adverse possessor had already obtained a right to be registered as proprietor by that date, registered land once again became immune to the process of adverse possession. But the political pressure for the change came from inner-city local authorities, who had been careless with their housing stock during the previous twenty years, and not from mortgage lenders, who had jealously guarded their rights. So it is still possible to bar a registered charge by adverse possession.[54]

There is an exception to the general principle where the registered proprietor does not object. A person who has been in possession of land for ten years may make a claim to be registered as proprietor of it,[55] if the registered proprietor does not object within three months of being notified of the claim,[56] or fails to do anything positive about it for two years afterwards.[57] In practice, of course, anyone who has been in undisturbed possession of someone else's land for more than ten years would be a fool to advertise the fact to the proprietor; hence the likelihood that 'shadow' unregistered estates, subsisting

Lord Radcliffe in *Fairweather* v. *St. Marylebone Property Ltd* [1963] AC 510, 541–3, and, in principle, those doubts were right, for, if there were a trust relationship, the registered proprietor would not have been able to reacquire title by adverse possession. Where the necessary period of adverse possession was complete on 13 October 2003, the effect of s.75 is preserved by para. 10(1) Sch. 12 Land Registration Act 2002.

53 Section 96 Land Registration Act 2002.

54 Section 96(1) Land Registration Act 2002.

55 Para. 4 Sch. 6 Land Registration Act 2002; rr.187-194 Land Registration Rules 2003.

56 Rule 189 Land Registration Rules 2003.

57 Para. 6 Sch. 6 Land Registration Act 2002.

behind the register and supported by estoppels, will become increasingly common.[58]

It was not, however, any part of the policy of the Act to rekindle cold boundary disputes. Boundaries in registered conveyancing are deliberately fuzzy in any event.[59] So it is still possible to obtain adverse possession of a registered boundary in a similar way to unregistered land.[60]

Possession of incorporeal hereditaments

An incorporeal hereditament is a burden on an estate in land.

Usually, the burden is negative. It prevents the estate owner, for the time being, exploiting the land in a particular way: for example, the burden of a right of way prevents the estate owner building on its route; the burden of a market or fair prevents the estate owner holding a rival market or fair; and the burden of a fishery prevents the estate owner fishing on the estate.

Sometimes, however, the burden is positive. It might require the estate owner to do something, such as to contribute towards the cost of repairing the chancel of a church.[61]

But, whether the burden is positive or negative, the benefit of most incorporeal hereditaments is automatically and irremovably attached to a corresponding corporeal estate in land. If that estate is subsequently severed, whether in time or space, the benefit of the incorporeal hereditament passes with each severed part. Whilst the benefit of it can be extinguished, without extinguishing the estate or the part to which it is attached, it cannot be alienated separately. So the benefit of an easement attached to the freehold estate of plot 'A' cannot be transferred to plot 'B'.

Incorporeal hereditaments of this type plainly cannot be possessed in any sense, for they have no independent existence at all. They are simply rights which are attached to some estate, and have become part of it, so as to be enforceable by the person in possession of it. The person in possession of the dominant tenement (the estate to which the benefit of the right has been attached) cannot ever complain about a 'dispossession' of the right, nor obtain an order to be put into possession of the right.[62] The

[58] See ch. 3. [59] Section 60 Land Registration Act 2002.

[60] Para. 5 Sch. 6 Land Registration Act 2002.

[61] Chancel Repairs Act 1932; *Aston Cantlow* v. *Wallbank* [2003] UKHL 37; [2004] 1 AC 546.

[62] *Territory of New Mexico* v. *US Trust Co. of New York* (1898) 172 US 171; Blackstone, *Commentaries on the Laws of England* (11th edn, London, Strahan & Woodfall, 1791), vol. 3, p. 206.

remedy is, instead, to sue in nuisance, complaining that the interference with the right is an interference with the use and enjoyment of the estate to which it is attached. This is why not every interference with the right will be actionable. In order to be actionable, the interference must be substantial, as with all other actionable nuisances.

Some incorporeal hereditaments are different, however, either because they exist 'in gross' (meaning that they are not attached to an estate in land at all) or because, although attached to an estate, they can be alienated in part to someone who has no interest in that estate.

A good example of an incorporeal hereditament which can exist in gross is an advowson, which is a right to appoint or present a cleric to a benefice. The circumstances in which this right can be exercised are now severely circumscribed,[63] yet, even when the right could be exercised freely, it was not protected by any of the possessory actions. If the bishop appointed his own cleric, the owner of the right could not bring an action for recovery of land, to evict him. The right simply was not corporeal enough for the possessory actions to be extended to it by analogy.[64]

The same is true of all other incorporeal hereditaments,[65] except for profits à prendre, such as a right to hunt, or to fish, or to cut turf.

Some profits are wholly alienable and 'without stint' (unlimited in extent). They exist in gross and may be sold or let to someone who does not own any land at all. Others are semi-detached. They can never be alienated wholly away from the estate to which they belong and the profit may only be enjoyed in such a way as would have been consistent with the servicing of that estate. But, subject to that, interests may be carved out of them in favour of strangers.[66]

Whatever the type of profit, in practice, the exercise of that right gives the owner of it a substantial degree of control over the burdened land.[67]

63 Patronage (Benefices) Measure 1986; see Mark Hill, *Ecclesiastical Law* (2nd edn, Oxford, Oxford University Press, 2001), p. 95.

64 The cause of action was *quare impedit* instead.

65 Blackstone, *Commentaries on the Laws of England* (11th edn, London, Strahan & Woodfall, 1791), vol. 3, p. 206.

66 In *Goodman* v. *Saltash Corporation* (1882) 7 App Cas 633, 658, Lord Blackburn said: 'The owner of the profit à prendre may take it in person or by his servants. But he may also, whether the profit is in gross or appendant to land, get the benefit of his profit à prendre, by selling or letting an interest in it, for a longer or shorter term, to any person capable of taking such an interest, and so long as that interest endures the donee has an irrevocable licence to take so much of the profit.' Similarly, in *Grove* v. *Portal* [1902] 1 Ch 727, Joyce J held that, in a fishing lease which authorised 'the lessee and his authorised friends' to fish, the lessee was entitled to sub-let two rods to strangers.

67 *Pole* v. *Peake*, *The Times*, 22 July 1998.

So, although, as an incorporeal hereditament, it is technically an 'interest' rather than an 'estate' for the purposes of the Law of Property Act 1925,[68] it has always been on the borderline of corporeality. A profit in gross can, for this reason, now be registered in its own right, as if it were an estate.[69] So, as we noted in chapter 1, the owner of a profit may bring actions not only in trespass and nuisance, but also in ejectment.[70] If dispossessed of the profit, he or she may bring an action to recover land to regain it.

But, although a profit à prendre may be possessed, it cannot be acquired by adverse possession. No incorporeal hereditament can be acquired or lost by adverse possession, even those that exist in gross.[71] A profit may only be acquired or lost by prescription.[72] Where a profit is lost by prescription, the prescription period ought to run against the owner of the right, in the same way as it would run against the freeholder if the rights had not been severed from the freehold.

68 Section 1(2) Law of Property Act 1925. Cf. s.205(1)(x).

69 Section 2(a)(iv) Land Registration Act 2002.

70 This does not extend to a common profit, because a right in common does not have the necessary degree of corporeality.

71 Section 38(1) Limitation Act 1980.

72 A profit in gross cannot be acquired by statutory prescription, because it cannot be occupied (s.5 Prescription Act 1832).

9

Possession judgments

Introduction

To explain the substantive law of possession is to tell only half the story. Enforcement is the other half.

For it is all very well to say that possession of an estate in land gives the possessor certain substantive rights, but those rights are valueless if they cannot be enforced. Indeed, to say that a litigant cannot enforce a right for a procedural reason, is to say that the wrongdoer has acquired a substantive right to commit the wrong.[1]

Sometimes, the problem is worse. It is little consolation for someone, who has just been compelled to give up possession by enforcement of a court order, to be told that, as a matter of law, he or she has the better right to it.[2]

In both situations, a book which dealt only with substantive rights would give a wholly misleading impression of the true position.

We have already seen, in the first eight chapters of this book, just how much the current substantive law of possession has been shaped and formed by the procedural rules of the past. This chapter is concerned with present procedural rules: it is about the nature of possession judgments, the methods and processes by which they are enforced, and some of the problems with those processes today.

[1] A legal right is nothing but a permission to exercise certain natural powers, and upon certain conditions to obtain protection, restitution or compensation by aid of the public force . . . Just so far as possession is protected, it is as much a source of legal rights as ownership is when it secures the same protection. Oliver Wendell Holmes, *The Common Law* (1963 reprint, ed. M. Howe, Boston, Little Brown & Co., 1963), p. 169.

[2] This is not a fanciful example: it happens all the time. A freeholder might grant a lease, and then conceal that when later mortgaging the freehold estate. The mortgage lender then brings possession proceedings against the freeholder, and the first the tenant knows about it is when the bailiffs arrive to enforce the warrant of possession. This ought to happen less often now for residential property, because CPR 55.10 requires the mortgage lender to write to 'the occupiers' giving them notice of the action fourteen days before the hearing date.

It has three main recurring themes: first, that the judgment is binding only on the parties and their privies, notwithstanding that enforcement is generally against the corporeal land itself; secondly, that the order usually fails to specify which estate in the land the defendant is to deliver up possession of to the claimant, so that it is easy to be deceived into believing that the order is dealing with the corporeal land itself rather than with an estate in it; and, thirdly, that restrictions on enforcement can leave the tenant in a legal limbo, as neither tenant nor trespasser, but rather something in between.

In rem or in personam?

A distinction is traditionally drawn between two types of judgment: a judgment in personam and a judgment in rem.

The first is a binding decision only between the parties to the action on their rights inter se. So far as strangers are concerned, the judgment is simply irrelevant. It is irrelevant even when what is in issue is whether one of those parties had a particular right against the other party, and, as between themselves, those parties have litigated that question out to judgment.

The second binds both the parties to the action and non-parties.

Some examples will make the distinction clear.

A judgment in debt is binding in personam only. A landlord might bring an action against an original tenant under an 'old' lease for the rent owed by the ultimate assignee, which is a claim in debt. In that action, the landlord might obtain judgment for the full amount as against the original tenant. But, if the landlord neglects to join the ultimate assignee as a party, and later thinks better of it, and decides to sue the ultimate assignee, then the debt will have to be proved afresh in that action; for the landlord cannot rely on the judgment obtained against the original tenant as proof that the rent is due against someone who was not a party to it. The judgment is binding only in personam, and so is *res inter alios* so far as the ultimate assignee is concerned.

There is nothing unfair in this. The original tenant might have had a perfectly good defence, which was not argued through ignorance, indifference or indolence. If the landlord later seeks to recover the same debt from the ultimate assignee, there is no reason why the ultimate tenant should be bound by what the original tenant did or failed to do.

A finding of paternity, on the other hand, is a judgment in rem. Once made, it is conclusive in all subsequent actions, whether or not the parties in those actions were also parties to the action in which the finding was made. If the court decides that a child is legitimate in one action, that decides the question for all purposes in all other actions too.

A possession order is an order in personam, but it is unusual for a personal action in that it requires the defendant to do something to a thing, namely, to give possession of it up to the claimant. That means, when it comes to the process of enforcement, that it looks a lot like a judgment in rem, for, when a bailiff or sheriff enforces an order for possession by writ or warrant for possession, everyone in occupation is evicted, and not merely the unsuccessful party to the litigation.[3]

Furthermore, a possession order is undoubtedly binding against successors in title. If, after judgment, the defendant transfers the land to someone else, then the possession order can be enforced against the transferee as if he or she had been a party to the action.

It might therefore appear that the possession order is really a judgment in rem.

Yet possession orders are true judgments in personam. Historically, the reason for this is that all possession actions are, by their very nature, actions for recovery of land; and an action for recovery of land is the action which, prior to 1875, was called the action of ejectment.

Actions in ejectment were, by their very nature, personal actions binding only between the parties, having been developed specifically for the purpose of short-circuiting the cumbersome 'real' actions, which did have effect in rem. Indeed, until the eighteenth century, the judgment in a possession action was not even binding between the real parties to the action, because the notional plaintiff was fictitious.[4] This meant that the same claim was often re-litigated between the same real parties, but with a different, fictional claimant in each action. William Woodfall, who at the beginning of the nineteenth century wrote the leading practitioners work on the law of landlord and tenant, commented on this as follows:[5]

> This in one respect may be deemed an advantage, because the parties are not concluded by one trial in case the real merits (from accident, partiality, want of evidence, which might be afterwards supplied, or the like) happened not to have been fairly tried between them; but in another respect, much mischief may result from it, as the spirit of litigation is thereby kept alive.

[3] *Leicester BS* v. *Shearley* [1950] 2 All ER 738; *R* v. *Wandsworth County Court, ex p. Wandsworth LBC* [1975] 3 All ER 390.

[4] See ch. 2 for the full history.

[5] *The Law of Landlord and Tenant* (2nd ed. London, Butterworths, 1804), p. 514.

In *Earl of Bath* v. *Sherwin*,[6] Mr Sherwin kept the mischievous spirit alive by making five successive claims, each of which he lost, until equity was persuaded to intervene, and an injunction was granted to prevent him trying again,[7] thereby taking the first step towards recognising that the judgment ought to be binding not merely between the notional parties to the action, but also between the real ones too.[8]

Nor does it make any difference to the personal nature of the judgment that a possession order can be enforced against non-parties. The nature of the judgment depends not on who might, as a practical matter, be affected by an attempt to enforce it, but rather who is bound de jure by it; in other words, against whom a plea of issue estoppel would succeed in a subsequent action.[9]

The essentially personal nature of a possession order, notwithstanding the method of its enforcement, can be demonstrated by considering the remedies available to someone who was not a party to the action, but who is nonetheless evicted by a bailiff or sheriff enforcing a possession order made in it.

If the order had acted in rem, there would have been only one course open to the non-party. It would have been necessary to apply to set aside that judgment, and to apply to be joined to proceedings in which the judgment had been obtained for that purpose; for, unless and until it was set aside, the judgment would have been binding.

[6] (1709) 4 Bro PC 373.

[7] See generally W. Holdsworth, *History of English Law* (London, Sweet & Maxwell, 1925), vol. VII, p. 17; W. Holdsworth, *Historical Introduction to Land Law* (Oxford, Oxford University Press, 1927), p. 173.

[8] By the end of the eighteenth century, common law courts were themselves refusing to permit a second action, if brought to try the same title, unless the costs of the first action had been paid: *Kene d. Angel* v. *Angel* (1796) 6 TR 740. See also Lord Mansfield's judgment in *Aslin* v. *Parkin* (1758) 2 Burr 665, 668: 'That the lessor of the plaintiff and the tenant in possession are, substantially, and in truth, the parties and the only parties to the suit . . . The tenant is concluded by the judgment, and cannot controvert the title . . . This judgment, like all others, only concludes the parties, as to the subject matter of it'. For more modern applications of the principle, see *Mcabe* v. *Bank of Ireland* (1889) 14 AC 413 and *Thames Investments* v. *Benjamin* [1984] 1 WLR 1381.

[9] In *Re Wykeham Terrace, Brighton* [1971] Ch 208, 209), Stamp J said: 'The second objection, and it is in my judgment a fatal objection, to the procedure which the applicants invoke is that an order made upon an ex parte application in ex parte proceedings will bind nobody. It is a truism that an order or judgment of this court binds only those who are parties to or attending the proceedings in which the order or judgment is given or made. This principle is blurred where the action is an action for the recovery of land by reason of the process by which the judgment is executed. The sheriff acting pursuant to a writ of possession will be bound to turn out those he finds upon the land whether they are bound by the judgment or not.'

But, because the order is only an order in personam, it is not necessary to do so. Non-parties may bring a separate action seeking to recover possession of the land without impugning the previous judgment at all. They may say that, even though, as a practical matter, the previous judgment might have been enforced against them, they have a better claim to be in possession than the successful claimant in that action; and they may say that, because they were not parties nor 'privy' to the previous proceedings, they are not bound by the judgment, and are therefore entitled to bring an action to be put back into possession, without impugning it.

It is also true, as the previous paragraph implies, that possession judgments are binding on 'privies' as well as parties. But, for the reasons explained below, that does not make them binding in rem either.

A party is anyone named in the claim form as a claimant or defendant.[10] A person is a 'privy' to a party, and so bound by the judgment, in three circumstances. First, if those who have an interest in land stand by, and allow someone else with the same interest to litigate out a dispute on their behalf, without applying to be joined, they will be treated as having been privy to it, and so will be bound by the result.[11] Secondly, anyone who claims an interest in the land which can be traced back to a disposition made by a party after the date of the judgment is a privy, and so bound by the judgment. Thirdly, anyone who claims an interest in the land as the result of a disposition made by a party after the proceedings were commenced, but before the date of judgment, is bound by the judgment too,[12] subject to statutory exceptions if the disposition takes place before the action has been registered.[13]

None of this in any way detracts from the personal nature of a possession order, for all orders in personam are binding on successors in title too.

[10] It is, in some circumstances, possible to bring possession proceedings against 'persons unknown': CPR 55.6. But, even then, the judgment does not act in rem. Everyone in occupation of the property is deemed to be a party to the action, and so is bound by the action, but it has no effect on the rights of anyone else.

[11] *Nana Ofori Atta* v. *Nana Abu Bonsra* [1958] AC 95.

[12] The rule was explained by Lord Cranworth LC in *Bellamy* v. *Sabine* (1857) 1 De G & J 566, 579, as follows: 'Where litigation is pending between a Plaintiff and a Defendant as to the right to a particular estate, the necessities of mankind require that the decision of the court in the suit shall be binding, not only on the litigant parties, but also on those who derive title under them by alienations made pending the suit, whether such alienees had or had not notice of the pending proceedings. If this were not so, there could be no certainty that the litigation would ever come to an end. A mortgage or sale might be made before the final decree to a person who had no notice of the pending proceedings which would always render a new suit necessary, and so interminable litigation might be the consequence.'

[13] Section 5 Land Charges Act 1972; s.87 Land Registration Act 2002.

Take, for instance, a judgment in debt. If a judgment creditor assigns the benefit of the judgment debt to a third party, the judgment is thereafter binding between the assignee and the debtor in the same way as it was between the original creditor and the debtor.[14]

The only difference between this and a possession order is that, under a possession order, successors to the burden of the judgment are bound, as well as successors to the benefit. But there is nothing odd in this. It is simply a consequence of the difference in the underlying substantive law. If, as a matter of substantive law, the burden of an obligation to pay a debt could be assigned, the judgment would be binding against successors in title to the judgment debtor too; but the debtor cannot, by his or her own voluntary act, transfer the debt to someone else, so the question does not arise.[15] Land, however, may be transferred subject to an obligation to deliver up possession to someone else. So the judgment is binding on successors in title to the burden as well as the benefit.

The rule, then, is clear. A possession judgment is binding between the parties named in the action, and their privies, and nobody else. If someone claims by title paramount, or by virtue of a disposition made by a party before the action was commenced, then, so far as he or she is concerned, the judgment is simply *res inter alios*. It does not decide anything about his or her rights; and, but for the risk of enforcement, it can be ignored, for it only decides the rights as between the parties and their privies.

It follows that there is nothing wrong, in principle, in having two inconsistent judgments, between different people, for possession of the same thing. The court, in an action between 'A' and 'B', might decide that the freehold in a property belongs to 'A'. In another action, between 'B' and 'C', it might decide that the freehold belongs to 'C'. But, as between 'A' and 'C', neither can rely upon the judgment which has already been obtained against 'B', except where the other is a privy of 'B'. Otherwise, as between 'A' and 'C', the ownership of the freehold simply has not been decided. This should not be surprising, for it is simply an aspect of the rule in *Asher* v. *Whitlock*[16] that all titles are relative.[17]

Nor is this simply an academic point. It has practical consequences. Two examples will help to illustrate the point.

[14] The assignee must apply for permission to enforce it (RSC Ord.46, r.2; CCR Ord.26, r.5) but that is given as a matter of course once the assignment has been proved.

[15] On an involuntary transfer, the transferee is bound. So a trustee in bankruptcy cannot dispute a judgment debt obtained against the bankrupt before the bankruptcy order was made, except by applying to set aside the judgment.

[16] (1865) LR 1 QB 1. [17] See ch. 3.

First, a boundary dispute may be determined between two adjoining freehold owners, but if the loser's mortgagor lender is not joined, and the lender subsequently exercises the power of sale contained in the mortgage (no doubt, after the loser has been made bankrupt for the costs of the action by the successful party), the judgment will not bind the purchaser.[18]

Similarly, a landlord may succeed in obtaining an order forfeiting the tenant's lease, but, if the landlord does not join the sub-tenant to the action, the order against the tenant is going to be of no use if the sub-tenant subsequently brings an action claiming that the forfeiture was unlawful. The sub-tenant is quite entitled to say that, so far as he or she is concerned, the judgment proves nothing; and that the landlord must prove that the forfeiture was lawful in an action in which the sub-tenant is a party, if the landlord wishes to recover possession free of the sub-lease. The reverse, of course, also holds true; a judgment against the sub-tenant does not bind the tenant.[19]

This might mean that the problems sometimes experienced by sub-tenants and mortgagees in obtaining relief after a forfeiture by action[20] within the relevant limitation period are entirely illusory.

The problem is that, if forfeiture proceedings are brought against the tenant alone, the sub-tenant or mortgagee might not find out about them until sometime later. In the meantime, the landlord might have obtained and executed the judgment.[21] Depending on the nature of the breach, the limitation period for applying for relief may expire either on execution of the judgment or six months thereafter. So the sub-tenant or mortgagee may be time-barred even before discovering that the lease has been forfeited. To start time running again, the advice that is usually given is that it is necessary to apply to be joined to the action in which the judgment was obtained, and to obtain an order setting aside that judgment, or at least its execution, for some irregularity or oppression, if that can be proved.

[18] In practice, mortgagees are rarely, if ever, joined to the action, because boundary disputes are about the people rather than the land.

[19] *Anon* (1699) 12 Mod 211.

[20] Peaceable re-entry is different. The limitation periods for claiming relief following a peaceable re-entry run from the date of re-entry, and the date of any subsequent judgment determining that the re-entry was lawful simply is not relevant for this purpose.

[21] In theory, if the premises are residential, the sub-tenant ought to find out, because the landlord is required to file an additional copy of the particulars of claim for the court to serve on the sub-tenant; CPR Part 56 PD para. 2.4. In practice, however, the copy tends to sit on the court file, unserved, because the court office is not used to serving documents on non-parties.

But, if the sub-tenant or mortgagee is not a party to the action, it is hard to see why the judgment should have any effect on their rights at all. They are surely entitled to say that the judgment is simply binding in personam between the parties before the court, and is not a judgment in rem binding on all those with an interest in the property. The landlord might succeed in obtaining a judgment against the tenant, deciding that the lease has been forfeited validly, but, if the landlord has not joined the sub-tenant or mortgagee to the action, then it decides nothing against them, for it is simply an order in personam. Time cannot start running, against them, for applying for relief, until the court has decided, as against them, that the landlord has lawfully forfeited the lease. If they are entitled to bring proceedings, notwithstanding execution of the judgment against the tenant, to recover possession on the grounds that the lease was never validly forfeited, it is hard to see how they can already be time-barred for applying for relief if it should turn out that it has been.[22]

Possession judgments: the land or an estate?

The standard possession order is made in form N.26.[23] There are other forms, which are all variations on the same theme, for use in different types of landlord and tenant claim.[24] Each form contains blank spaces, to be completed by the court when it makes the order. One of those spaces is for a description of the thing possessed which the defendant must give up to the claimant. It is customary to complete this by simply stating the address of the property. In ninety-nine cases out of a hundred, this causes

22 *Lord Hylton* v. *Heal* [1921] 2 KB 438, 449 per Rowlatt J. See also Warner J's explanation of *Doe d. Whitfield* v. *Roe* [1893] 1 QB 604 in *Ladup Ltd* v. *Williams & Glyn's Bank* [1985] 2 All ER 577, 583. In *Minet* v. *Johnson* [1886-90] All ER 586, 587, however, Lord Esher MR said that 'if Hartley had been a tenant of Johnson's of course he must go out'. It is unclear what, precisely, Lord Esher meant by this, but he probably meant no more than if Hartley's interest had been created since the commencement of the proceedings out of Johnson's, then Hartley would be bound by the judgment. See also per Lightman J in *GS Fashions* v. *B&Q plc* [1995] 4 All ER 899, 906: 'Confirmation or validation of a forfeiture by the lessee alone may not prejudice the entitlement of a sublessee or mortgagee to challenge the validity of the forfeiture and accordingly to maintain the continued subsistence of their interests.' Cf. *Rexhaven* v. *Nurse* (1994) 28 HLR 241.

23 CPR Part 4 PD Table 1.

24 N.26A (assured shorthold tenancies); N.27(1) (forfeiture for non-payment of rent); N.27(2) (forfeiture for non-payment of rent (suspended)) (which is not a form which is ever likely to be used: see *Inntrepreneur* v. *Langton* [2000] 1 EGLR 34); N.28 (order for possession, rented premises).

no harm. But it does make it appear as though the court is dealing with the physical land itself. Of course, it is not. It is dealing with an estate in the land, and, properly completed, the form ought to specify not only the address of the property, but also the estate in that property to which the order applies; whether that is a fee simple, a lease or a profit à prendre, and whether it is to be free of or subject to some derivative estate.

The process of enforcement

It is usually a criminal offence for anyone to use or to threaten to use violence to secure entry to any premises, where there is someone present on the premises who is opposed to the entry, and the person using or threatening the violence knows that to be the case.[25] Execution of a writ or warrant of possession by an officer of the court is excepted. For this reason, as an entirely practical matter, it is not normally possible to enforce a possession order by self-help, although the commission of the criminal offence does not make the act unlawful as a matter of civil law too.[26] But there are also various civil restrictions, which are largely contained in the Protection from Eviction Act 1977. The effect of those restrictions is generally to make it unlawful, as a matter of civil law too, to enforce a possession order against a residential occupier otherwise than by the process of the court. To use self-help in those circumstances is to commit an actionable wrong, even though the person in possession is defying a court order by continuing to possess it.[27] Non-compliance with the court order does not justify commission of the statutory tort.

In the county court, a possession order is usually enforced by a bailiff executing a warrant of possession.[28] As soon as the date for giving up possession specified in the order has passed, the claimant may require the warrant to be issued. The bailiff then fixes the date for it to be executed.[29]

In the High Court, the equivalent process is execution of a writ of possession by the sheriff.[30] Unlike in the county court, the writ normally

[25] Section 6 Criminal Law Act 1977, a statutory re-enactment of the Forcible Entries Act 1381.

[26] *Hemmings* v. *Stoke Poges Golf Club* [1920] 1 KB 720.

[27] *Hanif* v. *Robinson* [1993] QB 419.

[28] CCR Ord.26, r.17.

[29] Sometimes in order to speed the process up, the court gives permission to make the bailiff's appointment immediately provided that the date fixed for executing the warrant is after the date specified in the order for giving up possession.

[30] RSC Ord.45, r.3(1).

cannot be issued without permission from the Master,[31] but that is given as a matter of course.

Neither a warrant nor a writ of possession may be executed without permission more than six years after the judgment.

On the day fixed for execution of the warrant or writ, the bailiff or sheriff executes it by physically evicting all those found present on the land, using such force as may be necessary.[32]

A possession order is usually enforced by writ or warrant for possession only because it is relatively cheap and easy. The alternatives of committal, sequestration and appointment of a receiver by way of equitable execution are all slow, complicated and expensive.

Sometimes, however, there is no alternative but to use one of those methods, for a judgment may only be enforced by warrant or writ of possession where the court has ordered that a person be put into possession of an estate that carries with it an immediate right of occupation.

If the estate does not carry that right with it – for instance, if it consists of a reversion upon an occupational lease – then it cannot be enforced by warrant or writ of possession, for the judgment is that the successful claimant be put into possession of the reversion and not the lease, albeit that it will be a rare case where this is made explicit on the face of the order. There is no right, by virtue of the judgment, to evict the tenant, and any attempt to do so would be both a breach of the covenant for quiet enjoyment and a trespass upon the lease. All that can be done, by virtue of the judgment, is to require the defendant to deliver up possession of the reversion. So, if the defendant continues to demand rent, a receiver may be appointed by the court to collect the rents and pass them to the claimant.[33] Alternatively, if the defendant purports to exercise any of the rights reserved to the landlord under the lease, the defendant may be committed to prison for contempt, or suffer its assets to be sequestrated.[34]

31 RSC Ord.45, r.3(2).

32 *R* v. *Wandsworth CC, ex p. Wandsworth LBC* [1975] 1 WLR 1314.

33 CPR Part 69. It is not possible to obtain an interim possession order except against a pure squatter, but the same thing may be achieved by appointment of a receiver, for there is jurisdiction to require a litigant to give up possession, even if that involves giving up physical occupation, to a receiver appointed on an interim basis, notwithstanding that the right to possession is in issue in the proceedings: *Marshall* v. *Charteris* [1920] 1 Ch 520.

34 RSC Ord.46, r.5.

Setting aside possession judgments

A possession judgment might be set aside for one of three reasons.

First, an appeal court might set it aside, if the person against whom it was made successfully appeals the judgment.[35] Secondly, the court that made it might set it aside, if the person against whom it was made applies to the court to reconsider the judgment, on the ground of some procedural defect in the way that the claim was brought or the judgment given.[36] Finally, it might be set aside as against a third party, who wishes to intervene in the action.[37]

In practice, third parties claiming some interest in the land often apply to be joined to the action before judgment, or apply to be joined afterwards and to have the judgment set aside, even though, technically, they would not otherwise be bound by the result. In order that the court can decide at an early stage whether anyone else ought to be made a party to the action, the claimant is required, in the particulars of claim, to give details of anyone known to be in possession of the property.[38] Once judgment has been obtained, in the High Court a writ of possession cannot be issued unless it is shown that every person in actual possession of the whole or any part of the land has received such notice of the proceedings as appears to the court sufficient to enable that person to apply to the court for any relief to which he may be entitled.[39] There is no equivalent rule in the county court, although in practice the bailiff delivers a notice in form N.54 to the property a few days before the warrant is due to be executed.

The reason for this protection, and the reason why third parties often apply to be joined to the action, is that there is no tort of using the machinery of the court to enforce a judgment against a person who is not bound by it.[40] So, if a writ or warrant of possession is executed against a non-party, there is no remedy against the sheriff or bailiff, nor against the successful claimant in the action, except where separate authority has been given to the sheriff or bailiff to act as the claimant's agent.[41]

35 CPR 52.10(2). 36 CPR Part 39(3).

37 CPR Part 40.9, CPR Part 19. There is no jurisdiction to join a third party to a judgment after it has been obtained, so as to make the judgment binding against the third party: *Kooltrade* v. *XTS Ltd* [2001] FSR 158.

38 CPR Part 56 PD para. 2.1. 39 RSC Ord.45, r.3(3)(a).

40 *Metall & Rohstoff* v. *Donaldson Lufkin & Jenrette* [1990] 1 QB 391.

41 *Williams* v. *Williams and Nathan* [1937] 2 All ER 559; *Barclays Bank* v. *Roberts* [1954] 3 All ER 107; s.126 County Courts Act 1984.

That is not to say that it is necessarily lawful, as against someone who is neither a party nor a privy, for the executing party to remain in possession after the writ or warrant has been executed. Execution of the writ or warrant does not decide anything about the rights of those who are neither parties nor privies. Anyone in that position is quite entitled to bring an action afterwards, to be put back into possession, and to claim mesne profits in the meantime, on the grounds that he or she has a better right than the person who obtained the writ or warrant, for only the initial execution of the warrant is excused not the retention of possession afterwards.

A judgment might be set aside after it has been enforced. If it is, the enforcement does not, retrospectively, become unlawful simply because the judgment upon which it was based has been set aside.[42] If the court orders someone to do something, it is not wrongful to enforce that order using the process of the court, notwithstanding any pending appeal or application to set aside the order, unless the court has itself granted a stay of enforcement. But, if the order is subsequently set aside, then the court may impose terms doing practical justice between the parties, so as to restore them to the same financial position as they would have been in, had the judgment not been enforced in the meantime.[43]

So, if there is to be an appeal,[44] or an application to set aside, it is necessary to obtain a stay of enforcement, and, if it has already been enforced, and there is likely to be a delay before the substantive hearing, then it is necessary to apply to set aside the execution of the judgment on an interim basis.

Setting aside execution

Where a time limit is calculated from execution of a judgment,[45] the time limit will be extended if the judgment upon which the execution was based is set aside, for, if the judgment is set aside, the execution falls with it. Even if the judgment is sound, if the execution has been carried out in an oppressive or deceitful manner, then it is possible to set aside

[42] *Hillgate House* v. *Expert Clothing* [1987] 1 EGLR 651.

[43] *Rodger* v. *Comptoir d'Escompte de Paris* (1871) LR 3 PC 465.

[44] CPR Part 52.7.

[45] Where a lease is forfeited by court process, it is generally execution of the order that starts, or stops, time running for claiming relief. Execution also exhausts the court's power to reschedule arrears under a suspended possession order.

the execution alone, and thereby start time running again.[46] This applies generally, and not just to secure tenancies.[47]

Suspended possession orders

When the court makes an order for possession, there are normally three significant dates. The first is the date specified in the order by which the defendant is required to give up possession. The second is the date upon which the claimant is first allowed to make an appointment with the sheriff or bailiff to enforce the order by writ or warrant of possession. The third is the date fixed by the bailiff or sheriff to execute the writ or warrant by forcible eviction of all those present on the land.

At common law, if the claimant has an immediate right to possess an estate in land, then the claimant is entitled to an immediate possession order, and the court cannot refuse to make it.[48] Nor can it defer enforcement of the order, except in favour of a former tenant, or anyone else who entered with consent, in which events the courts have an inherent power to defer enforcement for a short time,[49] the exercise of which is now regulated by statute.[50]

The reality of judicial practice, however, does not always accord with the theory. Even in cases where there is no jurisdiction to defer enforcement, it is not unknown for Masters and District Judges to threaten to adjourn the final hearing of the claim, in order to extract some concession on enforcement. Provided that the threat is not to adjourn the final hearing for longer than it would take to appeal the decision to adjourn, they can do this with impunity, albeit with scant regard to their judicial oaths.

In some circumstances, the date upon which a person is required to give up possession is now regulated by statute. In a forfeiture action for non-payment of rent, the order cannot require the tenant to give up possession earlier than twenty-eight days from the date of the judgment.[51] If there is an application for relief, then, as part of the relief application, the court may defer it further.

More complicated is the jurisdiction that exists in respect of statutory tenancies regulated by the Rent Acts, and secure and assured tenancies

[46] *Peabody Donation Fund* v. *Hay* (1986) 19 HLR 145; *Hammersmith & Fulham LBC* v. *Hill* (1995) 27 HLR 368. See also *Croydon (Unique) Ltd* v. *Wright* [2000] L & TR 20.

[47] *Cheltenham & Gloucester* v. *Obi* (1994) 28 HLR 22.

[48] *Mcphail* v. *Persons Unknown* [1973] Ch 447.

[49] *Jones* v. *Savery* [1951] 1 All ER 820.

[50] Section 89 Housing Act 1989.

[51] Section 138 County Courts Act 1984.

regulated by the Housing Acts 1985 and 1988. In each of those case, where a possession order is made on a discretionary statutory ground, the court has power to make a possession order, but to suspend enforcement of it for a finite, but sometimes lengthy, period provided that certain conditions are met.[52]

Tolerated trespassers

A tenancy, which is being continued for the time being by a suspended possession order, terminates automatically as soon as the tenant commits a breach of that order.

Thereafter, there is always the possibility that the tenancy might be revived, with retrospective effect, by a further order of the court, for the court has jurisdiction to alter the terms of the suspension at any time before the order is executed.

If the tenancy is subsequently revived by order of the court, then the tenant is deemed always to have been a tenant, and may bring an action on any of the covenants in this lease.[53] In this respect, the tenant is in the same position as a tenant applying for retrospective relief from forfeiture, and, in considering the terms for any further order, the same principles (other than as to the time for payment)[54] ought to apply.[55]

But, subject only to that possibility, the tenant becomes a trespasser immediately the breach is committed. As soon as a breach is committed the landlord may issue and execute a warrant for possession without any further judicial intervention.[56]

In practice, however, landlords frequently continue to accept rent, even after the tenant has committed a breach of the order. Suspended orders are usually made in favour of social, rather than private, landlords, and not many social landlords are so unreasonable as to require a tenant who has committed a technical breach of a suspended possession order to give up possession forthwith.

[52] The same applies to residential instalment mortgages, where the mortgagee seeks possession on the ground of non-payment of the mortgage instalments, and will apply to forfeiture, if the Law Commission's Termination of Tenancies Bill is ever enacted.

[53] *Pemberton* v. *Southwark LBC* [2000] 1 WLR 1762.

[54] When granting retrospective relief from forfeiture, the usual order is that payment must be made within twenty-eight days: *Inntrepreneur* v. *Langton* [2000] 1 EGLR 34. But, where the court exercises its statutory power to make a suspended possession order, it may reschedule any arrears, over such term as it thinks fit. In practice, orders are often made allowing the tenant to repay the debt over many years.

[55] See ch. 4.

[56] *Thompson* v. *Elmbridge BC* [1987] 1 WLR 1425.

There is a conceptual problem in this, however, for normally, if a tenant who has no security of tenure holds over after expiry of the lease, and continues to pay rent to the landlord, which the landlord accepts, then the court is driven to the conclusion that the landlord has impliedly granted the tenant a new periodic tenancy, because the acceptance of rent, as such, cannot otherwise be explained.[57]

If that rule were to be applied in its full vigour to a breached suspended possession order, there would be this difficulty: it would be possible for a tenant, against whom an order had been made on the ground of arrears of rent, to say that, because he or she had subsequently committed a breach of the order, and because the landlord had accepted rent afterwards, it therefore followed that a new contractual tenancy had been created, and that the landlord had lost whatever right there might otherwise have been to recover possession for any breach of the former tenancy.

The judicial answer to this is the 'tolerated trespasser'.[58] For so long as there remains a possibility that the former tenancy might be revived by further order of the court, the court is not driven to the conclusion that the landlord has agreed to grant a new periodic tenancy at all. The payments can otherwise be explained on the premise that, for so long as there remains a possibility that the court might revive the former tenancy, the parties cannot have impliedly agreed to create a new tenancy.[59] There is no new tenancy; simply a tolerated trespass.

If, however, the tenancy is never revived, then the occupier is deemed to have been a trespasser from the moment that the order was first breached. A trespasser cannot enforce covenants in a lease, for there is neither privity of contract nor privity of estate between a landlord and a trespasser; and so it follows that an occupier, who has breached a suspended possession order and become a tolerated trespasser, cannot complain that anything which the landlord has done since is a breach of the covenants contained in the lease, unless the occupier has first succeeded in reinstating the lease.

The occupier is, nonetheless, 'in' possession of a leasehold estate, albeit as a squatter on the landlord's estate. As such, a tolerated trespasser is entitled to bring the possessory actions against third parties: if dispossessed by a stranger, the tolerated trespasser can bring an action to recover possession, and the actions of trespass and nuisance are available if a stranger intrudes or disturbs the tolerated trespasser. All of this is unproblematical,

[57] *Morrison Low* v. *Patterson* 1985 SLT 255.

[58] *Burrows* v. *Brent LBC* [1996] 1 WLR 1448.

[59] *Stirling* v. *Leadenhall Residential* [2001] 3 All ER 645.

because these are all remedies available to any squatter, and a tolerated trespasser is in no worse position than one who is not tolerated.

What is problematical is the decision of the Court of Appeal in *Pemberton* v. *Southwark LBC*[60] that a tolerated trespasser is entitled to bring an action in nuisance against the landlord. It is hard to see how this can be right, because it is a complete defence to an action in nuisance that the defendant has a better title than the claimant that the defendant is entitled to dispossess the claimant. The reason for this rule is clear enough: if the defendant has an absolute right to recover possession entirely from the claimant, at any time and for any reason, then the defendant must be entitled to intrude upon or disturb the claimant's possession in lesser ways too. That said, it is not hard to see why that rule was disregarded in *Pemberton*. The practical reality is that the courts created the concept of the 'tolerated trespasser' in order to prevent tenants, who are in substantial arrears with their rent, making unmeritorious claims to new tenancies; not to deprive those tenants of the rights which they had under the existing tenancies: and, whilst there is no escape route from the logical consequence that a 'tolerated trespasser' cannot make any claim on the covenants contained in the tenancy, the courts naturally balk at saying that such a tenant has no remedy at all, no matter how badly the landlord might have behaved.

[60] [2000] 1 WLR 1672.

10

Summary and conclusions

Meaning of possession

The word 'possession' is used, in English land law, to describe three different, related but inconsistent concepts. That is why it is so confusing.

It is primarily used to describe a relationship between a person and a legal estate in land: a fee simple, or a lease, or (notwithstanding that it is technically an 'interest' rather than an 'estate') a profit à prendre.

A person has a right to possess that estate if he or she has acquired a title to it which carries with it a fixed right to enjoy it now; that is, a title to it which is 'vested in possession'.

A person is 'in' possession of that estate if he or she (and not someone else) is, as a matter of observable fact, substantially enjoying the benefit of it; that is, taking the benefit of the estate, rather than the physical land itself.

But 'possession' is also sometimes used as a synonym for 'occupation'. A person is in occupation of land when physically present upon it, or when otherwise making some tangible use of it.

More rarely, nowadays, 'possession' is also used in a third, wholly fictional, sense, called 'constructive' possession. The law sometimes deems a person to be, or to have been, in possession of an estate in land, when, in fact, that is not, or was not, the case. This is constructive possession. Historically, this was very important to both title and procedure. But there are few circumstances now where that deeming process still takes place.

The key to solving most possession problems is to ask: In what sense is the word 'possession' being used?

Suppose that a squatter enters freehold land and then lets it to a tenant. The question 'who has possession?' is meaningless, unless we know what type of 'possession' is being referred to: for the paper title owner of the freehold retains a right to 'possess' the fee simple free from the lease throughout; the squatter, who is receiving rent from the tenant, is 'in possession' of a freehold reversion upon the lease; and the tenant, for the time being, is 'in possession' of the lease and in 'occupation' of the land.

If the right question is asked with sufficient precision, then the answer to most possession problems can usually be found within the coherent matrix of orthodox land law. If that is not done, then the result is inevitably to obscure the problem, rather than to solve it, and error is the result.

Protection of possession

The common law does not protect 'occupation' as such; or, at least, it only does so indirectly, by protecting possession of an estate, or the right to possess an estate.

It does so by three different causes of action: the action for recovery of land (formerly called 'ejectment'), the action of trespass (formerly called 'trespass quare clausum fregit') and the action of nuisance.

An action for recovery of land, by its very nature, is only available to a person who has a right to possess an estate in land, but who is not currently in possession of it. The complaint is that he or she ought to be in possession of it, but is not; and the claimant wants to use the process of the court in order to be put into possession of it, by ousting the defendant who is currently in possession.

The foundation of that complaint must be a title, but it does not have to be a paper title. Whether the land is registered or not, the claim can be based simply on prior possession of that estate.

The actions of trespass and nuisance, on the other hand, may be brought both by someone who is in possession of an estate in land, and by someone who is out of possession but who has a right to be put into possession of that estate.

They can also be brought against someone who is a mere occupier, or, indeed, anyone else; for, to commit those wrongs, it is not necessary that the wrongdoer should be in possession of, or have a right to possess, any estate in land.

The defence of *ius tertii* is never available in an action for recovery of land; for title is relative, the judgment is in personam, and the only issue in the action is: 'Who, amongst the parties, has the better right?' But it is available as a defence to the actions of trespass and nuisance if the wrongdoer would otherwise be at risk of having to pay twice for the same wrong.

It is always a complete defence to one of the possessory actions that the defendant, or someone under whom the defendant holds, has a better right to possess the estate in issue than the claimant, or has a right to possess another estate free of that estate.

Possession, title and freehold land

There is an intimate connection between possession and title. To say that someone has a right to possess a freehold estate is to say that he or she has a title to it; the better the right to possession, the better the title.

In unregistered conveyancing (leaving aside, for the moment, questions of adverse possession), the best evidence of title to a freehold estate is evidence of prior possession of it, either by the person claiming it or by someone through whom that person claims; and the older the act of possession relied upon, the better the title.

This is because our land law is still, at its heart, essentially feudal. There is no unowned land in England and Wales. The Crown is still the ultimate feudal overlord of the whole kingdom, and feudalism dictates that all private estates and interests in land ultimately owe their validity to a post-conquest Crown grant, taking the land out of the royal demesne. Without such a grant, the land must belong to the Crown absolutely.

In all but a tiny fraction of cases, however, it is impossible for a private individual to justify the use or occupation of land by producing such a grant. If the grant ever existed, it has probably been lost, and it probably never existed at all, for the Crown's ultimate title is a convenient fiction, not historical fact.

So the courts are willing to presume the existence of the grant from the next best evidence of it: prior possession. The older the act of possession, the better the evidence of the Crown grant.

That basic principle underpins registered conveyancing too.

Plainly, in practice, the longer a title has been registered, the less likely it is that someone will seek to upset it by producing an older, unregistered title. But, when one is produced, the previous registration regime allowed the register to be rectified, so as to register the better, older unregistered title; and it seems likely that the current registration regime will allow that too.

Even if it does not, the registered proprietor of an estate is not necessarily 'in' possession of it: nor is it necessary to be the registered proprietor, in order to bring any of the possessory actions and thereby to recover or protect possession of that registered estate; although, of course, the registered proprietor has a better title to it than anyone else.

Registration notwithstanding, prior possession is, therefore, truly still the basis of freehold title.

Leases and licences

A leasehold estate creating a tenancy is a mixture of contract and property. It is capable of being possessed because it creates an estate in the land. It is an independent property right.

A licence is, at the most, a contractual right only. It is not property, because the burden of it does not bind third parties. If it is not an independent property right, then there is nothing in the nature of an estate which is capable of being possessed.

Licensed land may, of course, be 'occupied', but it cannot be possessed in the same way as a leasehold estate can be possessed.

The 'touchstone' for the difference between a tenancy and a licence is whether it was intended that the power to control access to the property by strangers would pass from the grantor to the grantee. If that was the intention, then the intention must have been to grant an independent property right, which is only consistent with a tenancy; if it was not, then the intention must have been to grant a licence.

The three possessory actions – recovery of land, trespass and nuisance – are not available to a licensee, because the nature of a licence is that it confers no property right enforceable against third parties. A contract which creates an independent property right which can be protected and enforced against third parties is, by its very nature, a leasehold estate creating a tenancy.

The estate in a lease may exist after the contract has determined, but the contract cannot exist after the landlord has voluntarily destroyed the estate, for the contractual relationship is parasitic on the continued existence of the estate.

Where a lease is forfeited, it determines by entry, either actual or notional, and the landlord's reversion is accelerated from that moment. If relief is granted in the tenant's own name, it is retrospective, and the landlord is deemed never to have been entitled to possess the reversion free from the lease. But, if relief is granted by way of vesting order to a sub-tenant or mortgagee, the landlord is treated as having been entitled to possession free from the lease from the moment of re-entry until the moment when the vesting order is made.

Mortgages and charges

A secured lender does not have the right to take possession of the debtor's estate. Nor, when a secured lender takes possession, does the lender go into possession of the debtor's estate.

Instead, if the security takes the form of an actual mortgage term, then the lender has a right to take possession of the long lease, which the debtor granted the lender by granting the mortgage. But, if, as is more usual, the security takes the form of a legal charge, then there is no mortgage term; instead, the lender has all the rights and powers of a tenant of a long lease, created by way of mortgage term, without having the long lease itself. So the lender under this type of security does not take possession of an actual leasehold estate, only of the rights and powers attached to such an estate.

The lender under a legal security normally has the right to take possession of the security immediately. The lender under an equitable security normally has no such right, and, to obtain the right, must obtain an order from the court.

Until the lender enters into possession, the lender has no liability to third parties nor rights against them. The security interest is disregarded. Having taken possession, the lender is then put in the same position, so far as third parties are concerned, as if the lender had, on that date, taken an assignment of a long lease, created by the debtor when the security was created. If the lender goes out of possession again, then the lender is in the same position, so far as third parties are concerned, as if that lease had been assigned on.

There is an exception where the third party holds an 'old' lease for the purpose of the Landlord and Tenant (Covenants) Act 1995 and the lender holds a charge by way of legal mortgage. In that case, whilst in possession, the lender has all the rights of the landlord of that lease, but none of the liabilities.

Equity and trusts

The rules and doctrines of equity remain separate, distinct and different from those of the common law. Equity converts some rights which are personal at common law into proprietary rights. But equity also recognises personal and proprietary rights that have no counterpart at common law.

A person who has, in equity, a present fixed right to enjoy a common law estate (an equitable interest in possession) may bring any of the common law possessory actions, and may bring an action claiming any equitable remedy, in order to vindicate that right, simply by joining the legal owner of the estate as a defendant to the action too.

Someone with a lesser equitable interest in a common law estate may bring an action seeking any equitable remedy on the same basis, but has no right to join the legal owner of the right to the action as a defendant in order to make a common law claim. Only the legal owner can make that claim, and an owner of the equitable interest can compel the legal owner to do so only by bringing an administration action.

Someone who has an equitable proprietary interest with no counterpart at common law can seek equitable relief against the person interfering with the right directly, without the need to join anyone else, assuming (of course) that the equitable right is binding on that person as a matter of substantive law, but cannot do anything else.

The owner of an equitable right that is purely personal cannot apply directly against third parties for any relief. Again, the right can only be vindicated by bringing an administration action against the legal owner of the right, requiring the legal owner to bring proceedings against the third party.

But a person can always defend a claim on the strength of an equitable right, without joining the legal owner of it (if any); and a person who is, in fact, 'in' possession of a common law fee simple, lease or a profit à prendre, may bring actions in trespass and nuisance, irrespective of whether that person happens also to have some equitable interest in it too.

Where a lease is granted to a minor, the trust relationship means that the landlord cannot unilaterally determine that lease. The landlord must ask the court to do it, as a matter of discretion, on an application made for that purpose.

Birth and death, dissolution and insolvency

An estate can only be vested in an extant person, and that person can only be 'in' possession of it whilst extant.

A disposition to an individual who has never existed is void, but a disposition made to a person who has died is effective to vest the property in the deceased's personal representatives. A disposition made to a non-existent corporation is also void, but, if made to a company which has never existed, takes effect as a disposition to the person purportedly acting as its agent.

An insolvency frequently affects the right to possess an estate in land, but does not change who is 'in' possession of it, unless and until the right to possession is enforced, or until the person in possession ceases to exist.

Each of the insolvency schemes works differently. A private receiver is normally deemed simply to be acting as an agent for the debtor, but may become the agent of lender or even take possession of the estate as principal. A trustee in bankruptcy is a statutory assignee of the debtor's property, and is entitled to take possession as such. A liquidator always acts as statutory agent for the company in liquidation, and so never enters into possession in his or her own right.

But, whether those persons are in possession of an estate or not, they can all be occupiers, and it is no defence to an action for trespass or nuisance that the act was done on behalf of someone else in a particular capacity.

Where a statutory right of disclaimer is exercised, that destroys all rights and liabilities as between the disclaiming party and anyone else, but leaves intact all other rights and liabilities; the disclaimer is entirely disregarded, except where a claim is made directly by or against the person who has disclaimed.

A disclaimer of a freehold brings about an escheat, which destroys that freehold estate.

On dissolution, the otherwise undisposed of property of a corporation vests in the Crown as *bona vacantia*. But, on revival of a company, it revests, subject to any disposition that might have been made by the Crown in the meantime. A Crown disclaimer is not treated as a disposition for this purpose.

Adverse possession and prescription

Adverse possession and prescription are both rules that turn recent de facto enjoyment of land into de jure enjoyment. Adverse possession does it as a matter of substantive law. Prescription does it as a matter of the law of evidence. This explains some of the differences between them. But some are simply the accidents of history.

A person who is in possession of a fee simple or a lease is necessarily in possession of it adversely to anyone else who has a better title to it. But a licence cannot be possessed, so a person who currently intends to exercise the rights of a licensee cannot be 'in' possession.

Adverse possession creates no privity of estate, and so an adverse possessor cannot enforce covenants that run between landlord and tenant. But an adverse possessor is bound by, and may take advantage of, incumbrances, such as incorporeal hereditaments and restrictive covenants, which are attached to the estate, because adverse possession bars the title of the previous estate owner to the estate, and not the estate itself.

The only circumstance where two or more people can be 'in' possession of the same estate at the same time is where they are joint tenants. Otherwise, either none of them is in possession, or the others are all intruders on the prior possession of one of them.

Most incorporeal hereditaments are attached to a particular estate, and to derivative interests in that estate, and can never be alienated away separately. As such, they can never be possessed in their own right; although a substantial interference with the right is an actionable nuisance.

Others can exist in gross or can at least be partly alienated, but only a profit à prendre (not being a right in common) is sufficiently corporeal to be possessed, and is therefore capable of being recovered in an action for recovery of land and trespassed upon.

An incorporeal hereditament can never be acquired or lost by adverse possession. It can only be acquired or lost by prescription.

Possession judgments

An order for recovery of possession of land is an order in personam. It is a binding decision only between the parties to the action and their privies. It is not binding on anyone else, even as a decision about what the rights were as between the parties to it.

A possession order strictly relates to an estate in land, rather than to the physical land itself. But, if the estate carries with it a right of occupation, the sheriff or bailiff enforces the order by physical eviction of all those present on the land.

Anyone evicted in this way cannot complain that the act of eviction was, itself, a wrongful act, even if the judgment on which it is based is subsequently set aside.

But it is not a decision about the rights of third parties, and so third parties do not technically need to have the judgment set aside. They may, instead, make their own claims by fresh actions afterwards, in order to vindicate their substantive rights. More often, however, they will apply to be joined to the action before the judgment is obtained, and thereby ensure that no order is ever obtained which might be enforced against them, and the courts encourage this.

Where a judgment is set aside, any execution falls with it. But the court also has power to set aside the execution alone, leaving the judgment intact. That might be done because there are circumstances where time limits for remedies expire on or run from the date of execution.

Where a suspended possession order is made, the tenant is in possession wrongfully from the moment that the order is first breached. But an intention to create a new contractual tenancy cannot be inferred, simply from subsequent acceptance of rent, at any time when there remains a possibility that the court might make an order reviving the former tenancy. Unless and until it is revived, the former tenant cannot bring any action upon the landlord's covenants contained in the lease that fell due for performance after the breach, although, anomalously, the landlord cannot plead the unlawful possession of the former tenant as a defence to a claim in nuisance.

INDEX

For EU product safety concerns, contact us at Calle de José Abascal, 56–1°, 28003 Madrid, Spain or eugpsr@cambridge.org.

www.ingramcontent.com/pod-product-compliance
Lightning Source LLC
LaVergne TN
LVHW101502200926
848483LV00001B/200
9780521868990